NOVEL

AND JUSTICE FOR ONE
Copyright © 2017 by John Clarkson
All rights reserved.

Second Edition published 2017 by JOHN CLARKSON INC.
11 Schermerhorn Street, Suite 6WB, Brooklyn, NY 11201

ISBN 978-0-9992155-0-0   hardcover
ISBN 978-0-9992155-1-7   softcover
ISBN 978-0-9992155-2-4   e-book

1. The main category of this book – crime thriller – fiction.
2. Mystery/suspense – fiction. 3. New York – fiction.
4. Corruption – fiction. 5. Revenge – fiction. 6. NYPD – fiction.

Cover and interior designed by Anton Khodakovsky

Printing History:
Crown Publishers' edition /February 1992
Jove Book editions / September 1993

PRINTED IN THE UNITED STATES OF AMERICA

JOHN CLARKSON

AND JUSTICE FOR ONE

CONTENTS

*The most tolerable
sort of revenge is for those wrongs
which there is no law to remedy.*

—FRANCIS BACON

THIS ONE IS FOR MY FATHER

Author's Note

This novel was first published in 1992. I don't remember exactly when I began writing it. I do remember the two events that inspired the story. The first event occurred in 1976 when I visited an after-hours club in downtown Manhattan. The second event came in 1979. A six-year-old boy named Etan Patz disappeared on a spring morning in New York's SoHo district, igniting the worst fears of parents around the country. It happened during a two-block walk to his school bus stop.

Somewhere in the back of my mind those two events brewed for years. What if someone you loved vanished? What would you do to find them? And what if it turned out that the mysterious, hidden world of after-hours clubs had something to do with the disappearance?

At some point in the late eighties, those questions became the inspiration for my first novel. I hardly remember writing it. My sense is that it came out in a sudden rush. And selling it to a publisher happened quite fast. I landed an agent, George Wieser, very quickly. And as I recall, George sold it to Crown within a few weeks. Thank you, George! I do remember spending a very long time editing the book under the guidance of Peter St. John Ginna. He was patient with me. He made it a much better book. I still appreciate his efforts.

In the original author's note, I thanked my wife Ellen for her patience. A good deal of the research for *And Justice for One* started at four in the morning. All these years later Ellen is still patient with me, but more importantly, she still loves me, and I her.

The others I thanked in the first edition were "the people who made it possible for me to enter the world of after-hours clubs". One of them was a friend named Tommy Burns. When I asked Tommy how I should acknowledge him in the first edition, he said "Use T.B., 'Bartender to the Stars.'" Tommy rarely took anything very seriously.

Obviously, all the after-hours clubs described in this book no longer exist. But all of them except for one, which is a composite of three clubs, existed very much as described. It was a wild time in NYC. A time before cell phones and the internet and Uber. A time long gone.

So, what prompted me to re-publish *And Justice for One?* Since its publication in 1992, I have persisted in writing crime thrillers, despite a ten-year break after the first five. All of those novels are out of print, but readers often ask me how they can get them. This is an attempt to make that easier. It has also provided me with the opportunity to polish the book. Nothing substantive, but lots of nips and tucks. This new edition is still what I consider a raw, rather impetuous novel from an unformed writer just starting out. Maybe that's the best kind. Hope you enjoy it.

CHAPTER 1

The alarm clock shrieked a nasty little electronic beep.

It finally annoyed Jack Devlin out of his hazy, hung-over sleep. He kept his eyes shut hoping to suspend his awareness that it was someone else's alarm clock, that he was sick with a hangover, and that he had buried his father yesterday.

But it all came pounding back—the funeral, the reception at his brother George's house, the drunken night out.

The woman next to him finally reached over and turned off the alarm, but Devlin didn't open his eyes. He remembered the frenzied drunken sex, the kind only two strangers can have, but he didn't want to open his eyes and see her. He just wanted to stumble out of there while she slept and leave it behind. The alarm killed that chance. She was awake now. She gently attached herself to him. A long naked thigh nestled into his crotch. An arm wrapped around his chest.

Devlin had to leave, but she wasn't letting go. He had to go back to the apartment where he was staying and find his brother George waiting for him there.

He kept his eyes shut, cleared his throat, and asked, "Did you tell me your name was Helen?" knowing full well it wasn't.

"What?" She lifted her head. "What did you say?"

"Hold on a second. Where's your bathroom?"

"Down the hall."

Devlin gently extricated himself, swept the sheet off, and swung his legs to the floor. The room was air-conditioned down to a chilling cold.

He clenched his teeth, stood up, and squinted at the piercing pain in his head. It had been a long time since he'd drunk so much. With one eye half-open, he left the bedroom and walked into a short hallway that led to the bathroom. The hallway felt hot and stuffy after the air-conditioned bedroom. He ducked into the bathroom and closed the door behind him.

Devlin opened both eyes. The bathroom was cleaner than he expected. Very neat actually. Three string-bikini panties hanging on the shower rod were bright white.

He reached into the shower and turned on the hot water. The tub was sparkling clean.

He opened the medicine cabinet looking for something to ease his pain. She had a bottle of Excedrin. He swallowed four with a handful of water, hoping to get the pulsing spike out of his right temple.

He checked the contents of the medicine cabinet while he waited for the shower to warm up. There was a typical assortment of products, plus two vials of prescription medicine. One was a half-full bottle of Penicillin VK. The other was Valium, 5 mg. Both were for Daryl Austen from a Dr. Vincent Colonia. The address on each was 166 E. 63rd Street.

The shower water was steaming. Devlin adjusted it with cold water and stepped in. The soothing water washed over his head and face and ran down his muscled belly. He filled his mouth with water, swirled it around, and spit it out.

He lathered all over twice, shampooed his hair and shaved with a Lady Bic razor he found in the shower. He dried himself off with a clean, blue towel and walked back to the bedroom. The bare wood floor felt clean under his bare feet.

Daryl was sitting up in bed with her arms crossed under her breasts. In the dim light that leaked around the window shades, she looked a lot better than Devlin expected. A hell of a lot better. He sat in a chair next to the bed and looked right straight at her. Her breasts were nearly perfect. There wasn't an ounce of fat on a stomach just on the verge of showing some muscle. One long leg, uncovered by the sheet, was casually crossed over the other. The white sheet just about bisected her at the crotch.

She had a friendly, quizzical look on her face. A long, slim nose, full lips, and streaked blond hair that was permed into the crinkly style that made some women look sexy and others just look messy. On Daryl, it worked.

Maybe that's what you call a wry look, thought Devlin. He tried to see the color of her eyes in the dim light and decided they were probably blue.

Devlin liked the way she didn't seem at all bashful about being naked with a stranger.

"Did you ask me if my name was Helen?'

"Yes."

"You don't remember my name?"

"It's Daryl. Daryl Austen."

"Why'd you ask me, then?"

"I don't know."

"Were you thinking of someone else?"

"No. You get up this early every day?"

"Yes. Who was drunker last night, you or me?"

"I figure me."

"Did you tell me your name?"

"You don't remember my name?"

"No, are you insulted?"

"Yeah."

"Really?"

Devlin stood and began gathering his clothes. "No."

She asked, "How old are you?"

"You don't remember my age either?"

"You didn't tell me."

"How would you know?

"Come on," she asked. "How old are you?"

"Thirty-eight, how old are you?"

"Twenty-eight."

"I'm too old for you," Devlin told her.

"The hell you are, with that face and body. So what *is* your name?" He leaned over the bed and shook Daryl's hand. "Jack Devlin. She shook his hand and looked at his swaying cock. "Not too shy, are you, Jack Devlin?

"No."

"Guess you don't have to be, Jack."

"Guess you don't either, Daryl."

"Thanks. See, if we keep repeating each other's names, we'll remember them."

"I'll remember yours. Daryl."

"Is it too personal to ask where you got those interesting scars?"

"Yes." Devlin found his underwear on the floor and stepped into it.

"I see. Well, Jack, how about that tan? How did you get such a dark tan so early in the season? You look like you've got a white bathing suit on from behind."

"I was in the islands for a while."

"Doing what?"

"Vacation."

"Uh-huh." She waited for more from Devlin, but it wasn't coming. "Well, I see you've showered and all. A couple more minutes you'll be dressed, and you can get the hell out of here without any more morning-after chitchat."

Devlin looked to see if there was any anger in her, but she still had that crooked smile.

"I'm sorry, but I do have to leave."

"Well, don't leave before I tell you that I don't usually go to bed with strange men I meet in bars."

"I don't see why you'd have to."

"I don't."

"Why did you?"

"Because my fucking bastard of a boyfriend broke up with me, and I was angry and depressed, and I figured it would do me good to get laid."

"Did it?"

"Yes, but I don't like this hangover. And I don't like the feeling that you want to leave as fast as you can."

He told her, "It's not because of you."

"Why, then? You have to get to work?"

Devlin's face twitched. He picked up his pants from the floor and stepped into them.

Daryl watched and waited for an answer.

Devlin said, "No, I'm not going to work. I kind of ran out on my brother back at that bar. I want to catch up with him."

"That big guy you were with was your brother?"

"Yeah."

"And you said you two were out drinking because . . . " She stopped herself and put her hand on her mouth. Then she asked, "Were you telling me the truth about your father?"

"Yes."

"You really were?"

"Yes."

"Oh shit. I'm sorry."

Devlin was dressed except for buttoning his shirt. Daryl got out of the bed and walked quickly to her closet. She pulled out a robe and slipped it on with her back turned to him.

"Do you want any coffee or anything?

"No. Thank you."

"Come on. It'll take another five minutes."

"Okay."

She left the bedroom, suddenly seeming remote and far away from him. As he put on his socks and shoes, he kept thinking about Daryl Austin's smooth, sleek belly that curved so nicely down to the dark patch between her legs and her interesting quizzical smile that had disappeared so quickly when she remembered why he had been drinking so fiercely.

They didn't talk much while they drank the coffee, but Devlin was glad he'd stayed. Daryl didn't ask him any more questions or push at him. She was quiet and respectful of his loss. She said she was sorry about his father and even told Devlin he'd better hurry and see about his brother.

By the time Daryl walked him to the door, Devlin felt off balance. It had been a long time since someone had been so understanding. He started to say something, but Daryl told him, "Don't say anything. My number is in the book if you want to see me again."

He nodded once and turned to find the elevator. He didn't look back when he heard Daryl's door shut.

When he walked out onto the street it was 8:25 A.M. Traffic was already building on Third Avenue, along with the New York summer heat and humidity. It was the middle of July. A patch of hot, humid air had descended on the city that wouldn't leave. It just sat there getting foul with carbon monoxide and the hot breath of eight million sweating people.

Devlin slipped on a pair of sunglasses he'd worn during the funeral to fend off the glaring daylight while he hailed a taxi.

He sat in the cab and smelled stale cigarette smoke and sweat on his clothes. At least the hangover was subsiding under the coffee and Excedrin.

He hoped George had remembered to leave his keys under the doormat. At the pub on Second Avenue, somewhere uptown in the Seventies or Eighties, Devlin had tried to explain the convoluted instructions for opening the doors in the loft building, unlocking the elevator, and hiding the keys.

They had been fiercely drunk. Black drunk, like men can get when someone they love dies. The drinking had started right after the funeral Mass in the church up in Larchmont. They drank with the family and friends throughout the afternoon, then into the evening.

So many in the family hadn't seen Jack in so many years that his presence became almost as much an event as his father's death.

When everyone finally left, the brothers dropped their polite faces and sat together in George's backyard, still drinking but more slowly— without the urgency of sadness, or anger, or the pressure of guests and family standing around them.

They sat side by side on two mildewed chaise lounges in George's backyard and talked to each other with a bottle of Jameson Irish whiskey sitting on the grass between them. As the warm summer daylight seeped away, George's kids came down one by one in their pajamas. They each got a drunken kiss and a rough hug from their daddy.

George was so big, the kids seemed to disappear for a moment when he hugged them. Jack sat quietly and watched the nightly ritual.

Jeanine was six. Brian was eight. Mary Margaret was ten. Mary Margaret was old enough to know her father had been drinking. It made the child worry. She didn't like it, but she respected her daddy too much to say anything.

By the time the last kid was in bed, there was no more daylight in the July summer sky. George's wife, Marilyn, had come out twice offering them food. George waved it off. Jack gently refused it.

Jack admired Marilyn. She was one of the few people who had his respect. In his boozy reverie, he started to idolize her. It took a good, confident woman to let them keep drinking and not try to force or cajole them out of their misery. She let them wallow comfortably in their recollections. She let them share their alcohol-tinged memories of their father and their temporary brotherly camaraderie.

"Did you think much about Dad dying some day?" asked Jack.

George pulled himself up and answered, "Sure. Guy gets to be eighty you think about it."

"You felt close to him?"

"I guess. I saw him at least once a month. Half the time the old bastard insisted on driving himself over here from Jersey.

"Dad really loved you, George."

"He loved you, too, Jack."

"He thought I was okay, but he really loved you, George. You were such a damn good kid. Everybody loved you."

"Aw, come on. Dad was proud as hell about you.

"I know. He was one of the good guys, George."

"Sure was."

He was tough, but I liked him. I respected him. He was a gentleman. Worked hard all his life. Stuck with Mom. Sat next to her bed and took care of her for the whole year it took her to die."

George nodded. "He sure did."

He died well. Fast and neat. He hated worrying about needing someone to take care of him."

George asked, "You talk to him much?"

"Yeah, as a matter of fact." Jack reached over and clutched his brother's meaty shoulder. "I'm sorry I haven't kept in better touch with you."

"Ah shit, Jack, you don't have anything to be sorry about."

"No. It's not good."

"Why? You're running around working for that outfit of yours. I'm here with the family. How we gonna see each other?"

"I could call. When was the last time I called you?"

"I could call, too. I know you're out there if I need you. All I have to do is call that number for you, and your company finds you. Where were you?"

"Grand Cayman."

"When I called about Dad, they got you in less than an hour. I could call more. What the hell were you doing in Grand Cayman?"

"Sort of a working vacation."

Doing what? What does that company do?"

"Pacific Rim?"

"Yeah. What do they do?"

Jack waved his hand, "They use to call them detective agencies. Now they're 'security companies.' Pacific Rim has lots of clients based in the Pacific. Japanese, Korean, Taiwanese. Big electronics and manufacturing outfits. Lot of American clients, too."

George asked. "What do *you* do for 'em?"

Devlin shrugged, suddenly tired of all the whiskey in him. "Information. Protection. Security."

"You like working for foreign clients?"

"I don't work for the clients, really. I work for the guy who runs it. He's smart, and he's honest, and he has guts."

"Who's that?"

His name is William Chow. I met him when I was in Vietnam. He ran a supply service for the CIA. Had his own planes, trucks, the works. He never existed, but he knew everybody and everything."

"Hooked in with the spooks."

"Yeah, but not anymore. Not that I know of. He's got his own organization. At a certain point, you got to have an organization behind you."

"How come you left the Secret Service?"

"Had enough of the rules and regulations. Same with the military. They have tremendous power, George. Incredible resources. You wouldn't believe what they can do. And then a bureaucrat somewhere makes a policy decision, and it all goes to shit."

"That ain't the only place that happens."

"In your job?"

"Sure."

"What is it, Bristol-Myers?"

"Bristol-Myers Squibb now."

"They merged?"

"Yeah, like everybody else."

"So what do you do for 'em, George?"

"Information. Protection. Security."

Devlin laughed gently. He rubbed his face to push away some of the drunken haze. "Ah, George, we have to get together more often. We don't even know how each other earns a living."

"You'd be bored if I told you, and everything you do is a secret."

"Hmm." Devlin looked at the first stars appearing in the east, then turned again to his brother. "Mom's gone. Dad. It's just us now, George."

"I guess so." George took a thoughtful sip out of the Jameson bottle. "You going back to L.A.?"

"Soon."

"You staying in Manhattan?

"Yeah. A couple more days I guess. Got the company apartment."

George looked at his brother. "What are you so fucking serious about?" He reached over and put his big hand on Jack's arm and said, "I know you're there. You know I'm here. You've got your life. I've got mine. It's fine."

"I know it's fine. I know. You have a lovely life, George. You should be proud."

George settled his head back on the chaise. "Yeah, why not."

"You have those beautiful kids. They love you like a hero. Marilyn. She's great."

"It's just like a billion other families, Jack."

Devlin swept up the bottle from the lawn and thought about how soft his brother's voice had become. "I guess so, George." He took a burning swig and looked at his brother. "Last of the Mohicans, George."

George looked back at him.

Suddenly Devlin stood up. "Come on, George, let's get the hell out of here. I'm taking you to dinner."

"Shit. I can hardly stand up."

"Bullshit. Let's get the hell out of this backyard and just do something away from this goddamn funeral."

"The funeral's over, Jack."

"Not until I'm away from here it's not. I'm not letting you shake my hand, pat me on the back, stick me in a cab, and make some promise to stay in touch. We're going to spend at least one damn night together away from all this."

George blinked once and said, "Okay."

Devlin called a car service. He swore to Marilyn they wouldn't drive, and twenty minutes later they stumbled out the door and into the black limo waiting at the bottom of George's driveway.

Devlin took his brother to Palio on 53rd Street. They had a drink in front of the great Sandro Chia murals in the downstairs bar while they waited for a table. Their Italian dinner sobered them enough to prompt a new round of drinking that took them up the East Side through more comfortable bars.

They were two big men talking about a dead father they both loved and missed deeply. Two brothers bumping along down the street not caring very much about who didn't like it. Two sincere drunken men telling each other private things and making promises that both might later acknowledge but never actually keep.

And then, at the third bar, Devlin saw the blonde, and he was drunk enough not to ignore the sudden overwhelming urge for sex. He wanted to get close to her and take her home and strip and go as deep into her as he could. Go as deep as it took to turn aside the loss and stave off the emptiness.

There was so much power and energy in his good looks and boozy sincerity that when he asked, the girl just said, "Why not?"

He ambled over to George, who was playing darts with three other men. When Jack told him he was leaving, George at first looked confused and disappointed. But as soon as Jack pointed to the blonde, George smiled and slapped him on the back wishing him luck. George listened carefully while Jack gave him his keys and described how to get into the loft apartment.

In the hot light of the morning-after, the memory of George's big drunken smiling face haunted Jack. He willed the cab to hurry down Second Avenue.

The street door to the loft building where he was staying was open during the day because of the commercial lofts on the first two floors. Security started in the elevator. Each floor had a lock. Jack had told

George to leave the seventh floor unlocked. That way the elevator would take him to his floor, and George could hide the keys under the mat outside the apartment.

The taxi driver dropped him off, the lobby door was open, and Devlin stepped into the elevator. He punched seven at the same moment he saw the floor was locked.

"Damn!"

He stepped off the elevator and looked up at the lobby ceiling as if he could see through it and up to the loft on the seventh floor. He pictured George dead asleep in his bed.

He walked out of the small lobby and turned left on West Broadway. His watch said ten minutes to nine. The hell with it, he thought, I'll just have to wake him up.

Five rings and the answering machine came on. After the beep, Devlin yelled into the phone, "George, it's me, Jack. Wake up!"

Nothing.

"Come on, George, wake up. I'm locked out. You have to let me in, George. Come on!"

Nothing.

He thought about it. The answering machine is in the living room. He's in the bedroom. Maybe the door is closed.

"Shit."

Devlin yelled louder, "Come on, George, wake up!"

People across the street stopped and looked at him. He stuck his head farther into the half-phone booth. "George!"

Nothing.

He could see his seventh-floor window halfway down the block. It seemed very far away. Nobody is in there, thought Devlin. Now what the hell do I do?

CHAPTER 2

By nine o'clock, Marilyn Devlin was thinking the same thing. Her call had put her through the same anxious progression. From a first attempt to gently rouse the brothers, to an angry shout at the answering machine, to worry and confusion.

In the end, she decided to sit and wait. The kids were in school until three o'clock. George was taking the day off after the funeral. She didn't have to be anywhere until three when she had to pick up the children. She couldn't imagine not seeing George or at least hearing from him by then.

#

Devlin sat in the Elephant & Castle restaurant on Prince Street getting annoyed at the Mozart playing softly in the background and sipping his tea. He didn't touch his omelet. He carefully ticked off the logical explanations in his head. Whatever explanation he came up with ended with him calling George's house. But what if George wasn't there? Marilyn would be going crazy.

He got up and went to the payphone in the entrance foyer to the restaurant. He had to call information for George's number. Marilyn answered on the first ring.

"Yes?"

"It's Jack."

"Where are you? I've been worried sick. There's no answer at your apartment."

George wasn't there. "I know. I'm locked out."

"What happened?"

"I gave George my keys. We got separated. I think he's up there sleeping, and he forgot to put the keys under the mat for me."

"What do you mean you got separated?"

"Look. Don't worry, Marilyn. Sit tight. I'm going to call a locksmith and get in there. I'll call you from the apartment."

"Jack, I don't understand. What's wrong? What's going on?"

"Marilyn, don't worry. I'll call you back."

He hung up before she could say anything more.

#

The locksmith pulled up in front of the building an hour later. He was in his fifties. His disheveled black hair flecked with gray. He had on green khaki pants and a cheap short-sleeved shirt. He looked as if he had seen a million broken doors and busted locks. "You Devlin?"

"Yeah."

"Tough night, huh?"

"Yeah."

"Lost your keys, huh?"

"Right."

"I should ask you if you have any verification that you have the right to enter the premises I am about to break into."

The words sounded serious, but the look on the locksmith's face wasn't. It was a pro forma sentence he recited to protect himself. Devlin took out his wallet and showed him a driver's license.

"That ain't even a New York license."

"It's a company apartment."

The locksmith shrugged. "Well, you look like a citizen. Don't worry about it."

Devlin said, "You got a license in case anybody asks?"

The locksmith looked at Devlin with a mixture of surprise and pleasure. "Absolutely. In nineteen goddamn years, no one has ever asked to see my license. Once somebody asked me what I was doing drilling and pounding and banging open doors. And that one time all I said was 'I'm a locksmith,' and they backed right off. Never asked to see my license."

He pulled out a well-worn wallet and started to thumb through a fat pocket filled with cards and papers. "You know I carry a copy of my license, figuring some cop or some super is gonna ask me for sure, but no one ever does. Well here you go, pal, licensed by the State and City of New York to wreak havoc on any and all locks that stand in my way."

The license was copied on old Photostat paper, the kind copy machines used fifteen or twenty years ago. Devlin looked at the thick oily piece of paper. It had been folded in a wallet so long it would never flatten out. He peeled it open. Devlin had only asked as a joke, but now he wouldn't dare not look at it. The locksmith's name was Alphonse Lettieri.

"Well, Mr. Lettieri, it looks official to me. Let's go."

"Fuckin' right it's official."

Lettieri drilled out the cylinder lock on the elevator and the Medeco lock on the front door in minutes. The inexpensive lock above the door handle gave him the most trouble. The drill started to turn the whole cylinder, and Lettieri had to pry away the collar protecting it and then pull out everything.

Devlin stood watching wondering he would do if his brother wasn't in there, already knowing he wasn't. Not even George could sleep through this break-in.

A quick look around the apartment told Devlin that George had never been there. It was 10:48 A.M.

A cold flash of anger and worry hit Devlin's stomach. He walked quickly to the bedroom and saw the telephone answering machine blinking with messages.

He pushed the button, impatient for his brother's voice to come on and tell him where he was and what happened. The machine beeped and played back his own voice and Marilyn's instead.

"Christ, now what?" Devlin muttered to himself.

He sat on the edge of the bed. He wanted to start calling hotels, but he knew the first calls should be to the police and hospitals.

Lettieri came back from his truck with a new set of locks for the front door. Devlin had an absurd urge to ask him what to do. Lettieri looked at Devlin and knew something was wrong. "What happened?" he asked.

"My brother was supposed to stay here last night. I gave him my keys. Apparently, he didn't make it here. Might have decided to stay at a hotel instead."

"Guy doesn't show up in this fucking city, you've got to start checking."

"I'd better get on the phone."

Lettieri ambled back to the front of the apartment. Jack reached under the table next to the bed and pulled out the White Pages. He turned to the back. A map showed the boundaries of each police precinct.

The last bar they had visited was in the 19th Precinct. He dialed the number. A woman's voice answered mechanically, "Nineteenth Precinct, Collins."

Devlin asked if there were any reports or contact with a man named George Devlin. When asked why, he explained that George Devlin was missing. He was connected to another officer who took Devlin's information and put him on hold.

Lettieri walked back into the bedroom.

Devlin asked, "Done?"

"Yeah."

He handed Devlin a set of keys. "Here's your new keys."

"How much do I owe you?"

From his back pocket, Lettieri pulled out a rectangular metal case. He took out a form and tore off the first copy. He handed it to Devlin, stowing a pink and yellow copy in the back of the case. Devlin looked at the total—$401.60.

Lettieri saw his expression and said, "Expensive night out."
Devlin started to read the itemized entries. The locks, keys, labor,
collars, tax. It added up. He took four one-hundred-dollar bills and
a fifty out of his pocket. Just then the voice from the police precinct
came back on. He held the bills and listened.

"No report on any Devlin. If he doesn't show up in two days you
can file a missing persons report."

"Two days?"

"Right."

"Okay, thanks. If you get any information, can I give you a number to contact me?"

"Yes, but until a missing persons report is filed any number you
give me won't automatically cross-check with the computer reports,
so it won't do much good."

"Okay. Thanks."

Devlin hung up the phone and handed the bills to Lettieri. "Here
you go."

Lettieri started to fish for change. Devlin told him, "Keep it. I
appreciate the fast service."

"You're welcome. Hey. It'll work out. He'll turn up. He's probably
sleeping it off in some broad's apartment."

Devlin looked at Lettieri and realized the whole thing was so
goddamn typical even the weathered locksmith had figured it out.
Trouble was, he had the wrong brother shacked up in some broad's
apartment.

CHAPTER 3

Susan Furlong's apartment was cold. The air conditioner was set too low. No one else was there to turn it up, and the cold kept her wrapped up in her bed. Outside it was 91 degrees at four-thirty in the afternoon.

In the last eight years, she had been Susan Franklin, Sandra Frost, Susan Frisch, and Sarah Freund.

Susan Furlong was a brunette, as was Susan Frisch. Sandra Frost was a light redhead. Sarah Freund had been blond, which was closer to Susan's real color—light brown.

And the real Susan was Susan Ferlinghetti. Although the problem right now in the twilight moment from sleep to consciousness was whether or not there was a real Susan Ferlinghetti anymore.

Sometimes Susan had to stop and convince herself she had it right. That happened too often, and it never failed to remind her of the day not too long ago when she woke up with a nose bleeding from snorting too much cocaine, not knowing the name she was using, where she was, or how she got there. And not being able to completely sort it out for almost five minutes. That was truly terrifying.

That was the day she determined that she would never let her life slip so far away from her again. It had only taken about four years for it to get out of control. But the process had started a long time before that. Probably at the moment she first realized she was so beautiful, so extraordinary that with the right smile or raising of an eyebrow or direct gaze with her piercing green eyes, she could get most of what she wanted.

By the time she was twelve, Susan knew she had an almost frightening power over boys. There wasn't one of them in the entire seventh grade who would refuse her anything. The smart ones gave her their homework and answers to tests. The tough ones gave her protection from anyone who would dare bother her.

Susan was the kind of girl that boys would stare at and not care if they got caught. She was the kind of girl who drove Sister Mary Agnes Theresa crazy. The nun constantly yelled at her for being brazen. She snatched at the belt on Susan's school uniform, pulling it and loosening it so it wouldn't emphasize Susan's figure, which was already fuller and more stunning than many women's.

And Susan was just there, not even trying. She took her looks and her body just as they were. She accepted the power she had without really thinking about it. She had other things to think about. She had her mother, Marie, who had to work like a slave because her worthless husband was either gone, or drunk when he did show up. And she had her sister Rosalie, who was the smartest kid in school but was also skinny and nervous and frail. And she had Cecilia.

In those days, kids like Cecilia weren't called special kids or disadvantaged or Down syndrome kids. They were called Mongoloids, or just dummies.

Ceece never meant to cause any problem or pain, but even when Susan was twelve, she knew that someday, someone would have to take care of Ceece.

And Susan loved Ceece too much to let anything bad happen to her. Susan had loved Ceece from the day she was born. She was so cute. So sweet. Susan and Rosalie would play with her for hours. And for years, Ceece stayed tiny and playful and funny. Like a little monkey. A toy. A doll. Susan used to think, if Ceece could have only stayed that way, so tiny and cute, someone would always love her and care for her.

The nuns let Ceece stay at St. Cornelia grammar school through the eighth grade. Most of the time the kids treated her well. While

Susan was in the school, no one dared make fun of Ceece. If anybody made Ceece cry, there were plenty of older boys ready to prove to Susan no one could get away with that. Ceece had her place in the school and the neighborhood for a good long while. After grammar school, Ceece stayed home with Marie. And after Marie . . . Susan knew it would be up to her to find a place for Ceece.

By high school, Susan was very pragmatic about her beauty. She used it to cultivate the right guy. Get to the right parties. Ride in the best cars. There was always a look that made every boy sit up and do her bidding.

But Susan knew that was kid's stuff. She knew that someday her body and her face and piercing eyes and shining hair would have to earn enough to take care of Marie and Ceece. Especially Ceece.

When she was sixteen, Susan figured her best shot was to become an actress. A movie star. When she told her mother her plan, Marie treated it like everything else . . . just something happening at the moment that would soon pass. Rosalie wanted to get on American Bandstand, Ceece wanted to fly in an airplane, Susan wanted to be an actress.

"Fine," said Marie. "After you finish high school and enough college to earn a living, then you can be an actress."

Susan was too smart to argue. She sat and listened to her mother, but she knew what she was going to do whether her mom liked it or not.

Susan did finish high school. Then she enrolled in Manhattan Community College, and Marie let her get an apartment in the city. Within six weeks she stopped going to class and started working full-time.

By January she had enrolled in the American Academy of Dramatic Arts on Madison and 36th Street, and she was on her own, pursuing her dream.

Too late for Marie or anybody else to do anything about it because Susan had her own place and her own money and she made sure to send fifty dollars of it back home every month no matter what. If she had to survive on one can of tuna fish a day and pay the rent late and wash her clothes by hand, she sent Marie and Ceece that fifty dollars.

The dream kept her going. It seemed so easy to make that dream start to happen. She remembered exactly how she felt when Lloyd Cuttler, the director of the Academy, told her she had passed her audition and handed her the contract to fill out. A contract. She was already signed up to be a star. February 1979. The movie just hadn't hit the theaters yet.

She was so excited the day she enrolled that she had to sit down at a Chock Full O'Nuts on Madison and order a cup of coffee. She glowed. She wanted to laugh. She couldn't stop smiling. The waitress who served the coffee stared at her.

The dream and the excitement lasted about two months before it all started to turn sour.

Her apartment was on the sub-ground floor of a townhouse on 38th between Lexington and Third. When you first walked in, it could almost seem charming, but after you'd lived a couple of weeks in the gloom, the charm was gone.

And the money to pay for it was difficult to accumulate every month.

Susan worked as a waitress, a sales clerk at Macy's, then at Bloomingdale's, then as a waitress again. She worked all day. Hard. Then she went to classes at the Academy four nights a week.

It didn't take her long to realize that just about anyone who could walk and talk would have passed that *audition*.

And for some reason, her instructors seemed to make a point about not letting Susan think she was special. She purposely held back directing the "look" at her instructors. She wanted to be recognized for her talent. She knew they watched her. She knew they were looking at her face and her body, but it seemed they were paying less attention to her because she was beautiful. It was as if the ugly girls were going to be the real actresses, and she was just going to be some bimbo.

Her classmates were even worse.

Susan worked hard in her acting classes, but she always felt as if she were struggling upstream against a constant flow of egos. Every gesture, every word, before, during, and after class was from someone trying to get attention. No one had any desire to pay anyone else any attention because they wanted it all for themselves. It was very different for the girl who had always been the center of attention without really trying.

Outside, of course, there was plenty of attention paid to Susan Ferlinghetti. Outside the men were there, and that saved Susan and condemned her at the same time.

In the restaurants where she worked owners, bartenders, and waiters came on to her. As did the customers. At Macy's and Bloomingdale's, it was male bosses and customers. The men who tried too hard to meet her while she was waiting on them were usually the most fun—and the biggest pains in the ass. The bosses were generally good for the best meals. Fellow workers were invariably the worst.

During that first year, Susan carefully picked out a steady set of three men. One was William, a wealthy married man who bought her the best meals, lots of clothes, and sometimes even jewelry. Once in a while, a weekend away.

Richard was her second steady. He was the most beautiful man she had ever seen. She picked him up. He was dining alone and reading a book while he ate. Richard turned out to be gay, which was a relief.

She never had to sleep with Richard, but he was always willing to keep her company. Richard taught her more than any man she had ever been with.

Their dates were generally Saturday or Sunday afternoons. Parts of the week that Susan hated to be alone. They went to museums, galleries, and theater matinees. She learned how to gossip with Richard. She learned who was in, what was hip, and how to make the right cutting remark or shrug something off. Susan even learned how to read *The New Yorker* from Richard.

The third steady was Bruce. He appeared to be normal. He was single. He was handsome. And there was no reason at all that Susan shouldn't relax and enjoy being with him. Unfortunately, Bruce was an alcoholic who refused to admit it.

Dates were Knicks games or movies or dancing in the latest place. But every date started with dinner, and every dinner ended with Bruce drunk enough to keep himself firmly separated from reality. Bruce even mixed a half-pint of Jack Daniel's with his Coke in the movies. Bruce was the only one who was really exciting in bed. He would do anything. The booze made him wild.

Interspersed with her steady three were occasional flings with men who could provide her with what she needed at the time. A meal. A ticket to a play she wanted to see. A limo ride home. A gram of coke. Entree to the hottest club. Sometimes a couple of hundred-dollar bills. She had to pay the rent after all. And send money to Marie and Ceece. And pay Ceece's increasing medical bills. And fill out applications for state schools. And hope Marie would hang in with her arthritis and congestive heart and swollen ankles for long enough until Ceece got into a good state school. They said the waiting list was five years.

Eventually, Susan stopped her acting classes. She gave up on the endless auditions. And gradually gave up real jobs. Without thinking about it or planning it, Susan Ferlinghetti had become a soft hooker. And if she had any doubt about that being the hard truth, Robert Wexler taught Susan what she had become once and for all.

Susan checked the clock next to her bed. The red digital numbers said 5:27 P.M.

Wexler would be coming to pick her up for dinner around eight-thirty. They would eat at some restaurant by ten. After dinner, Wexler would visit various clubs and nightspots until about three in the morning. By three-thirty, Susan would be in place as the hostess in Wexler's after-hours club. By that time, he would essentially be done with her, and she would have consumed a sufficient amount of alcohol to greet the guests. She knew the alcohol had replaced the cocaine habit. But she told herself she was controlling it. And she wouldn't get a hole in her nasal septum from drinking.

Susan Furlong got out of her bed and began the ritual of putting herself together for Robert Wexler.

CHAPTER 4

Devlin sat where Lettieri had left him and worked the phone. Bellevue Hospital, New York University Hospital, Lenox Hill Hospital, and Beth Israel had no George Devlin admitted in the last twenty-four hours. Neither had Mount Sinai, Columbia Presbyterian, Harlem Hospital, St. Luke's-Roosevelt, or Gouverneur.

Six hotels hadn't either.

Marilyn called him twice while he was looking up phone numbers. He'd kept her at bay. He didn't think he could do it a third time.

He threw the phone book on the floor and turned on the answering machine with the speaker on high so he could hear if George called, while he took a quick shower with the door open and changed into fresh clothes. The last vestiges of the night before were left in a pile on the bathroom floor.

His big brother who didn't have a mean bone in his body, and who had taken care of him more than once when they were growing up, was gone. Why? If someone had hurt his brother, Devlin was going to find out who, why, and make them pay for it. He was very good at doing all three.

#

Devlin met NYPD Detective David Freedman in a small park surrounded by constant traffic. It was in Abingdon Square in the West Village. A play park that would be crawling with little kids by early evening when their yuppie parents returned from work. But now at three in the afternoon it was empty except for a few homeless bums and two Jamaican ladies airing out infants and visiting with each other.

Years ago, Freedman had helped Devlin on a case that ended with a lot of people being killed but had made the NYPD look as if they'd solved a major crime. The case had also made Freedman a First Grade Detective, but he never wanted to live through anything like that case ever again.

Freedman approached Devlin with a deprecating smile and a shake of his head. He was a short, wiry man with kinky black hair and the tough manner of a New York cop who had lived in the town all his life. He stuck out his hand, and Devlin shook it. Freedman's first words were, "I see you're still alive, Jack."

"So far. How are you, David?"

"Still fighting the good fight."

"I appreciate you coming. And so soon. I know you must be busy."

"Yeah, yeah. You look like you've been hiding on a beach somewhere."

"On a sunny beach."

"Nice. Why are you here instead of there?"

"My father passed away. I came home for the funeral."

"Oy, shit. I'm sorry. It was sudden? How old?"

"Heart attack. He was eighty."

"He was healthy until then?"

"Yes. It was quick."

"I guess that's good. But it's a loss. I'm sorry."

"Thanks."

Freedman became the tough cop again. "So what the hell you want with me that won't get me into too much trouble?"

"I have a problem, David, and I want your advice."

Devlin told the cop about the post-funeral drinking with his brother, picking up Daryl, staying the night with her, and losing George.

Freedman shook his head slowly, "Wonderful. Perfect. Death, booze, and a blonde."

"Yeah. Reminds me of why I don't drink very much."

"I presume your brother is not the kind of guy who disappears for a while."

"No way. He's a citizen. Wife, kids, career, house in Westchester. The whole normal everyday scene. I've called hospitals and hotels. No record of any George Devlin."

"This isn't good, Jack. Not in this fucking city. What can I do to help?"

"Just answer a couple of questions, so I don't waste time."

"Shoot."

"If I file a missing persons report with the police, will anything much happen?"

"Not much. Certainly not before at least forty-eight hours. If there's crime involved, they might do something, but you don't know that yet. Or if the missing person is a retarded kid or something. Something that would make the *Post* come up with an interesting headline, like 'Retarded Blind Mute Yeshiva Student Lost in Harlem on School Trip.'

"Otherwise, the report gets entered into the computer, and the information basically sits there until something happens to wake the computer up and make it spit out a notice of some sort. Like if the missing person gets arrested. When they enter the name at Central Booking, it will kick out the missing persons on them.

"Otherwise a couple of days go by and the missing persons report gets assigned to a detective team who already has too much to do. The good teams will somehow remember the names and descriptions, and if they stumble across someone they'll go back and check and find out that yes, they remembered right and so-and-so is being sought after by such-and-such.

"You aren't going to have twenty-three thousand cops looking for your brother, but filing the report could do some good, and it certainly can't hurt you."

"Should I file it in the precinct where I lost him?"

"Yes. Although it's not like he lives in that precinct, so that complicates things. Where was it?"

"The one-nine. We were in a bar somewhere on Second Avenue in the upper Seventies."

"Know the name?"

"No. It was some Irish place. I'll be back there to find it tonight. Think it's important for the report?"

"Not really. I tell you what I'll do. You give me the information, and I'll file the report up in the one-nine. I'll make sure it gets into the channels fast and really gets assigned instead of just added to some guy's list."

"Thanks."

"I'm sorry there's not much else I can do."

"One other thing," Devlin said. "If I'm going to really canvass the hospitals and hotels I'll need some help. He could be registered under a different name or as a John Doe waiting in a crowded emergency room somewhere. I need someone who can get around and see if anybody matching my brother's description was admitted. Do you know a reliable private detective?"

"Yeah, but what about your people at Pacific Rim? They must know someone in New York. You could get professional rates or something, right?"

"Yes, but I'd rather not have them involved unless I have to. At the moment, things are a little strained between us."

"What things?"

"I think I've been trying to avoid doing the work, David. I don't feel right about some parts of it."

"The killing part."

"Yes. The killing part."

"But if something happened to your brother I'll bet you'd almost enjoy killing that person."

Devlin stared at Freedman. The detective had a tough, uncompromising look. Freedman had long ago decided some people deserved to be killed and made no apologies, but Freedman was smart enough to know that he was implying George might be dead, and he apologized.

"Hey, I'm sorry. That was stupid. The main thing is to find your brother. Especially now. My father died two years ago. It wasn't a good feeling. I got a brother and a sister. Believe me, we're closer now. This ain't the time to lose your brother.

"I know a guy who can help you. A good, honest detective, if there is such a thing. His name is Sam Zitter. He's getting to be a crotchety old fart, but he knows what he's doing, and he gets around. He'll give you a full day's effort. He has a lot of contacts which more than make up for his age slowing him down a little bit. He's right near here, too. Go see him. He's over on Eighth Avenue, just below Fourteenth Street. The name of the place is Intrepid Investigations. Give his receptionist my name. Otherwise he probably won't see you."

"Okay. Thanks, David."

Freedman stood up. "Let me know if you need anything else."

"I will. Take care, David."

"You, too. Let me know how it turns out."

"I will."

"Sorry for your troubles, Jack."

Devlin watched him walk away and knew that David Freedman was genuinely sorry for his troubles. They both knew the troubles were far from over.

CHAPTER 5

Robert Wexler lived most of his life after dark. So he was just finishing the routine that began his day when Devlin was ending his meeting with Freedman. It was a routine Wexler greatly relished because it provided the opportunity to enjoy his possessions, alone, without distractions. Waking up meant enjoying his silk pajamas, showering meant caressing the ivory inlays of his custom shower faucets, eating breakfast gave him the chance to enjoy his sterling silverware and English china.

Wexler even enjoyed breathing the cool air pumped out by his air conditioners. Robert Wexler bought and paid for those things. He owned them. He used them. They were his to do with as he pleased.

After his late afternoon breakfast, Wexler dressed in light cotton khaki slacks from Paul Stuart, a crisp, blue Turnbull & Asser shirt with a conservative striped silk tie, and a tropical weight blue blazer made for him by a custom tailor on Fifty-seventh Street.

He checked the slim Tag-Heuer watch on his wrist and saw it was precisely 8 p.m. Robert Wexler, five-ten, nicely graying hair, a trim 165 pounds, attractively tanned and perfectly groomed, was ready to step out into the cooling end of a hot summer New York evening.

He didn't have to call his Sutton Place building's garage. He knew that when he descended from his apartment on the twenty-fifth floor, his car and his driver would be waiting for him in front of the building.

Wexler knew the gold Mercedes 560 SEL would be glistening, and his driver Randy would be standing at the back door ready to open it. Once, not too long ago, Randy had lost track of time and was sitting in the front seat reading the newspaper when Wexler came downstairs.

Without a second's hesitation, Wexler informed the driver that he was fired. He told the stunned young man to get out of the car. He then got behind the wheel and drove off himself. But that was just the beginning.

The next day, there was an eviction notice nailed to the door of Randy's apartment. The same day his bank informed him there was a lien filed on his checking and savings accounts for money owed the corporation that had hired him. The following day Equitable Insurance sent him a notice he would have thirty days to renew his health insurance at his own cost. And the Taxi and Limousine Commission sent him a notice to appear for a disciplinary hearing or his chauffeur's license would automatically be revoked.

A competent law firm would have successfully fought all the actions for Randy if he had thousands to pay them. But, of course, he didn't. His only alternative was to call Wexler and beg. Which he did.

Wexler held the phone to his ear and thought about making Randy grovel even more, but decided it was a pleasure he would postpone for some time in the future when he would fire him once and for all without any reprieve.

For the time being, he told the chauffeur, "All right, Randy. Perhaps you've learned your lesson. Meet me with the car at the usual time tonight."

The nightmare stopped. The legal actions stopped. His health insurance continued.

Now when Randy parked the Mercedes in front of the building on Sutton Place, he immediately got out and stood by the back door. Even if he was ten or fifteen minutes early, Randy got out and stood by the door. He never, ever sat in the car waiting. He did what he was told. Wexler owned him.

\#

Susan Furlong glanced at the small electronic clock on her dressing table. The digital numbers read 8:11. Wexler's key would be turning in the lock sometime between 8:15 and 8:30, but Susan never had any warning. Wexler was never announced by the doorman. He simply appeared and walked into the apartment. He owned it. And as far as he was concerned, Wexler owned Susan, too.

Her duty as his chattel was to be beautiful, to be dressed attractively, and to be ready to greet him when he walked in.

And as soon as he sat down, she had to excuse herself and fetch Wexler a perfectly chilled glass of Mimosa made from fresh-squeezed orange juice and a newly opened split of Moet & Chandon Champagne. That was the routine. Of course, Susan had been manipulating men for much too long to let Wexler control her completely. She played Wexler's domination game, but with just enough defiance to let him know there wasn't any guarantee she would always do as she was told. She kept telling herself that challenging him just a little meant she wasn't totally his. Unfortunately, Wexler enjoyed the lurking defiance that was in her. He liked the challenge. It was an insidious and dangerous game. And like most gambles, the more Susan played, the more chance she had of losing everything.

With very little time left, Susan had three more nails to paint, the orange wasn't squeezed yet, and she was down to her last split of champagne. The clock said 8:13. She dashed off a slash of Revlon red sherbet on the nail of her little finger, carefully closed the bottle and put it away because Robert did not like a messy bedroom and rushed into the kitchen.

On the way, she willed a vision of cabs and trucks blocking his way, and she screamed. It was a loud, shrieking yell that helped release some of the agony and tension.

She took out a large Sunkist orange from the vegetable bin in her refrigerator. It was the last one. She cut it in half in one stroke and pushed it down hard on the Braun electric juicer and watched as the juice flowed slowly into the champagne glass she had placed under the spout. It barely filled a quarter of the glass. She took the second half of the orange and watched it produce enough juice to fill the glass to just above the halfway mark. Enough.

And then, she heard it—the sound of a key in her door.

She quickly placed the glass of juice into the freezer section. It had to be chilled.

Then she literally ran to the front door. Thank God Wexler insisted on two locks being engaged at all times.

She was in place just seconds before the door opened. But she was still a good enough actress to make it look as if she had been waiting there for five minutes.

She hoped the smile wasn't too tight. She hoped Wexler couldn't see the small beads of moisture at her hairline. She hoped he didn't want a second mimosa as he sometimes did.

"Robert darling, how nice to see you this evening."

Wexler paused and observed. It was all right. Barely. And then he examined Susan's captivating smile and let himself be absorbed into the moment. Her eyes were glistening with the tension and ferocity he enjoyed. Her high, well-defined cheekbones set off the classic line of her nose. Her mouth was closed and turned down in a slightly arrogant smile. He looked at her mouth, her neck, the skin of her chest, the rise of her full breasts under her light summer dress. He looked all the way down her calves to her shoes. Perhaps they needed a shine, but by then Susan's body and beauty had captured Wexler. The pleasure of Susan was exquisitely incomplete. Wexler was smart enough to know that he didn't own her totally and completely yet. Not as long as he couldn't accept the thought of losing her.

"Susan, how nice to see you."

The evening charade had begun.

CHAPTER 6

It was a short walk from the park where he had met Detective Freedman to the office of Sam Zitter. It occupied a storefront on Eighth Avenue near 13th Street. The entire front window was painted over. The background color was dark yellow. A large blue insignia bore the words "Intrepid Private Investigations" wrapped around a star that looked like a sheriff's badge.

Devlin entered and found himself in a small foyer that ran the width of the office. There were three chairs against the left wall. They were covered in faded, green Naugahyde. The floor was linoleum tile, also green. The walls were covered in dark wood paneling and green plaster. Facing the front door and running along the width of the room was a partition made of the same wood paneling. Into the partition was cut a large bulletproof Plexiglas window and a tin-clad door. Devlin didn't see any receptionist behind the Plexiglas.

Next to the door was a small sign. It said to ring the buzzer and be seated.

Devlin rang the buzzer and sat on one of the green chairs. He noticed the video security camera trained on him from a corner of the ceiling.

He waited five minutes, got up and rang the bell again. After five more minutes, he heard a rapping on the thick Plexiglas window. Behind it was a man who appeared to be in his late fifties. He looked as though he had been chopped out of a large block of stone. He was a chunk of a man, about six feet tall. He had thick short-cropped salt-and-pepper hair. He shouted through the Plexiglas, "You Devlin?"

Devlin stood up and said, "Yes."

The door opened, and Sam Zitter extended his hand. "I just got off the phone with Freedman. You sound like quite a character. Come on in."

Devlin never thought of himself as a *character*. He followed the stocky man through an office area with two desks, down a small corridor to a back office. Zitter was wearing a green sport jacket over blue pants. He had on a button-down beige oxford shirt with no tie. Devlin wondered if the man was color-blind.

Zitter's office was clean, uncluttered, and neatly arranged. There were no papers or files piled on his desk. The floor was carpeted. The furniture old but not beat up.

Zitter settled his considerable weight into a high-backed executive chair behind his large desk and told Devlin, "Sit down. Sit down. Tell me what I can do for you."

"How much did David explain?"

"Nothing about your problem. Just about you. I like to have a background on the people I do business with, if possible. You have a pretty goddamn interesting one. New York cop for all of six months. Military police in Vietnam. Secret Service. Now with some security outfit on the West Coast. Pacific Rim," he said.

"Yes."

"I've heard of them. Oriental fellow runs that."

"Yes."

"Tell me, how come you quit the force after six months? Number one in your class and all that.'

"I didn't want to go on the pad. And I didn't want anybody being suspicious of me because I wasn't.

"Seems kind of extreme."

"I tended to be a little all or nothing in those days."

"Sounds like it. Maybe you saved yourself a lot of grief."

"What made you quit?"

Zitter shrugged. "I had a different beef."

"What rank did you make?"

"Detective First Grade."

"That's as good as it gets."

"About par for the years I put in."

"What did you work?"

"After uniforms, I worked burglary and safes for a number of years. Then mostly on homicide squads. Passed civil service exams up to Lieutenant. Moved out of the Detective Division and ended up the whip of the one-oh."

"Kojak's precinct."

"Right. You know we used to get goddamn Japanese tourists showing up wanting to see Kojak?

"I heard that."

"It's true. Anyhow, what's your problem, Mr. Devlin? How can I help you?"

Devlin quickly told him about his missing brother. Zitter listened with knit brows. He shoved on a pair of reading glasses to jot a couple of notes on a yellow legal pad, then tossed the pen and the glasses on the desk. Devlin figured he must go through several pairs a year.

When Devlin was done, Zitter asked, "So you've filed a missing persons with the cops, but you want me to get involved."

"I didn't file a report. Freedman offered to file it for me. But I can't wait for the cops. I want to find my brother now, and I can't do it all by myself. I need someone to make the rounds at hospitals and hotels. I've done what I can on the phone. But George could be in a hospital as a John Doe. And I only checked hospitals in Manhattan. The only way I'll know for sure is if someone goes to emergency rooms and checks it out."

"What are you going to be doing instead?"

"I'm going back to the bar I left him in and start from there."

Zitter thought about that for a second but didn't comment.

He slipped his glasses on and looked at his notes. "You say he's about six-six, two-sixty?"

"Right."

"That's a big man. Even bigger than you."

"George has a couple of inches and forty pounds on me."

"It shouldn't be too hard to find him even if he got admitted without identification. I know people in some of these emergency rooms he might have ended up in."

"Good."

"What was he wearing when you left him?"

"Dark suit. White shirt. Blue tie. Black tie shoes. Funeral clothes."

Zitter jotted notes. "You've got no idea what might have happened?"

"None."

"Your brother isn't the type to disappear on his own, is he?"

"Mr. Zitter—"

"Sam. Call me Sam."

"Sam, we both know anything is possible. But I just don't see my brother doing that. At least not this way. Not at the end of a drunken night out with me. Not the day we bury our father. It's a hell of a lot more likely that he got mugged, or maybe smacked by a car or something."

Again, Zitter stared at Devlin for a couple of seconds without saying anything. Then he leaned back and asked, "What's your brother like?" Devlin watched Zitter and thought that he would have asked that question, too.

"Does anybody know what another person is really like? As far as I know my brother is a regular guy. He's got a wife and two kids. Lives in the suburbs. Has a good job. It's absolutely typical. But what else is there? It would just be guessing. If you talked to Freedman, you know there are people in this town who would want to hurt me. But as far as I know none of them have any idea that I have a brother.

"What else? He's bigger than ninety-five percent of the people you meet. But that never seemed to cause him trouble. It never made him a bully or anything like that. In fact, just the opposite. He always went out of his way *not* to take advantage of his size."

Zitter asked, "He's not an all-or-nothing guy like you? Not a hothead?"

"The only time something ever makes him lose his temper is if things are unfair."

"For instance."

Devlin had to think for a moment to come up with an example. "The last time I saw him get really mad at something was when we were kids. We were playing football in high school. The other team gets off this school bus and walks out onto the field. A big Puerto Rican kid comes up to me as I'm sitting on a park bench waiting to head over to the field. Asks me what position I play. I tell him fullback. He says, 'Let's see you run with a broken toe,' and he stomps right on top of my foot with his spikes. Wham! Hurt like hell. He takes off, running over to his team. I start limping after him, but he's got a good lead on me. My brother, my big brother George, saw what happened and he was just in the right position to cut him off. He gave that kid a forearm that almost took his head off. Then he picked him up and started beating the shit out of him. It took three grown men, coaches, to pull him off. Almost started a riot with that other team. But that was my brother. Once he saw that, nothing was going to stop him. It wasn't fair."

"How was your toe?"

Devlin shrugged. "The football shoes took most of it. I scored three touchdowns that day. We whipped their asses. Pushed 'em all over the field. They were big and mean, but they didn't have any decent coaching. No technique. We beat 'em without my brother. The other team refused to play if George was allowed in the game."

"Really. How'd he take that?"

"Didn't bother him at all. He'd done what he wanted. We were winning. He spent his time cheering everyone on and helping the Waterboys. But listen, so what? It's just a story. I happen to think my brother is the nicest guy in the world, but what difference does it make? I can run lots of scenarios in my head about what might have happened and why. But I still don't know. We have to check the obvious answers and start from there."

Zitter leaned forward in his chair and put both elbows on the desk. His questions were over. "You're right. I'll get to work. The rate at my agency is seventy-five dollars per hour. On a job like this, I usually contract a ten-hour retainer. Plus expenses, which should be minimal for this."

"Fine. Can you start tonight?"

"I can."

"Good. How can I keep in touch with you?"

Call my beeper number. Zitter handed Devlin his business card. When you hear a tone, punch in a number where I can reach you."

"I'll be on the move," said Devlin.

"So will I. Stay at a payphone or whatever for five minutes. If I don t call you back in five minutes, try me again later."

"If you find him before I call you, I'll want to know right away. How can you reach me?"

Zitter reached into a desk and pulled out another beeper. He checked the number on the back and wrote it on his legal pad.

Here, you carry one, too. Stick it in your pocket. These don't beep. I don't carry anything that beeps. Put it where you can feel it. When it vibrates look at this readout here on the top. Then call me at that number within five minutes."

Devlin put the beeper in his pocket. "Okay."

"I'll work until about one or two, but that's it. At my age, I gotta get some decent sleep, or I fall apart. I'll start with the Manhattan hospitals the EMS guys use most of the time. If I don't find him, I'll start checking hospitals in the other boroughs and maybe some hotels tomorrow. That's going to be a lot harder. . . . "

"We'll talk about that when we get there."

Zitter gave Devlin another thoughtful stare. He didn't much like being interrupted, but he let it go.

"Okay. We'll take it step by step."

Devlin stood up and put out his hand. Zitter shook it with a meaty hand went with his thick body. Devlin took out eight one-hundred-dollar bills and laid them on the desk.

"Here's for the ten hours and some expenses."

"Let me give you a receipt."

"Give it to me with the final bill."

Please, Mr. Devlin, it'll just take a minute. I don't want to have to worry about any confusion. And I want you to sign my contract and release."

Zitter quickly filled out a receipt and a standard contract. Devlin pocketed the receipt and signed the forms without looking at either of them.

He thanked the burly ex-cop again and left.

Devlin figured he had a couple of hours to kill before he tracked down the Irish bar. He wanted to get there when the late-night bartender was on. Enough time to eat, grab some sleep, and call Marilyn. She must be going crazy by now, thought Devlin. He sure as hell didn't want to have to make any more calls without something more to say than, "I'm still looking, don't worry."

#

Dinner for Susan and Wexler that night was at a small Italian restaurant in Chelsea. The food was expensive, the waiters effusive, but it seemed to Susan to be one of the few places where the meal was worth the high price. She had never eaten Italian food that was served so nicely and tasted so refined.

She started the meal with a vodka martini. For dinner, Wexler ordered a Mondavi Chardonnay, which she helped drink. She ended the meal with coffee and a Grand Marnier.

For most people that much alcohol would be consumed during a leisurely evening meal that would end a long day. For Susan, it was the beginning of her day. It was like drinking through breakfast.

The night would continue now, on into the morning, until almost noon. The alcohol would continue, too. Never enough to make her sloppy drunk, but always enough to keep things in soft focus so that she was insulated from the sharpest pain of being treated like Wexler's servant.

After dinner Wexler would visit four or five clubs or restaurants with Susan. He enjoyed the impression he made when he walked in with Susan, but his appearance with or without her always commanded the right level of attention because each place they visited was owned by Wexler. They would be shown to a quiet table. When Wexler deemed it appropriate, Susan would be sent to tell the manager to visit Wexler's table. No matter how imperious Wexler's managers were when they dealt with the public, when Susan told them Wexler wanted to see them, the men immediately stopped what they were doing and quickly reported to his table.

Susan was not allowed to return to the table until Wexler was finished. Occasionally, Susan would watch Wexler conduct his business. Wexler mostly listened. The little bit he did say made the person listening nod his head quickly. A few times Susan spotted Wexler receiving the thick envelopes of cash that were discreetly passed to him.

When Wexler dismissed the person at his table, Susan could return. It was demeaning to step and fetch for Wexler, but at least Susan didn't have to entertain him with compliments or conversation. Once the evening started, Wexler rarely spoke to Susan. In his opinion, hardly anyone merited his attention. They were either too stupid or too unimportant. And so it went. A night with Robert Wexler.

CHAPTER 7

It took Devlin a little longer than he expected to find the bar. Which was another reason to curse himself for being so drunk the night before.

His alcohol-impaired memory told him the bar was in the Seventies, so he had started walking on the east side of Second Avenue at 69th Street. He didn't find the bar until 82nd Street. It was called O'Callahan's. An upscale version of an Irish bar—dark woods, brass, and marble. Wooden bar stools, wooden booths, and sawdust on the wooden floor. There were two waitresses serving meals and drinks to the booth patrons in the front and to more people at the tables in the back room. Two bartenders were busy behind the bar. One bartender took care of the customers, the other concentrated on supplying drinks to the waitresses.

It was ten o'clock, and the place was busy.

It didn't stop Devlin from quizzing the bartender he recognized from the night before.

Devlin smiled at him and asked, "Bartender, what's your name? A young Irishman with unruly brown hair and a quick smile offered his hand and said, "Brian, sir. Good evening."

Devlin shook his hand and said, "Hello, Brian, I was in last night,

The bartender spoke with a thick Irish brogue. "Yes, sir, I remember you. Late it was. You and a big fellow. He was playing darts with some of the boys."

"Yes. That was my brother."

"Uh-huh."

"Do you remember what time he left?"

Someone called for a drink, and the bartender apologized and turned away to serve his customer. Devlin waited patiently as he filled three more orders.

When the Irishman returned, he apologized again. Devlin wondered why he was so polite. Someone working a New York bar at the peak of business didn't owe anybody a lot of time.

"So, let me think now—what time did your brother leave? I'm not sure, but it was almost closing."

"You close at four?"

"Yes, but after one or two o'clock if it gets slow we close up. Your brother left just about the time I was going to ask the fellas to wind up their game."

"So they finished their game?"

"Yes. That was it. They'd had enough to drink, let me tell you. After the game I told them I had to close up. No one else was here."

"Did they all leave together?"

"Did they leave together? Well, I guess. I can't really say for sure. They all left at about the same time. I don't know if they stayed together or not. I don't imagine there would be many bars open at that hour if they wanted to continue with their drinking."

"About what time was that?"

"What time? Well, it had to be close to three. When I closed up and left, it was near to three-thirty."

The way the bartender said it, it sounded like "tray-terty."

"Thanks, Brian."

"Certainly, can I get you a drink?"

"Let me have a glass of club soda."

Devlin sat sipping the club soda. He was trying to decide why he didn't like the bartender. Too polite. Too many of his questions repeated, which is one way liars give themselves time to think up answers.

Devlin glanced at his watch. It was 10:45. His next move was to either wait and see if any of the dart players showed up or start checking other bars in the area.

He finished the club soda, left five dollars on the bar, and turned to leave. Just then Daryl Austen walked in. She was wearing blue jeans, suede half-boots, and a dazzling white shirt.

Devlin had the feeling she had intentionally dressed down, but jeans and a white shirt on her body looked sexy and attractive and smart. She had on a simple pearl necklace, and the white shirt was unbuttoned just enough to show the beginning of her lovely cleavage.

She walked directly up to Devlin as if they had made an appointment to meet.

"I was wondering if you'd be back here tonight.

"I didn't expect to see you."

"Oh. I thought that was why you came back."

"Uh, no."

"Why then?" she said. "That's why I came."

Devlin didn't respond.

"Hey what's the matter, Devlin? I thought we left on pretty good terms this morning. Did your brother get home okay?

"No."

"No? What happened?"

"I don't know. That's why I'm here. I'm trying to track him down."

"God, this is terrible."

"Do you know any of those guys he was playing darts with last night?"

She stopped to remember, then her face brightened, and she said, "Yeah, as a matter of fact. One of them is a guy named Richard Meisner. He comes in here a lot. He's a funny little guy. I get a kick out of him because he does this routine where he tries to hit on me, and when I ignore him, he makes believe that's my way of coming on to him. It's impossible for me not to laugh. He even did it one night when I was with Bill. I guess he figures nobody's going to hit him because he's so short."

Devlin asked, "Bill is the guy you split up with?"

"Yes."

"Did this Meisner give you his phone number?

"About fifty times. He used to write it on bar napkins, but I just kept throwing them away."

"Is his number listed?

"Let's find out. I think he said he lives in the Fifties somewhere. I'll call information."

Devlin watched her as she walked to the payphones at the back of the bar. Her tangled blond hair came down to the middle of her back. The jeans fit her long legs and round derriere perfectly. Devlin noticed he wasn't the only one in the bar watching her walk to the phones.

She was back quickly. She sat on the bar stool next to Devlin and told him, "He said he'd be here in fifteen minutes."

"He wasn't kidding, was he?"

"No, I told him about the problem. He knows I'm serious."

Devlin frowned but didn't say anything. He motioned for another club soda.

Daryl asked, "What's the matter?"

"I'm not sure I want you getting involved in this."

"Why?"

"I don't know."

"You're not pissed that I came looking for you tonight, are you?"

"No. I guess I'm glad you did. You've saved me time, finding one of the guys he was with last night."

"So how come I didn't hear a 'thanks' or something like that."

"Thanks."

"That doesn't sound like thanks."

"Look, I'm sorry. The thought that something happened to my brother is making me crazy."

"Well, what do you think happened?"

Her question stopped Devlin. Not even Zitter had been as direct and to the point as Daryl Austen.

Suddenly Devlin asked, "Where are you from, Daryl?"

"Pittsburgh, why?"

"You don't sound like a New Yorker."

"Are you avoiding my question?"

"Yeah. I don't like running down the answers in my head."

"Devlin, are you a cop or something?"

"What makes you ask?"

"I don't know, you sound like you've been through this before."

"I'm not a cop. I guess I'm a 'something.' I work for a private security company on the West Coast. Yeah, I have been through this before."

"Private security? What's that? Like a detective agency or something?"

"Sort of."

"Well, I'm sorry about all this shit that's fallen on you. Your father. Your brother. I just wanted to help."

"I know. Thanks. Really, thanks."

You're welcome. Buy me a beer while we wait."

Devlin ordered a Sam Adams for Daryl and another club soda for himself. Meisner showed up before they finished their drinks. He was short and skinny with slicked-back dark hair. He had on a white shirt and canary-yellow Bermuda shorts that were too big for him. He walked with his head down and seemed to bounce with each step. He approached Daryl and put his hand on her shoulder.

"Daryl honey," he said.

Daryl swiveled around on her bar stool and stood up. She was a full head taller than Meisner. He looked at Devlin, who also stood, and said, "This isn't some trick to get me down here so this giant can kick my ass for bothering you all your life, is it?"

Daryl answered, "No, Richard, we really do have a problem.

Devlin introduced himself and asked Meisner if they could talk at a table in the back of the restaurant.

"Sure. Anything you say, big fella."

The three of them settled in at a table. As soon as they sat down, Devlin tried to make Meisner feel at ease.

"I'm sorry we rousted you out to come down here, but I've got a problem. Daryl has been kind enough to help me, and I wanted to ask for your help, too."

Meisner squinted in an attempt to look concerned and said, "Yeah, sure. What the hell's the problem?"

"Last night I was in here with my brother. Late. Remember that big guy you were playing darts with?

"Uh, yeah. That was your brother?"

"Yes.

"Nice guy."

"Thanks."

"You left, and he stayed here and played darts."

"Right. I left before him."

Meisner gave Daryl a quick sidelong glance just to let her know he knew who Devlin left with.

Devlin continued, "The problem is, my brother has disappeared."

"What do you mean?"

"He was staying with me in the city. He lives up in Larchmont. He was supposed to meet me at my apartment, and he never showed up."

"Never?"

"No. I've got to find him. Or find out what happened to him. Did you guys stick together after the game?"

"Man, that sounds weird. No, we didn't stick together. I mean, I didn't. After the game, we had a round of drinks, and then I left. It was pretty late. I had to get home and get some sleep. Your brother and the other two guys were still here when I left. Still going at it pretty good, too."

"Who were those guys he was with? Do you know them?"

"No. Never met them before. I think they were Irish, maybe one was a Brit. They were together. Me and your brother— George . . .?"

"Yeah."

". . . me and George teamed up against them."

"Who won?"

"They did."

"Were you playing for money?"

Meisner shrugged. "Yeah. Five bucks a game. We lost five bucks each. No big deal."

"No bad feelings?"

"Nah. No way. We each paid 'em the five, and they bought the drinks after the game. Everybody was real friendly. Unless your brother got into some beef with them after I left. But I really doubt it."

"So who were these guys? They live in the neighborhood?"

"I don't know." Meisner's brow furrowed in concentration. "I think maybe one of 'em did. I really don't know."

"You remember their names?"

"One was Sean. What the hell was the other guy's name?"

Daryl urged him, "Come on, Richard, you're good with names."

Devlin gave her a look that told her not to interrupt.

Meisner looked at Daryl and seemed to lose his train of thought, then announced, "Bill! I think his name was Billy. Seemed like the other guy called him different names, like William and Billy or Robert and Bob. I don't know. I was half in the bag myself."

Devlin searched his own memory. He hated the fact that he had been too drunk to even notice who his brother was with, much less remember their names.

"So as far as you know, my brother was here with the two Irish guys when you left."

"Right. Still here. Still drinking. Still going strong."

"No idea of where these guys live?"

"Nah, I never asked 'em where they lived."

"All right. Thanks, Richard. I really appreciate it. Can I buy you a drink or something?"

"Well, I don't know. I start drinking here with Daryl, and she gets wild, you know. I gotta watch out."

Meisner couldn't help himself. Daryl gave him a stern look, and he stopped. "Sorry. Didn't mean to kid around. No thanks, Mr. Devlin, I'll take a pass. I should go back home. I was doing some work."

"Thanks again."

"No problem. I hope your brother turns up okay."

Daryl thanked him, too, and even let him shake her hand. He held her hand and stared into her eyes as if he were communicating an intimate feeling they both understood. Despite herself, Daryl started to roll her eyes and smile. Having succeeded in coaxing a smile out of her, he said, "See you, honey," and walked out of the bar with his bouncy walk.

Daryl asked Devlin, "Now what?"

"There's not much I can do between now and when this bar closes."

"What happens when the bar closes?"

"I'm not sure."

"You're not sure, or you're not telling me."

"I'm not telling you."

Devlin knew exactly what was going to happen. Meisner's information had achieved one thing. Devlin knew for sure Brian the bartender had lied to him. He hadn't hustled the dart players out so he could close up. He had kept serving them drinks long after the game was over.

"Well, if you're not telling me what you're doing will you at least walk me home?"

Devlin hesitated for two seconds, then said, "Yes."

CHAPTER 8

The world of after-hours started for Susan at about three o'clock in the morning, when she and Wexler arrived at the Starlight Club. The club opened at three-thirty, but they arrived early to set up.

After-hours meant after the licensed bars closed in New York. No bar could legally serve drinks after four. But that didn't mean people would stop drinking. For some, the real night started when the legitimate world's night ended.

When the after-hours crowd began drifting into the Starlight, they were screened by Bernie, a six seven, 240-pound black man who decided who entered.

The club was in an old loft building on lower Broadway near Grand Street. The lobby of the building was small and dingy, exactly like the lobby of a cheap-rent commercial building should be. During the day factory workers, messengers, Spanish women who operated sewing machines for sweatshop wages, truckers delivering boxes and crates—all passed through the lobby with the cracked tile floor and dingy walls and none of them had any idea that an after-hours club operated on the sixth floor.

But in the early morning hours, the lobby took on the fleeting glamor of something forbidden. Bernie stood behind a podium like a maitre d' and greeted the patrons as they entered.

Many of them had membership cards. The cards were red and bore the logo of the club—a fine-line pencil sketch of a woman with her forefinger to her lips. No telephone number. No address. Just the name **STARLIGHT** in white letters and the face of the woman. Card members were directed to the small self-service elevator. People without cards had to talk to Bernie. He judged them by their clothes, how drugged they were, their attitude, who had referred them. Some he let enter. Most of them were told there was no after-hours club in the building. Very few ever argued the point.

Once in the elevator, the patrons headed for the sixth floor, where they ran into Joe and Eddie, Wexler's prized team of bouncers.

Seeing Joe and Eddie quieted even the most boisterous drunks. Joe was 265 pounds packed onto a frame of heavy bones just under six three. Eddie was even bigger—280 pounds, six five. Both were in a constant contest to see whose arms, chest, calves, neck, or other body parts were bigger.

But it wasn't so much their bodies that quieted people as it was their faces. Joe and Eddie looked crazy. Whether it was the steroids they couldn't give up or just general psychosis or both, Joe and Eddie didn't look at people, they glared at them. They didn't smile, they grimaced. One look at Joe and Eddie and the natural reaction was to get away from them as soon as possible.

The two bouncers stood on each side of the final doorway to the Starlight, mammoth, barely controllable, filled with steroids and violence.

Joe and Eddie were seldom needed inside the club. But occasionally an argument or fight broke out, and they were unleashed. Wexler had given explicit orders that if they handled anyone they should do it with a degree of brutality that would impress and intimidate. But whatever they did had to be done outside the club. Wexler would not tolerate the slightest damage to himself or his property.

And the hostess of the Starlight was Susan Ferlinghetti. Wexler had strategically placed her in the club's foyer. After the guests had made it past the brutish presence of Bernie and Joe and Eddie, Susan was the visual prize that rewarded them. Her exotic beauty told them they had made it into someplace special.

Joe and Eddie threatened people, Susan welcomed them. They avoided looking at Joe and Eddie, but they couldn't stop looking at Susan. It was just the right combination of danger and attraction that Wexler wanted for the night crawlers who came to the Starlight Club.

\#

When Devlin agreed to walk Daryl home, he knew what would happen. But this time when Devlin and Daryl made love they were both sober and thoughtful.

There was no hiding in the alcohol. Both were careful with what they did because both knew the other person would miss nothing.

Daryl was open without being wanton. She was secure and natural in her lovemaking. Because her body was so flawless, she had no problems with showing it or letting Devlin enjoy it. She took the pleasure she wanted from Devlin, and because he let her, she was eager to give pleasure back to him. Daryl gave him the trim muscularity of her body, her long legs, firm buttocks, and perfect breasts. She kept moving into him, stroking his chest and back and neck. Kissing him all over and gently holding his balls while she licked and sucked his cock.

She liked the fact that Devlin was a big man. She kept holding him and embracing him tightly as if she could bury herself in his large, muscular body.

After it was over Daryl gently stroked Devlin's face and chest. She stared at the scars on his torso but didn't say anything about them. Then she suddenly scooted up on her knees and told him, "It's been a long time since I felt like that. If ever."

"That's nice to hear."

She lay right back down next to him as if she didn't want to let his body get away from her and asked, "What are you going to do? Do you want to stay?"

"I can't. There's something I have to do."

"So late?"

"It has to be in the dead of night."

"Really?"

"Really."

"What time is it?" she asked.

He looked at his watch. It was one o'clock. He resisted the urge to call Zitter. Then he realized the vibrating beeper had been away from his body for the last hour. He gently eased away from Daryl and asked, "Can I use your phone?"

"Sure."

He called the number Zitter had given him, hung up, and waited patiently next to the phone. In three minutes, it rang back. He picked up and quietly said, "Devlin."

"Zitter here. Nothing yet. I'll check one more hospital then start again in the morning."

"Okay. Thanks."

He gently replaced the phone and stretched out next to Daryl. "Who was that?"

"A detective I have helping me."

"Looking for your brother?"

"Yes."

"Has he found anything yet?"

"No."

"Are you sure you don't want to sleep and start again in the morning?"

"I'm going to sleep for an hour and then get out of here. Will that bother you? I'll be quiet."

She snuggled up to Devlin and told him, "No. I want to fall asleep next to you. I'll just make believe you got up early and went to work."

"That's what I'll be doing."

"On one hour of sleep?"

"It'll have to do."

She was already drifting off. "If you say so."

Devlin set his wristwatch alarm and closed his eyes. He thought about asking her what time she had to wake up, and if she had to get to work and what kind of work, but he put it all aside because right now that wasn't important. He closed his eyes and was in a deep sleep in less than three minutes.

When he woke to the softly beeping alarm, he was quickly wide awake. Daryl was still plastered against him with one arm and one leg draped over him. He liked the warm feel of her skin and breasts and crotch against him. She was tall enough to fit nicely against his tall frame. He eased himself away from her. She rolled over and curled up by herself. He got out of the bed and walked quietly to the bathroom, showered quickly, dressed, and left.

By 2:30 A.M. he was standing in the shadowy entrance to a hardware store across the street from O'Callahan's bar.

It was a quiet night. Warm but not hot. The city seemed to be finally cooling down from the day's heat. Devlin stood without moving, feeling the air, sensing the quiet. Maybe the humid spell was breaking, he thought.

He watched the last two patrons leave the bar. Brian, the bartender, began cleaning up the place. Fifteen minutes later, the cook and two young boys left the bar. All three speaking Spanish to each other.

Another fifteen minutes went by, and the bartender was finally at the bar's doorway. He turned and switched off the neon sign in the window, closed the front door and locked it. It looked as if he were about to hail a cab, but then he started walking uptown on Second Avenue.

Devlin quickly crossed the street and trailed behind him about ten feet back.

Devlin wondered how he should do this. He felt too visible on Second Avenue. At the moment, there was no one else in sight, but there was plenty of traffic moving down the avenue.

As they approached 84th Street, he quickened his pace. Just before they reached the corner, he closed the distance and quietly called out, "Brian."

The bartender hesitated then turned to look behind him. Devlin backhanded him across the face with a sharp, brutal slap. It was enough to knock the Irishman back a few steps, but Devlin quickly grabbed the man's shirt, pulled the bartender toward him, and smashed his left elbow into his temple.

Devlin watched the man's eyes glaze as he teetered on the edge of consciousness. The bartender had no control of his legs and looked like a man too drunk to walk.

Devlin was surprised at how much anger he felt. He observed it as one would analyze the symptoms of the flu. It had curled over him and enveloped him like a wave. He suddenly wanted to beat his fists into this man who had lied to him.

What had pulled such rage out of him?

Was it fear about what might have happened to his brother? Was it anger because he was so powerless to change what happened after he had left his brother?

Devlin knew he had to get off the street before he lost control. At that moment, the anger filled him with such strength he could have scooped the bartender up with one arm. He grabbed him around the waist and looped the man's left arm over his shoulder.

He turned and walked out into the street looking for a cab. There were two empty cabs coming his way, and he hailed one of them.

As they struggled into the backseat, the driver looked as if he were about to tell Devlin to get the drunk out of his cab. In a clear, sober voice Devlin assured him, "Don't worry, I'm taking him home."

As Devlin slammed the cab door with his left hand, he shoved his right elbow into the bartender's sternum with such force that he nearly cracked it. The slamming door covered the sound of the Irishman's body absorbing the blow. He was paralyzed into unconsciousness.

Devlin gave the cab driver the address of the loft downtown.

Back at the loft, Devlin sat in the living room, waiting until he felt the moment was right. The bartender was in a small room in the back. Devlin had shoved him, still half-conscious, into a straight-backed chair. Devlin had taped the man's wrists together behind him and his ankles to the legs of the chair.

The only other piece of furniture in the room was a table placed a few feet in front of the chair. The bartender's wallet, keys, money, and address book were laid out on the table. On the wall behind the table were photocopies of all the bartender's identification: New York State driver's license, green card, union card. It was as if his life were laid out for anyone to see and do with as they pleased. Also on the table was a closed attaché case.

Devlin felt deathly tired. The hour of sleep at Daryl's wasn't enough. He looked at his watch. It was ten minutes to four in the morning. A hell of a time to start work.

Devlin knew the bartender had lied to him. He knew the bartender would continue to lie if given a chance. Devlin assumed that people would lie to him. And in this case, he had no information to catch the bartender's lies. He knew virtually nothing, yet he had to find out the truth. He had to find his brother.

Devlin stood up. There was only one way to do this, and he didn't relish doing it. He walked back to the small room, opened the door, and walked in.

The bartender looked up and said, "You!"

Devlin stepped forward and immediately slapped his face hard. The bartender started to yell, and Devlin slapped the other side, this time harder.

The Irishman shook his head and spit blood on the floor. "What the fuck do you think you're doing, you bastard?"

Devlin squatted in front of him and looked him in the eyes. He pointed his finger at the man and spoke very quietly. "Don't talk. Don't dare ask me a question. Keep your mouth shut and listen. Listen very carefully, or you will be hurt very badly.

"It's just you and me. No cops, no friends, no lawyer. No chance anyone will find you and help you. The only way you're going to get out of here alive and in one piece is if you tell me the absolute truth. You've already lied to me. Don't do it again. You only get one warning."

Devlin looked into the bartender's eyes. He wanted to see fear. He saw anger, confusion. But fear? He wasn't sure yet.

Devlin stood up, turned his back to the bartender, and looked at the driver's license on the table. The man's full name was Brian McGinty. He lived at 340 East 98th Street.

He turned back to the bartender. Brian yelled at him, "Who the fuck are you? Are you crazy?"

Devlin muttered something too softly for the bartender to hear. Reluctantly, Devlin turned to the table and opened the attaché case. It was filled with a jumble of items—none of which belonged in an attaché case. Devlin pulled out a small round sponge and a roll of adhesive tape.

He moved behind the bartender with surprising quickness. McGinty had no time to look behind him before Devlin wrenched back his head so suddenly it forced his mouth open.

Devlin stuffed the sponge into his mouth, held his head back, and slammed the inch-wide strip of adhesive tape across his lips.

Devlin walked to the table again, tossed the tape in the attaché case and picked up an iron pipe about a foot long and a half-inch in diameter.

He walked over to the chair, and without a second's hesitation, Devlin smashed the pipe into the shin bone of the bartender's right leg.

The sponge and tape muffled most of the scream.

Devlin then turned the pipe deftly and punched it down hard on top of McGinty's left knee cap. McGinty's entire body jerked with searing pain. Devlin moved swiftly and gave a smart rap with the pipe on McGinty's right wrist and then the left wrist.

None of the blows were hard enough to break anything. But the pain was terrible. The bartender screamed into the sponge and tape across his mouth.

Again, Devlin crouched down in front of McGinty. He switched the pipe to his left hand and held his right forefinger to his lips to motion for silence. Tears of agony seeped out of McGinty's eyes. It took him a few moments, but he managed to stop yelling.

When he was quiet, Devlin reached out and pulled the tape off. It ripped a layer of skin off the bartender's lips, causing more pain, but McGinty didn't scream.

Devlin left the sponge in his mouth. He leaned closer and spoke to him again, pointing the pipe at the man's face for emphasis.

"Once more. Tell me the truth, and I won't hurt you. If you don't do that, I will start again. And I won't stop for a long time. I will start breaking bones, my friend. And if you think you hurt now, wait until I break the small bone above your wrist and start pounding on it."

Devlin paused to let the threat sink in, and let his rage wash over him. Then he snarled his first question, "Now do you fucking understand me?"

McGinty nodded. This time Devlin saw the fear in his eyes.

A small wet stain spread from the bartender's crotch. He somehow managed to stop just before he soaked himself.

Devlin stood up and pulled the sponge from the man's mouth. He turned back to the table and dropped the pipe into the case. He picked up a pad of paper and a pen and turned back. He rested against the edge of the table and paused.

"Are you ready?" Devlin asked quietly.

McGinty croaked, "Yes."

"Good. What are the names of the two that played darts with my brother?"

"Uh, Richie ..."

"I know his name. Richard Meisner. I want the names of the other two."

McGinty blinked once and then seemed to resign himself to his fate. "The names are Sean and Billy McKay."

"Brothers?"

"Yes."

"Where do they live?"

"They live in Washington Heights. I think on 168th Street. I swear I don't know the address. I've never been there."

Devlin noticed that most of the bartender's Irish brogue had disappeared.

"What's their phone number?"

"I'm not sure."

"What's the number you call when you want to tip them off to come to the bar?"

"It's a beeper number, I think. 555-2 ..."

"Come on," Devlin said gently.

"I think it's 555-2268."

"You *think* that's it?"

"That's it."

"How do you work the hustle?"

"It's different. Sometimes they work it with the dart game. If they can get the guy into big money, they do it that way. If not, they just keep the guy drinking. I serve them drinks with hardly any booze. I load up the other guys. They can usually get somebody so drunk they don't know what they're doing.

"The mark takes out his wallet to pay for drinks. They distract him, get ahold of it, take most of the money. They never take it all. Never pull any rough stuff. They usually end up putting the mark in a cab and giving the driver money to drive the guy home.

"He wakes up the next morning, and most of his money is gone. A couple of hundred bucks. Maybe his credit cards. No big deal. He could have lost it. Who knows. Neat. Clean. No hassle."

"What's your cut?"

"Ten percent."

"Seems hardly worth the trouble."

"Sometimes they score pretty good. Five, six hundred bucks."

Devlin paused, letting the bartender wonder if he believed his answers. Then, slowly, he asked, "Where is my brother?"

"I swear to God, I don't know."

"Are you lying to me again?"

"No. I swear."

"You're telling me these guys hustle people at darts. Or if that doesn't work they drink them under the table and rip them off."

"Yes. It's a hustle for money. They don't strong-arm anybody. I don't know what happened to your brother. I told the truth about them leaving."

"Why would they leave?"

"It was past four. Closing time. Your brother wasn't drunk enough. He didn't drink like a fool. Just kept at it, steady, steady. He was too big to play around with so they had to keep at it for another hour or so. Or maybe they just quit and left him. I don't know."

"Where were they going to take him if they were going to keep drinking?"

"I don't know. Probably an after-hours club."

"Where? In that neighborhood?"

"I swear I don't know. They're all around the city, those places. I haven't ever been to one. I swear I don't know. They would've had to take him someplace if they were going to keep drinking. I don't know where."

Devlin turned away from the frightened man and closed his eyes. He was almost sure the bartender was telling him everything he knew but almost wasn't good enough.

He picked up the small iron pipe and turned back.

McGinty stared at the vicious piece of metal and could already feel the pain. He yelled, "Don't hit me, for God's sake, I told you the truth."

"Maybe," said Devlin. "But I'm going to have to make sure. Now we go through it again. But this time I want every single detail. Let's start with the time you called them ..."

CHAPTER 9

It was a typical night for the Starlight Club. More accurately, a typical morning.

By four A.M., the people who couldn't quit until well after daylight started to arrive. Most came in groups of three or more. Some singles. A smattering of couples.

Past big Bernie in the lobby. Past the twin monoliths Joe and Eddie into the serene welcome of Susan.

Once past Susan, they entered the front room. Subdued lighting and heavy drapery made the club look opulent. But if anyone had ever turned the lights on full, the Starlight would have looked ratty and slightly dirty under the facade. Like a well-dressed whore who hadn't showered very recently.

Of course, the lights would never come on at the Starlight. The drapery covered all the walls and all the windows. The outside world didn't exist in the Starlight Club. There was no starlight, moonlight, or daylight allowed in the club. Nothing was allowed to intrude on Wexler's perverse hideaway.

On the right side of the first room was a small bar with eight stools. There were small couches and chairs opposite the bar. In between the bar and the seating area was a floor space covered by a fake Oriental rug.

There was only one bartender in the front room. Beyond the front room was another large room. In this room, there were two slot machines and five backgammon tables. High-stakes gambling on backgammon was continuous. A host in a tuxedo monitored the games and collected a hundred-dollar house fee from each person who wanted to play.

Once or twice a month Wexler would unveil a craps table or roulette wheel, or sometimes a blackjack table in the game room. Running the casino games was not easy. But the illegal games provided another reason to come to the Starlight.

To the left of the game room were two large communal bathrooms. There was no designation for sexes. You opened the door and walked up two steps to enter a thickly carpeted room of about fifteen square feet. Mirrors and sinks on one side, three stalls on the other. Never knowing whether a man or woman would come out of a stall, and never knowing the condition they'd be in was another one of the attractions of the Starlight Club.

The bathrooms often became cocaine central. Lines would be laid out on the marble sinks. The sounds of noses sniffing up the drugs would mix with the watery sounds of both sexes using the toilets. For some, it was fun to hear a strange woman or man pissing a few feet away.

On the other side of the game room was a wide archway that led to the largest room at the Starlight. It looked like a small nightclub. There were about twenty tables around a parquet dance floor. Theatrical lighting illuminated a small raised stage. Hard-edge rock music blared out of speakers for anyone who felt like dancing.

A long bar ran alongside one wall in the big room. A small kitchen was behind swinging doors on the far side of the room.

A Vietnamese chef, called Wong because no one bothered to learn his Vietnamese name, worked in the kitchen preparing hors d'oeuvres. Each plate of hors d'oeuvres cost twenty-five dollars, and nobody used credit cards at the Starlight. No one wanted a record of attendance at the Starlight. It wasn't supposed to exist. And because the Starlight didn't really exist, it didn't matter what you did there.

If someone wanted to sell vials of cocaine, they did it. If a woman wanted to let a breast fall from her evening dress, she did it. If a man wanted to be masturbated under the table and his partner, male or female, obliged, it happened.

And if a group wanted to sit at a table and talk and drink as if it were a family reunion, they did that, too.

About the only thing you couldn't do at the Starlight was damage the place. Anyone who became boisterous enough or violent enough to break glassware or furniture was swiftly and painfully removed by Joe and Eddie.

There were many violent and dangerous people at the Starlight, and in an extreme emergency the two bartenders in both rooms had 9-mm semi-automatic pistols behind the bars. But so far, the weapons had never been used. No one had ever stood up to Joe and Eddie for more than a few seconds.

Amid all the frenzied activity, Wexler calmly sat at his special place—a bar stool at the far end of the long bar, just near the service area. This was Wexler's office. On the bar was a small leather-covered notebook that he had taken from his breast pocket. Occasionally he would enter numbers, make calculations on a small calculator, enter more numbers. Everything in the notebook was cryptic. No names, no explanation. Only Wexler knew what the notebook meant. When he wasn't keeping track of his business, Wexler was carefully orchestrating the activities at the Starlight.

This night the crowd was noisy and wild, but Wexler looked completely unruffled in his crisp summer clothes. He sipped from a cold glass of Mumm Champagne.

Despite it being the middle of the week, there were almost two-hundred people in the club. Wexler well understood that cocaine, sex, and alcohol fueled his club's success.

The cocaine was everywhere. Dribbling from noses and lapels and spread on teeth and gums. It charged up his patrons so that sleep was impossible, and the thrill of being in this forbidden place was irresistible.

At one table a Wall Street commodities trader sat with his jacket off and his brightly colored suspenders blazing against his white shirt. His bow tie had been undone hours ago by one of the two women with him. She was blond, wearing a black strapless evening dress with thousands of tiny flat plastic disks sewn into the material so that any available light sparkled off the surface of each black disk. She had a dark tan, sparkling white teeth, and enough cleavage to attract attention even at the Starlight.

The Wall Streeter's second companion was the opposite of the blonde. She was small, dark-haired, in a white version of the black dress the blonde wore. She had on deep, dark red lipstick and lots of dark eye makeup. She looked evil.

All three were drinking champagne and sniffing the long lines of cocaine the Wall Streeter had laid out on the table.

Every few minutes he would lean over to one of the women and kiss her in the most lewd and salacious manner possible. Lips, teeth, tongues—every part of the orifice was put to task.

And then the woman partner who wasn't anointed by the man would immediately kiss the other woman in an attempt to outdo the man.

At another table, two black couples sat. All four were dressed in loose-fitting, comfortable but expensive clothes: slacks, silk blouses, sweaters, gold chains, and big rings.

The two men were drinking Chivas Regal and milk, the women huge snifters of Remy Martin. The men were cutting a deck of cards for a hundred dollars a cut. Each time the cut was made the loser would pay the winner from a pile of crisp hundred-dollar bills about an inch high.

On the dance floor, thirty or forty people sweated and inter-twined. Every combination and sexual preference were represented. In the midst of the dancing crowd, one tall redhead was doing a slow strip. Someone was yelling for her to show some hair. She laughed and pulled up her skirt to reveal high-cut black lace panties.

Wexler knew the cocaine and alcohol were essential to the success of the Starlight. But Wexler knew the most important part of the club's attraction was sex. It was lust that powered the Starlight. And Wexler was a master at fueling the flames to just the right fever pitch. The Starlight was by far the most profitable of his enterprises, so Wexler was determined to work the operation for every cent it could produce. It was time to present the morning's first piece of entertainment designed to keep the juices flowing.

Her name was Hedda. She had presented her act in several of the shady sex clubs that had dotted Manhattan in the past few years. The House of O. Hellfire. The Paddle Club. Plato's. Most of them had closed for one reason or another, so Hedda found herself performing at private parties and after-hours clubs.

This was Hedda's first appearance at the Starlight Club. Hedda's act was basically a striptease with an S&M air. She was confident the crowd would like her, but she made the mistake of thinking she was going to be in control on stage. Wexler had other plans for her. A nasty little surprise that she would never forget.

The lights dimmed. The dance music stopped. Those on the dance floor drifted back to their tables. The patrons at the outside bar slowly headed into the main room.

The stage was completely dark. Slow, sensual music came on and suddenly a spotlight illuminated the stage, revealing the tall figure of Hedda standing stock-still.

Most of the crowd turned to look at her. She was an imposing figure. A little over six feet, well over six-four in her spiked boots.

Her white-blond hair was cut into bangs that fell just above her eyes and just below her ears. It looked like a platinum helmet.

She wore dark eye makeup and blood red lipstick that set off her white skin.

She had on the expected leather outfit. Black leather choker with studs and black leather corset with bra cups. The corset tightly bound her waist. Under the corset, she wore a black leather G-string.

On her long legs were black leather boots.

There wasn't much to strip off, but when she did begin to show the body bound under the leather, everyone was impressed.

Her breasts were large, but the skin tone and muscles would have kept them uplifted without the corset cups. She took her time bending and twisting, showing off her plentiful cleavage. Her skin was deathly white. In the bright white spotlight, small blue veins could be seen tracing their way below the bra cups of the tight leather corset.

Slowly she unlaced the corset as she undulated toward the crowd with one long leg extended.

Just as the corset was about to fall off, she turned her back to the crowd. The leather garment slid off, revealing her muscular back, which was glazed with sweat.

She fondled her breasts and nipples with her back turned to the crowd. From the way her head bent forward the viewers could tell she was licking and biting her nipples. And all the time she was doing it, her hips and ass ground and rotated in deep, sensuous erotic thrusts. It was as if Hedda's body had pulled her into a deep sensuous trance. She couldn't resist the urges this body forced on her. It was as if her mouth and hands were at the mercy of each erogenous zone.

Even the jaded patrons of the Starlight Club were getting restless. They couldn't see what she was doing, but they could see enough to know she was working herself into a deep ecstasy.

Hedda felt the erotic tension in the room and teased them even more by bending over straight-legged and showing them her perfect pear-shaped ass bisected by the thong of the leather G-string.

She slid her hand inside the string and purposely thrust her middle finger deep into the crevice, letting them wonder whether the finger was going into her vagina or anus.

Then suddenly, when the crowd was almost squirming, she whirled around with her right arm cupped under her luxurious breasts.

Both nipples were pinched between silver nipple clips, which were attached to either end of a short silver chain. Hedda held the chain in her teeth. As she threw her head back the clips at the ends of the short chain pulled her nipples taut, lifting her breasts and making the crowd squirm with a mixture of apprehension and titillation.

Now she was shaking her head back and forth, pulling the nipples first in one direction then the other. Her hand thrust under the small black patch of her leather G-string and the crowd could see clearly that she was masturbating herself.

A sheen of sweat appeared on her stomach, and one drop slid between her breasts.

The music tempo increased. It seemed to be all bass and drums now, with trills of synthesized sounds skirting in and out of the insistent rising beat.

Suddenly she tore off the leather G-string. She dropped into a half-crouch. The long muscles on the front of her thighs stood out. Her blond pubis thrust toward the crowd and she spread her vaginal lips revealing her pink inner skin and a swollen clitoris.

She thrust her tongue out, licking and sucking on the silver chain.

Suddenly, from one of the tables, a black girl seemed to glide toward the stage and then accelerate toward Hedda as if she were being drawn by a huge magnet.

She wore a short black skirt and a white silk blouse. Before anyone knew what was happening, including Hedda, she slammed her head into Hedda's crotch, knocking the blond S&M goddess on her back. The woman grabbed both of Hedda's trembling white thighs, gaining more leverage and pulling Hedda's crotch firmly against her mouth.

The assault panicked the big stripper. It hurt. It felt as if some animal had attached itself to her soft tissue and clitoris. Desperately, Hedda pushed against the black woman's forehead with one hand while using the other to help her crawl backward away from the sucking, clutching mouth that would not let go.

But no matter how hard she tried to get away, she couldn't. The black woman was clamped onto her vagina. Hedda became frightened, then frantic. She screamed out, "No, stop it! Stop!" She writhed from side to side. She dug her heels into the carpet on the stage and tried to twist away. She pushed against the woman's head with both hands, but now the woman had locked her hands behind Hedda's lower back and nothing could pry her away.

Suddenly Hedda screamed out in pain. The black woman had bitten her. Hedda stopped trying to push away the head, and the black girl returned to licking and sucking furiously.

Someone in the crowd yelled, "Yes!

Another cried out, "Go, baby!"

Everyone was now riveted to the stage. The danger and animal magnetism of it had completely captured the crowd.

Hedda continued to writhe and twist, but her attacker rode with the movements. The black woman was flat on her stomach. Her long legs were spread for leverage and her short skirt had ridden up above her ass revealing that she was naked under her skirt.

Hedda's two hands grabbed fistfuls of the girl's jet-black hair. But now she seemed to be holding on rather than trying to pull or push the girl's head away from her crotch. Now that she had weathered the initial shock and discomfort it was obvious that Hedda had succumbed to the pleasure of the cunnilingus.

Hedda yelled out, "You fucking bitch!"

It only fueled deeper tonguing and licking. The girl sensed she had her victim under control, and she pulled her head back, giving her room to let her long pink tongue lick the entire area between Hedda's legs. She let one hand come from behind Hedda's back and pulled open her blouse so she could rub her own swollen nipples. Then she pulled up her skirt and started to manipulate her own clitoris.

Now she was titillating rather than attacking, and Hedda began to grind her hips in anticipation of orgasm.

But the girl was prolonging it. She wanted to pleasure herself while she was teasing Hedda.

The crowd was seething. Suddenly a tall man with a huge erection projecting from his unzipped pants jumped on the stage and started masturbating over the two writhing women. The crowd began to chant in unison, "Go, go, go . . ."

Wexler, watching it all, pushed a button concealed under the edge of the bar where he sat. It signaled Joe and Eddie to come into the room. He had this crowd worked to a fever pitch, but he had to make sure no one started pushing aside tables and chairs to start an orgy.

As soon as they entered, Wexler signaled them to stay in the back. As the crowd teetered on the edge of orgy and violence, Wexler titillated himself by letting it go further and further.

He was ready to send Joe and Eddie to the front of the room when the black girl began to approach the edge of orgasm. She buried her head in Hedda's vagina, this time sucking the blonde's clitoris into her mouth and sucking and sucking until Hedda screamed and writhed in a crashing orgasm.

The man finished himself, sending streams of his ejaculation pumping into the air. Streams of it fell across Hedda's heaving stomach and breasts. The man dropped to his knees, Hedda's head fell back against the carpet. The black girl rolled on her back.

The flash point had passed. The crowd dropped into a stunned silence. Wexler signaled for the music to end, and the lights dimmed into darkness.

CHAPTER 10

It was close to six in the morning by the time Devlin was satisfied the bartender had told him everything. Devlin was tired to the bone. The night before had given him very little sleep. This night only an hour.

The bartender was at the begging stage now. "Please, Mister, I didn't mean any harm to come to your brother. My mates never hurt anybody. Ever. Just a soft hustle, that was their game. Let me go, I'll help you find him."

This was where Devlin wanted him. He had to seal the alliance now. "I know you will, Brian."

He stood up and came behind the chair. He flipped open a small folding knife and cut through the tape binding McGinty's wrists. He stood back as the defeated bartender's hands dropped away from the chair.

Devlin stepped in front of the chair and quietly told him, "Undo your legs, now."

McGinty shook his hands to get the blood back into them and managed to pull the tape off his ankles. He remained seated.

"Stand up."

Slowly he got to his feet.

Devlin pointed to a door. "There's a cot in there. Set it up and sleep if you want."

"Man, I've got to piss something terrible."

"There's a jug with a handle in there, too. Use it. Don't get any on the floor."

Devlin watched as Brian shuffled to a small closet behind them. He pulled the cot out and found the urine bottle. Brian stood inside the small closet and relieved himself into the bottle. He was careful not to drip any on the floor.

If he had any fight left in him, Devlin knew this would be one of the moments it would come out. An angry man with a jar full of urine could do some damage. But McGinty carefully set the container on the floor against the wall.

Without another word, he set up the cot and lay down on it. Devlin told him quietly, "Get some sleep. I'll be back, and we'll figure out what to do next."

"Yes, sir."

The bartender closed his eyes. Devlin gathered everything on the table and dumped it into the attaché case. He closed it, walked to the door, and left. The door automatically locked behind him.

Devlin spent the next half hour showering in steaming water, trying to wash away the strain and tension of terrorizing a petty hustler into submission. He let his mind step through the plans for his next moves.

He set his alarm for 10:00 A.M. Four hours of sleep would have to do.

The call came from Zitter at 9:45. The sound of the phone hit Devlin like a bucket of ice water. He knew before he reached for the phone that it was Zitter.

He muttered, "Devlin."

"I found him."

"Where?"

"Goddamn Gramercy Hospital on the East Side."

"Near the park?"

"Yeah. Last fuckin' place they should take a John Doe. I don't know how the hell they got him there. Must have been some half-ass private ambulance service. Couldn't have been any of the EMS people. They would have taken him to a city hospital for sure."

Zitter couldn't stop talking. He was too wound up from hitting the end of the search.

"Sam, tell me what happened. How is he?"

"Nobody knows what happened. The doctors can tell you what shape he's in better than I."

"You tell me."

"All right. I'm not good at this, for chrissake, so just listen. It's bad. Intensive Care. I conned a nurse into letting me see the chart." Zitter paused to look at his notes. "He was admitted at eight-eleven yesterday morning. No identification. Found by a cab driver near the turnaround by Battery Park. I imagine the cabbie called into his dispatcher who got some damned private ambulance service to pick him up, figuring he could get a cut or something. The emergency room notes say he was unconscious from a head trauma. Lot of other bangs and bruises. Three broken ribs. Swollen testicles. Busted hand. Somebody did a number on him. They sent him to surgery. Neurologists did some sort of operation to relieve the pressure from the head injury. I looked at the surgeon's notes, but I can't read the fucking things. The bottom line is, your brother's in a coma. I only saw him from outside the ICU, near the nurses' station. Only family members can get in there. All I could see was a lot of tubes coming out of him and a lot of bandages."

"You sure it's him?"

"Yeah, it's him. I went down to the patients' property room and asked the clerk to show me the inventory. No wallet, money, or keys, but same clothes you described and same shoes. School ring. Wedding ring. And the physical description matches. It's gotta be him. I'm sorry, Jack."

Devlin sat on the edge of the bed picturing his brother in a hospital Intensive Care Unit.

"Okay, Sam. You did what you were supposed to do. I'll get down there and find out what I need to know. I'll be in touch. Thanks."

"Listen, Devlin. I'm not off this until you don't need anything that I can do. This is shit. I don't know who did this to your brother, but

I'll help do whatever it takes to find out. You let me know, hear?"

"Yes. I will. Thanks. I have to get going. I'll call you."

Devlin stood up. He clenched his teeth against the rage. No matter how much cruelty and senseless violence he had experienced in his life, it never failed to anger him. He could never accept it. And now it had touched and brutally hurt his own brother. He'd experienced this blinding fury many times in his life, and so this time, once again he was able to keep the rage in its place. He had long ago learned that the best thing was to use it as fuel. This time all he could do was contain it and force the next moves to click into place in his brain.

Coffee, Marilyn, the bartender, the hospital.

#

Gramercy Hospital was a place it seemed everyone had forgotten.

It was a small hospital left behind by a city whose demand for medical care had grown beyond control. The immense complex of Bellevue Hospital, New York University Hospital, and the Veterans Administration hospital that spread along First Avenue to the east gobbled up tons of people who needed medical care, from the indigent to the wealthy.

That left Gramercy to mop up the leftovers—patients of its ever-decreasing medical staff and AIDS cases.

When Devlin walked into the ICU, he saw seven beds. Five were occupied with terminally ill AIDS patients—young men in their twenties and thirties. One bed held an Italian man who seemed to be at the end of eighty-plus years of smoking. And in the corner bed was George.

He walked quickly to George's bedside. All he could see was an approximation of his face. That alone was enough to make Devlin want to stop looking. Both eyes were swollen shut with dark, ugly purple bruises surrounding the area under the eyes and the bridge of the nose. The nose was so badly broken that both nostrils were swollen shut.

Taped into George's mouth was a thick, oval-shaped respiration tube. Two ugly strips of adhesive tape were wrapped around his mouth and back of his head to hold the respirator tube in place. The tape pulled George's mouth into a strangled grimace. George struggled to breathe on his own, but each breath was augmented by the mechanical force of the respirator, making the spectacle even more grotesque.

George's left arm lay outside the sheets. The hand looked puffy and inflamed from IV needles.

George was so far from being awake that Devlin didn't even try to talk to him.

He moved to the head of the bed. The monitors and breathing apparatus seemed to close in on him, incessantly repeating their small accusing electronic noises.

He put his hand on his brother's shoulder and said, "I'm sorry, George. I'm so sorry."

CHAPTER 11

Devlin sat with George for two hours while he waited for Marilyn to come in from Larchmont. The struggled breathing, the constant push and pull of the respirator, the cruel tape that disfigured his face – it all began to make Devlin feel so pressured and tense that he couldn't see straight.

The nurse working the ICU told him the resident doctor in charge would be by at one o'clock and he could better explain George's condition. Visiting hours in the ICU were unrestricted for family members, so Devlin was permitted to wait.

At 12:25 P.M. the nurse came for Devlin and told him that Marilyn had arrived. They had kept her in a small waiting room outside the ICU, knowing that Devlin should see her first and try to prepare her.

When Devlin entered, Marilyn sat hunched over on the edge of a small couch the color of oatmeal. There were two other people in the room. Two men, both gay, each wrapped in a private envelope of grief. Neither man spoke much to each other. They looked as though they had been waiting in that room and rooms like it for years.

The smaller man, in jeans and a light blue polo shirt, chain-smoked Marlboros as if to tell the world he didn't have AIDS, and he could do whatever he wanted with his body.

The other man wore a neatly pressed seersucker suit and a bow tie. He sat quite still. They were also waiting for the doctors' midday rounds. They would talk with the doctors, then leave with some reassurance their lovers wouldn't die that day. Being there at the moment of death was the most important thing they could do now. Unfortunately, they had to be very lucky to time it right.

Marilyn stood up as Devlin entered. She looked confused and hurt. Devlin held out his hands as if to embrace her, but she wouldn't allow it. She stood back from Devlin and demanded, "What the hell happened, Jack?"

Devlin stiffened. He was in no mood to be reprimanded. His face turned hard and remote, and his eyes receded into flash points of anger.

He hadn't wanted the anger to pull him back so far from her, but it did. He watched Marilyn's face go blank, and for a split second he saw fear in her eyes. She had forgotten who she was talking to. She was too accustomed to being a wife and a mother who could reprimand a child or a husband. Devlin was neither, and the look on his face frightened her. Devlin held himself in check for a moment, and the danger passed away from them. Marilyn tried to speak again, "Jack, I . . . I'm upset, I didn't mean to—"

Devlin interrupted her. "I know. Just listen to me. George has been hurt very badly, Marilyn. I don't know how it happened or why. There's not much purpose to talking about that part of it now. The doctor in charge of him will be here soon. He should be able to tell us more."

Marilyn looked up and steadied. "Is he all right? I mean, how bad is it?"

"It's bad. You won't want to see what he looks like now. He's bruised and swollen. His face . . . everything. But you have to get past that."

"Oh, Christ."

"The way he looks isn't the problem. He's unconscious. He's had a head injury. They had to perform surgery. Part of it is the injury, part of it is the drugs they gave him, but he's still unconscious."

"Why? What happened?"

"We'll find out more when the doctor comes. In about a half hour. I'll wait here. You don't need me in there when you see him. Try and look past all the bandages and mess around him."

Devlin walked with Marilyn toward the ICU. At the entrance, she closed her eyes and breathed slowly. The deep mothering instinct and iron will that was somewhere in all women came up inside her, and she turned and walked into the Intensive Care Unit.

A few minutes after one the resident appeared at the nurses' station. Devlin intercepted him before he entered the ICU. The doctor's nameplate said Dr. Yi Min Wu, M.D. Devlin explained about George being his brother. The doctor looked up at Devlin with a frown, as if knowing the identity of his patient were bad news. He wore steel-rimmed round glasses, a blue shirt, and a stylish Giorgio Armani tie. He had on a short white jacket instead of a long lab coat.

When they shook hands, Devlin felt smooth, soft skin.

"Mr. Devlin, I am the neurosurgical resident on staff. May I discuss your brother's condition with you after I finish my rounds?"

"How long will that be, Doctor?"

"About one hour."

Before the hour was up, Devlin, Marilyn, and Dr. Wu stood in the corridor a few feet down from the nurses' station. It was somehow private despite the traffic of hospital personnel and visitors that flowed past them.

Dr. Wu spoke in a soft voice. He had a trace of a Chinese accent and occasionally dropped articles like a foreign speaker.

"Your husband, brother, is in critical condition. It won't be easy to hear details. You sure you want me to explain?"

Devlin let Marilyn answer first, "Yes."

"Yes."

"Okay. He had very serious injury to his head. Lots of other trauma, but none as serious as the head. Fortunately, we think he was found relatively quickly. The swelling was not life threatening when they brought him in, but quickly heading in that direction.

"Okay, two types of injuries to head. First from a direct blow. If the blow is severe you get a certain kind of bleeding and swelling at the site. Brain stays in one spot, head moves away fast because of blow, then when brain catches up to head, it sheers away blood vessels between it and skull and bangs into skull. You get bleeding, hematoma, swelling. Depend on how severe the blow.

"Second kind of injury is when you fall and hit your head. Or you are moving forward and hit your head. In this case, injury at point of contact is usually minor, most of the serious injury is at the opposite point of contact because the brain bounces back and impacts the skull.

"We think your brother was hit hard from behind, injury number one, then fell forward and hit his face and head on the ground causing second type of trauma to brain. His nose was broken, front teeth chipped, and forehead bruised . . . so first injury is compounded by second type of trauma, both at same site. That's the worst."

Marilyn was squinting in discomfort. Dr. Wu was over the hard part so he kept on.

"Again, fortunately, the surgeon who performed this operation is one of the best in the city. I came specifically to this small hospital to study because Littinger occasionally does surgery here. He was available the morning they brought your brother in. Very fortunate for your brother.

"As I witnessed the surgery, it was flawless. Littinger relieved a great deal of pressure, removed a major clot and did everything right. I say rear head injuries are better than front, but none is good. How much damage and how much, if any, is going to be permanent I can't say until Mr. Devlin regains consciousness.

"Right now, this coma is partially induced by the drugs we use to prevent further swelling. My guess, and don't hold me to it, is he will be unconscious another two, three days. When he wakes up he'll certainly be disoriented. We won't know how much permanent damage was sustained and how much therapy he will need, if any, until about a week after he regains consciousness.

"Naturally, we have to watch very carefully for any recurrence of swelling or complications. He has a lot of other injuries, but they are treatable. The broken ribs are serious. We hope they didn't damage his lungs or heart. Preliminary tests show they didn't. Anything else I can tell you?"

Marilyn was speechless.

Devlin asked, "How did this happen?"

"I don't know."

"You must be able to tell something by the injuries."

"No point speculating. It might have been useful to know if this was a car accident or a fall or whatever. But at this stage knowing that doesn't matter anymore, and no value for me to guess."

"Doctor, I want to know what you think happened to my brother."

Devlin wasn't asking. Wu looked at Devlin's eyes and decided not to oppose him. "Okay. I think two, maybe three strong men beat up your brother. He's a big man. He probably put up pretty good fight. Knuckles on both hands are badly cut and bruised. Knuckles on one hand broken in two places. I think they hit him in head to down him, and then kick and beat him until they were tired of it. It's not a car accident or a fall down the stairs. I'm sorry."

Marilyn turned and walked away from them.

Devlin said, "Thank you. How can I reach you if I need to ask something?"

"Call the hospital."

"No other number?"

"No. Look, I can see you're very angry. That won't help your brother."

Devlin didn't respond.

"If it's any consolation I can tell you that your brother will never remember any of the pain of what happened."

Devlin looked at the doctor and quietly said, "What happens when he wakes up? Tell me he won't have to live with pain when he wakes up. Tell me he'll walk straight. Tell me he won't be terrified to be on a street at night, or forget his kids' names, or be in a fucking wheelchair and not be able to feed himself or dress or wash."

"Please . . . "

"Tell me none of that can happen to him now and I won't be angry. Tell me whoever did this to him is just as beat up and hurt as he is instead of walking around laughing about it now, and I won't be angry."

Devlin turned away from Dr. Wu and walked out of the hospital before he hit someone.

CHAPTER 12

In the cab back to the loft Devlin concentrated on his breathing. He tried over and over again to clear his mind of everything. But the image of his beaten, swollen brother crumpled in that bed, struggling with every breath pushed into him by that goddamn respirator tube taped into his mouth, kept tearing at him.

His only thread to the people who almost killed his brother was the bartender locked in the loft. He wanted to grab a fistful of the man's hair and drag him to the bedside and shove his face in front of George's so he could see and hear and smell what he had done.

But if he did that, he'd never find the others. So he kept breathing and concentrating and pulling himself away from the rage so that he could act like a machine and get this done. Because Jack Devlin knew goddamn well that this was not going to vanish into the constant current of violence that swirled around a city out of control. What had been done to George was his fault, and he wasn't going to drop it.

The bartender was a mess when Devlin unlocked the small room. He was sitting on the edge of the cot, holding his head. His fingers were buried under his tangled hair. He needed a shave, and he stank of urine and body odor.

Devlin told him, "Stand up."

McGinty stood up slowly and asked, "What now?"

"Right now, you have three things to do in life. Get home, get into work tonight, and make sure those friends of yours are in that bar by ten o'clock."

"What if I can't find them?"

Devlin slowly took McGinty's throat in his hand. He squeezed the throat only hard enough to get a grip on it, but he knew the bartender could feel the power in his hand and arm. "You don't want to be the only one I hold responsible for this. You don't want to be the sole target."

The bartender struggled out an answer. "All right. All right. I'll get them there."

Devlin released his grip. The bartender gently rubbed his throat and told Devlin, "Just take it easy, please. I told you we never hurt anyone. It's a soft hustle. No one ever gets hurt."

Devlin punched him once, hard, in the solar plexus. The same spot he had hit him in the cab. McGinty's breathing was paralyzed, and he crumpled into unconsciousness.

By the time McGinty came fully awake, he was in a cab with Devlin heading up Lafayette Street. At Cooper Square, Devlin told the cab driver to pull over. Devlin turned to McGinty and said, "Four things. Get home. Get to work tonight. Get your friends there by ten. And don't ever say another word to me about nobody getting hurt." Devlin got out and slammed the door.

McGinty leaned forward and told the driver his address. Pain seared through the center of his chest. He realized he had to have cab fare and checked his pockets. He had his keys, his address book, and his wallet. He took the wallet out of his back pocket. His money was in the wallet, but instead of his cards and identification, the two photocopied pages that Devlin had taped to the wall were neatly folded and stuck into the wallet.

He had no idea where Devlin had taken him, or who Devlin was. But he knew for certain where Devlin would be at ten o'clock that night.

#

The first time Susan met Robert Wexler was at Regine's. It was about a week after the cocaine binge that made her finally quit.

There were two reasons Susan was able to stay away from the drug. She was ruthlessly truthful about what the drug had done to her. And she would die before she would let cocaine make her unable to watch out for Ceece.

While Susan was doing coke regularly, her mother received a letter from the Suffolk School for the Handicapped notifying the family that they expected an opening for Ceece to come due sometime within the next six months.

They had waited almost four years for the opening. Marie and Susan visited the school. Marie cried most of the time, but Susan knew immediately that this was the best they could ever hope for.

The school was run by the State of New York. The residents lived in rooms for two. The school had job training, complete medical facilities, and the grounds were clean and well kept. The wards and dorm rooms were neat and pleasant. And the staff seemed to genuinely care.

Once Ceece was accepted, her Social Security disability benefits would pay for everything. Ceece would be taken care of and protected for the rest of her life. All Susan had to do was hold things together another six months. Keep off the coke, keep up her *dates*, and keep the money flowing to Marie and Ceece every month.

The man who had taken her to Regine's that night was a friend of a friend. Susan realized she was at the stage where she was being passed around by a circle of self-important but basically sleazy men. A year before Susan wouldn't have even considered being seen with them, but for now, they were a necessity. They provided meals, entertainment, sometimes clothes, sometimes money, and most of the time she could avoid sleeping with them.

Susan may have been cash poor, but she looked rich. She still had her clothes and her body and her striking face, and in the dim light of New York's clubs and restaurants, she looked flawless.

Shortly after they arrived, Susan's date brought her over to Robert Wexler's table. He wanted to show her off. Susan was curious about the distinguished-looking man who held himself in such reserve. He was so carefully groomed with his full head of graying hair and impeccable clothes, and he held himself so much above everyone. As if he knew something they didn't. As if he were smarter, better, more deserving than anyone else.

She found Wexler's attitude and manner annoying. But at the same time, she had the desire to make him want her so that she wouldn't be treated with the same disdain he treated others. When they were introduced, she acknowledged the introduction, but then made sure to ignore him. She also made sure to sit straight and turned herself so that Wexler had a good view of her lush body and classic features. Not having much money had taken about five pounds off her and she was undeniably at her peak.

It was the perfect strategy to make Wexler want her. And, of course, for Wexler wanting meant owning.

He knew exactly what Susan was doing by ignoring him. And he knew it was working.

After about fifteen minutes, a third man appeared at the table, and Susan's date left with him to snort lines of coke in the men's room. Wexler asked Susan, "You don't indulge?"

"I'm on the wagon."

"Which one?"

"The one that doesn't carry any coke."

"Then you need a drink."

"Yes. Absolut and club soda with a piece of lime."

Wexler signaled for a waiter and ordered the drink. "How long have you known your date, Mr. Rubinstein?

Susan continued to look away from Wexler. "About three hours," she answered.

"That man's a fool to leave you sitting here. Why are you out with him?"

"Because I want to be. Why are you insulting him?"

"Because I know him, and I think you deserve better."

"Doesn't everybody?"

"No. Everybody doesn't. But you do, Sarah." Her name that night.

"And I suppose the next thing you're going to say is that I should be with you."

"Why say what you've obviously figured out for yourself?"

Susan waited for the proposition, but the actual offer came as a surprise.

Without any lead-in, Wexler told her, "I'm opening a club. I need an assistant. Someone to help me. Someone to host it. I think you'd be perfect."

"I'd *be* perfect, or *look* perfect?"

"Both. Are you interested?"

"No."

"Why not?"

Susan shrugged as if she had become tired of the conversation. She looked around for her date, but couldn't spot him.

Wexler gave her a winning smile and said, "It seems you've already learned an important lesson."

"What's that?"

"A person rarely loses money by saying no."

"Really."

"Yes. Really. You've just said no to me, so I've got to make it worth your while to consider my offer."

"And how will you do that?"

"By giving you one thousand dollars to come and listen to my offer in more detail. Your time is worth money, so I'll pay you for it. Call me tomorrow. We'll have dinner. You'll earn a thousand dollars just for listening to my offer."

Wexler handed her his card, stood up, and said, "If you think it's worth the trouble, call me after four o'clock, and we'll arrange dinner. Have a pleasant evening."

Susan knew she was going to call Wexler before she even looked at the card.

The discussions were gradual. The first meeting was over a late dinner. It was quite businesslike.

Susan kept finding ways not to say yes for as long as she dared, but eventually Wexler's offer was much too good to pass up.

By their last meeting, Susan had a monthly salary of $6,000 in cash, an apartment, and a job as the hostess of the Starlight Club.

She also had the cold realization that although it was going to cost Wexler a great deal of money, she would soon have the job of being his mistress, too.

She kept telling herself it would only have to last a few months. Six at the most. Ceece would be safe and secure. She'd have enough money saved to get out of New York and start over. Maybe even move to L.A. and get back to acting school. Move someplace where men with disposable incomes and short memories didn't know her name. Whatever that name happened to be.

She felt sure she could play Wexler for her own ends. Until the morning she saw what Wexler did to people who crossed him. Then she wasn't so sure at all.

It happened to a waiter who had been fired at the club. He was a young man, no more than twenty-five. Particularly handsome with blond good looks. He was slightly effeminate and obviously high-strung.

The club had closed at ten-thirty that morning. The last patrons had drifted out about an hour earlier. Wexler was seated in his usual place at the end of the bar quietly making entries in his small leather notebook. Susan was sitting a few stools away from him. She was drinking coffee and sipping Grand Marnier.

The waiter appeared rather suddenly. Susan didn't even see where he'd come from, but she got the impression he had been waiting until everything quieted down before he confronted Wexler. His anger had been brewing. He sounded shrill and overwrought. Everything burst out in a loud rush. "Mr. Wexler, I have to talk to you. I don't know why you fired me. I do my job. I deserve to at least know why I'm being fired."

Wexler looked up from his notebook. In a calm, icy voice he told the man, "You *don't* do your job. You don't deserve to know *anything*. Do not yell at me. I'm tired, now go away."

It was too much. The waiter cracked. He stepped toward Wexler and screamed, "You can't treat me like shit!"

Without a hint of warning, Wexler turned the ballpoint pen in his hand, twisted on his stool, and plunged the sharp point directly into the waiter's left eye.

The man's head snapped back. He staggered backward and started to scream in pain. He dropped to his knees and bent his head over with his hands shaking in front of his eye.

Because Wexler had shoved the pen upward from his seated position on the bar stool, the pen hadn't penetrated the man's eyeball. It had skimmed over the top and lodged between the eye and the socket. It stuck out at a strange angle. Everything had happened so fast that Susan couldn't believe what she was seeing. It took a moment to realize what was sticking out of the man's eye.

Wexler was on his feet, still talking in that eerie, icy voice, enunciating every word. Without hardly raising his voice, Susan could hear every word Wexler said, despite the waiter's screams.

"Don't tell me you aren't a piece of shit. You *are* shit. You are a piece of dirty little shit, and I will treat you any way I want to."

The man's screams brought Joe and Eddie running into the main room. Eddie straddled the waiter from behind and grabbed him by the shoulders. Joe stood in front of him with his fists clenched and ready to strike. Both Joe and Eddie gritted their teeth in maniacal grins.

Wexler took a step toward the man who was now screaming in gasps. The waiter couldn't bring himself to touch the pen that was sticking out of his eye socket. His open hands shook in front of his face.

Wexler slightly raised his voice so Joe and Eddie could hear him over the sobbing screams. "Shut him up."

Joe viciously kicked the waiter in the stomach. The blow stopped the screaming and the man's breathing. Joe grabbed a handful of hair and pulled the waiter's head back again so he couldn't double over.

Susan wanted to look away. She felt a wave of nausea, but she couldn't stop watching. In a strange way, she felt the waiter had to know someone other than Wexler and his bodyguards were seeing this happen.

Susan had no idea what to do, or what Wexler was going to do. As she struggled to think of some way to stop it, Wexler sneered and said, "I want my pen back." And as quickly as he had stuck it into the man's eye, he grabbed the pen and wrenched it out.

The waiter made a horrible grunting noise and passed out. Suddenly, Susan felt the vomit rising in her throat. She turned away from the bar spewing the bile and contents of her stomach toward the wall. Some of it hit her leg and knee, and she felt the warmth and stench cling to her.

The room was suddenly deathly quiet. "Get him out of here," Wexler ordered.

Joe and Eddie each grabbed the waiter under an arm and started to drag him out as they would a heavy piece of furniture.

They dragged him away, face down, but Wexler put up his hand and said, "Stop!" The behemoths turned and looked at him. As if he were explaining something to young children, Wexler said, "Turn him over so he does not bleed on my carpet."

Eddie, the bigger of the two giants, looked under the dragging head and saw the blood coming out of the eye socket. He half growled, reached over, and snatched the other shoulder away from Joe, twisted the body around, and threw the waiter onto his back. Then, as if he were vying with Joe for a piece of meat, Eddie slammed Joe in the center of his chest and slapped him on the side of the head.

Joe growled back and smiled at him, reached down and picked up the body, spun it around completely and slammed it back on the ground.

Wexler interrupted them. "Stop playing with him and get him away from here. Far away."

Eddie smiled at Joe and yelled, "Far away!"

Joe yelled back, "Yeah. Far fucking away!"

They reached down and each grabbed an arm and hauled off their prize.

Susan never saw the waiter again. No police ever came. Nothing happened. She never heard about any repercussions whatsoever.

Two months later, during one of their late evening dinners she felt the moment was right and asked Wexler, "Remember that waiter you fired?"

Wexler grinned and looked up from his meal. "The one I used for a pen holder?"

She felt stupid for asking him if he remembered. Then she asked straight out, "Whatever happened to him?"

"Curious, are you?"

"Yes."

"Well, I think the charming Joe and Eddie took him to Harlem and dumped him in a trash basket. They have a very droll sense of humor, those two."

"Weren't you worried there might be some reprisals?"

"What kind of reprisals?"

"I don't know. The police? Something."

Wexler put down his fork and began to talk in a condescending tone of voice that said, "All right, I'm going to take the time to teach you something.

"Let's examine the possibilities. First of all, with regard to the police. In a word, it's his word against mine. And Eddie's and Joe's, and, of course, yours. We never saw any of that happen. So what are the police going to do? Nothing.

"Should we consider some personal act of revenge? That requires personal courage and quite a bit of skill, neither of which he has. What other possibilities are there? Powerful friends? The wherewithal to hire somebody? No, no, he doesn't have either. Believe me, dear, I've made worse enemies of better men than him and never lost a wink of sleep."

Susan had watched him during his speech and saw how much he enjoyed it.

Wexler watched her for a reaction, and Susan knew she had to be very careful. She gave him a whisper of a smile and said, "How nice to have such confidence."

Wexler looked her in the eye and said, "Anyone stupid enough to go against me deserves whatever happens to them."

CHAPTER 13

After he left the bartender in the cab, Devlin went back to the loft and called Zitter.

"You still want to help?"

Zitter told him, "Yeah. But just so we're clear, I'd like to do it for free, but I can't afford to."

"That's fine. Just keep track of your hours and ask me for the money when you want it."

"Okay, what do you need?"

"I've got a line on two guys who may have set up my brother for a beating, or done it themselves. I've got it arranged for them to show up at a bar on the Upper East Side. Ten o'clock. I'd like you to back me up.

"Fine. I'll come armed?"

"That would probably be a good idea."

"What about you?"

"Yes."

"Okay. You want to tell me about all this now, or later? I want to know whatever there is to know before I walk into that bar."

"Meet me at nine o'clock. Pick a place around Eighty-second. I'll fill you in. Buy you dinner, too, if you'd like."

"Why not? There's a place on Eighty-ninth called Juanita's. Decent Mexican food. Not too expensive. How's that?"

"Good. See you there at nine."

Devlin hung up. He needed sleep. And he wanted to think over the possibilities as he drifted off. He knew that he couldn't really plan what to do until he saw the Irishmen. But he knew his subconscious would sort out some of the possibilities while he slept. And when he saw them, the right move would happen without too much planning.

He stretched out on the bed and was asleep within three minutes.

\#

At Juanita's, Devlin told Zitter everything that had happened at O'Callahan's and with the bartender while he watched the old cop eat his meal faster than he had ever seen anyone eat.

Zitter finished the last swig of his Dos Equis beer and sat back in his chair. This time he had on a yellow shirt and a brown sport coat over gray slacks. His tie looked like somebody else's. It was a regimental number with blue and red stripes. Zitter's ample stomach strained against a wide brown belt that didn't go with the gray slacks.

Devlin was barely halfway through his chicken poblano.

Zitter rubbed his face and announced, "I still want a cigarette after a meal. Especially a meal with a few beers."

Devlin asked, "When did you quit smoking?"

"Five years ago. You ever smoke?"

"Cigars, sometimes."

"I figured if I was going to quit something it might as well be smoking. Can't quit eating, that's for sure."

"It's tough."

"You look like you haven't got an ounce of fat on you."

Devlin pushed away his plate of chicken poblano. "I can't stand eating past a full stomach."

"That's a fucking gift from God, my friend."

"I guess," said Devlin.

"I never threw away a piece of food in my life."

"Depends on the food, doesn't it?"

"Hell no." Zitter swallowed and asked, "So what do you want to do about these mutts who are supposed to show up tonight?"

"All right . . . the way I see it, these guys are either going to be there around ten or never be there at all. I don't know what line the bartender fed them to make sure they show up, but I don't guess it matters too much."

Zitter said, "They sure as shit wouldn't come if they knew you what you did to that bartender."

"Not necessarily. If he told them what I did, they might show up to kick my ass."

Zitter looked at Devlin's hard face and said, "I got a feeling you'd like that."

"In a way. I'd get some satisfaction, but I'm not sure I'd find out what really happened to my brother."

"Then again, if that bartender told them everything, they should know they can't fuck with you, and they probably won't show up."

"Yeah, well, let's not go in circles. Here's the point—we have to get them in there and keep them in there until I'm done with them, or until I decide to take them somewhere else."

"Okay."

Devlin opened and closed his hand. "So we open the box and close it."

Zitter decided to give his advice. "Fine. You set your ass inside. I'll come in after you and sit at the bar. When they come in, I'll move to cover the front door. They won't get past me unless you say so. Simple as that."

"I don't know anything about these guys, Sam. They might be armed."

"I'll have my gun out first, believe me. If they draw on me, I'll shoot first. I didn't retire from the force to get killed by some punks in a bar. If you want to shoot from behind them, just make sure you don't hit me."

"You have a vest on?"

"Not yet. I got a nice Kevlar in the car that don't show too much under my shirt. I'll have it on. And I'll have a nine-millimeter Browning under my armpit and a Charter Arms Pug on my ankle."

"What's the Pug? Twenty-five millimeter?"

"Yep. What are you holding?"

"Forty-five. Caspian Arms. Custom."

"That's a big fucking cannon. I assume you know what you're doing with it?"

"It's taken me quite a while to figure that out."

"What does that mean?"

"It means I can shoot exactly where I want to, and I'm not killing anyone with it."

"If you had the choice between letting me get killed and killing someone, would you still hold to that rule?"

"I wouldn't let it get to that point."

Zitter shrugged, letting the topic go. "The hell with it. Everybody does what he's gotta do."

Devlin picked up the check, laid down cash, and they left.

#

Devlin walked into O'Callahan's deciding he wanted to know right away if they were coming.

He walked up to the bar and called out, "Brian." The bartender stopped what he was doing and came over quickly, despite a pronounced limp.

Devlin asked, "They going to be here?"

"They said they would."

"What did you tell them?"

"I told them some guy was coming in they should meet."

"What did you say when they asked why?

"I said they'd find out when they get here."

Devlin asked, "They think it's some kind of a score?"

"I let them get that impression."

"Good. You tell them to be on time?"

"Yes."

Devlin checked his watch. It was ten minutes until ten. "Tell them to see me at that back table."

O'Callahan's was fairly quiet. There were empty stools at the bar. One booth in the front and one table in the back were occupied.

That left five empty tables. Devlin sat at the one farthest to the rear. He only had to wait fifteen minutes before they arrived. It seemed like a long time. He couldn't stop thinking about that goddamn adhesive tape pulled across his brother's face to hold in the respirator tube.

He saw them as soon as they walked into the bar. He recognized the taller one, but really didn't remember the other. They were both thin and wiry. Friendly and easygoing, moving loosely, as if maybe they were already drunk. Both had thick brown hair, both had prominent white teeth. Devlin thought they looked like a cross between the Gibb brothers of the Bee Gees and Jack and Bobby Kennedy. They were perfect guys to spend an evening with in a bar.

Their innocent looks made Devlin even more furious.

McGinty drew them pints of thick, foamy Guinness and motioned back toward Devlin.

Zitter still hadn't shown, but it didn't break Devlin's concentration on the two brothers. Just as they got up from the bar with their pint glasses of stout, Zitter walked in.

As the two approached him, Devlin stood up from the table. The taller one had on a light green sport coat, a short-sleeve plaid shirt, and jeans. The smaller brother had on black jeans and a red pullover knit shirt. Their clothes seemed cheap and foreign. The clothes made them look a little poor. A little less threatening.

Zitter hiked his leg over a stool and took a seat at the bar near the front door. Knowing that Zitter would prevent them from leaving, Devlin came out from behind the table and greeted the two brothers. If they decided to bolt when they saw him, Devlin was sure he and Zitter could stop them.

If the sight of Devlin concerned them, it didn't show. The taller one held out his hand. "Sean McKay."

Devlin shook his hand and felt the compact strength thin men often have.

"Jack Devlin."

The smaller brother introduced himself. "William McKay. Devlin, aye? Son of the sod, I take it."

Devlin wasn't interested in small talk. He motioned for them to sit at the table so they would be facing the front of the bar and said, "Have a seat."

Devlin sat in the chair facing the back wall. That put his back to the front of the bar and blocked the view of everyone else in the place.

As soon as they all sat down, Devlin carefully took out his .45. He laid it flat on the table with the barrel facing the brothers. The gun looked huge.

Both brothers stared at the gun. Devlin carefully laid a napkin over it in case the waitress came by.

Then he spoke quietly to the brothers. "Both of you put your hands on the table, and don't move, or I'll shoot you." He pointed to Sean and said, "You I'll shoot in the eye," then to William he said, "You I'll shoot in the fucking teeth."

The taller one, Sean, spoke first. "Take it easy, lad. I know you, you know me, no need for this now, is there?"

"That depends on you two. Now listen to me very carefully. Sean, open your jacket slowly and show me there's no gun in there."

Sean did as he was told.

There didn't seem to be any bulge under William's shirt. Devlin told them, "Don't either of you move your hands an inch from this table."

Sean said, "Yes, sir. You're the boss. There's no need for that gun now, you know. Terrible, fearsome, horrible things."

Devlin looked at the two men and thought they should be more nervous.

"Here's what's going to happen. I'm going to ask you some questions. You answer me, and I won't break your hands so bad you'll never throw darts again."

Sean, the taller brother stared back at Devlin. He answered, "Well now, sir, am I supposed to be terrified?

"I don't give a damn what you are. All I want you to do is listen to me and answer my questions. If you move or try to leave, you'll be hurt."

"Ask your damn questions then, and to hell with your threats. I've been threatened by better than you, so leave off. What are you in an uproar over? Your brother? I remember you. You were in here with that big sod the other night. Both of you drunk as skunks. What happened? He get home without a few dollars?"

Devlin reached across the table and grabbed the shorter brother by the back of the head and slammed his face onto the table. The sound of his nose breaking sounded like a huge knuckle cracking. A man eating at a table nearby turned to see what made the noise. Several people at the bar turned as William came up off the table with his hands to his face. The blood streamed from between his fingers, but he held in any reaction to the pain. It happened so fast that no one really knew what had occurred.

Devlin glared at Sean and said, "If you'd like your brother hurt some more, keep it up. I'll beat him to a bloody mess before anybody stops me because that's exactly what somebody did to my brother. Now I'm going to find out who did it. And if you think you can stop me, keep acting the tough guy."

William had a napkin to his face, trying to keep the blood off his red sweater. Devlin was impressed with the way he took the pain.

Without taking his eyes off Devlin, Sean very quietly told his brother, "Billy, go to the bathroom and stop the bleeding. Then come back and sit down. This man and I are going to have a conversation."

Before standing up, the smaller brother looked at Devlin. Devlin nodded, and William stood up and left with a napkin hiding most of his face.

Sean said very quietly, "We never laid a finger on your brother. If you tracked us down to it, then you know our game. We drink and give a fella a good time until he's too drunk to see straight. Then we take his money and maybe his credit cards. We always leave him enough to get home. We never deal in any rough stuff. If a mark gets loud or tough, we walk. If we spend all night at it and it looks like we'd have to hurt someone, we walk."

"I hold you responsible for my brother. What did you do to him?"

"Nothing. We took him to an after-hours joint, thinking we could wear him out. We couldn't do it. He was a goddamn ox. We had to drink alongside him by then. No one was serving us weak stuff like in here. We couldn't keep up. We boosted a few bills from his change, but that was it. Period. We left him. On his own. Alone. You want to make us your brother's keeper, fine. We did the same thing to him you did. We left him in a fucking bar."

Devlin rubbed his face and eyes. He looked into the Irishman's face. There was a matter-of-fact toughness about the man that Devlin didn't expect. He seemed to be telling the truth not because he was afraid, but because he didn't care to say anything else.

Sean started to reach into his pocket, and Devlin told him tiredly, "Don't move. Keep your hands on the table."

William returned from the bathroom. He walked carefully and took his chair beside his brother. He had toilet paper stuffed into his nostrils. The paper was turning red.

Sean asked, "How are you then? Better?"

"Been worse."

The brothers looked at each other and seemed to reach an understanding of some sort.

Devlin looked at them and said, "I don't know what the hell you're up to, but we're going to start with last night, and you're going to tell me everything that happened until you left my brother. Where you went, who you saw, what happened. Start talking."

Sean looked over Devlin's shoulder and told him, "I think not, sir. I think we've told you all we're going to."

Devlin followed his gaze and looked over his shoulder. He saw a young policeman entering the bar. He had red hair and freckles. He looked like a grown-up version of Howdy Doody.

Out on the street, Devlin could see the back end of a police car double parked.

Sean smiled and said, "It looks like our ride is here."

Devlin saw Zitter staring at him. He gave Devlin a quick shake of his head that told him not to try to stop the police officer.

The cop walked straight toward the table. Devlin slowly placed the .45 back in his armpit holster. The cop approached and said, "What's the problem here, gentlemen?"

Sean answered, "No problem officer. We were just leaving."

Devlin remained seated as the two brothers stood up. Sean bent over and said to him, "If you found us, you'll find where your brother went, but it won't come from me. The people who run those places can cause me a hell of a lot more trouble than a broken nose. Good night, now."

The brothers turned to leave as the cop stood over Devlin.

Devlin stood up and said, "Wait a minute. Aren't you going to introduce me to your policeman friend?"

Sean stopped and turned. His smile showed his big white teeth. He stepped toward Devlin and the cop. "Certainly, son. This is Officer Donovan. Officer, this is . . . what did you say your name was, sir?"

"Devlin. Jack Devlin."

"Mr. Devlin, Officer Donovan."

Devlin shook the cop's hand and said, "If you're a cop, what the hell are you doing protecting scum like this?"

The cop dropped Devlin's hand and said, "What the fuck are you talking about? You looking to have your ass beat and thrown in jail?"

"Yeah! Throw me in jail. Go ahead. I broke that little bastard's nose there. Did he tell you that when he called?"

The cop said, "What, are you crazy?"

Devlin said, "Here, let me show you." And before Sean could move out of his reach, Devlin grabbed him behind the head with his right hand and smashed his left elbow into his nose, breaking it. In a split second, he had his face right into the cop's.

"Go for it, you fuck. Go for your gun. I'll stick it right up your ass and pull the trigger. I'll face any judge before I let a rogue cop push me around."

The cop told him, "You're fucking crazy."

Devlin said, "Maybe so. Maybe so," and then turned and walked toward the front of the bar. For a second, he wondered if the cop was going to shoot him in the back. Then he saw Zitter slide off his stool and stare at the young cop so it would be harder for him to shoot Devlin.

As Devlin passed Zitter, they ignored each other, and Devlin headed for the door. He made it out of O'Callahan's, walked behind the parked police car. Donovan's partner was sitting in the driver's seat. He had no idea of what had just happened inside. Devlin hailed a cab coming down Second Avenue, jumped in, and was gone.

CHAPTER 14

Devlin took the taxi back to Juanita's and waited at the bar for his beeper to vibrate, or for Zitter to walk in the door.

He drank a cup of coffee and fought off the urge to have the bartender throw a shot of Jameson in it. He sat and thought about why the urge to drink nagged at him. Too many goddamn bars, he thought.

Before he finished the coffee, the beeper vibrated in his pocket. He fished it out and squinted at the digital number that appeared on the small screen. He slid off the bar stool, found the phones in the back of the restaurant and dialed the number. Zitter picked up the phone on the first ring.

"Where are you?"

"Juanita's."

"I'll drive by in five minutes. Don't come out until you see my car. You've got to get the hell out of this neighborhood. If that cop and his partner get themselves together, they'll be looking for you."

"If they wanted to arrest me they would have done it."

"They might just want to shoot you, for chrissake. Stay out of sight till I get there."

Zitter hung up without another word. Devlin went back to the bar and settled his tab. He watched out the window until he saw Zitter's green Dodge Dart appear. He ducked into the car and Zitter immediately turned off Third Avenue and headed east.

Zitter told him, "Scrunch down in that seat. I don't want to shoot it out with those boys and their buddies."

Devlin hated doing it, but he couldn't drag Zitter into suffering for his rage.

Zitter said, "Tell me what happened back there."

"They beat me, Sam. I didn't scare them for a second."

"No? It looked like you got your licks in."

"Not enough to stop them.

"How did the cop show up?"

"When I slammed the shorter one's face, they asked if he could go to the bathroom to stop the bleeding. I shouldn't have let him out of my sight. I guess there's a payphone by the restrooms. The bartender didn't do it, did he?"

"No. No way. He wasn't near a phone."

"Damn it. They must have some deal with that cop for protection."

"You think so?" asked Zitter.

"Yeah. The cop knew those guys. He didn't come in there to see what was happening or to arrest me. He came to get them out. He wouldn't even take me down when I challenged him. He didn't want anyone to know he's connected to those two."

"It's not the first time cops helped some crooks. Maybe those two are snitches he's trying to protect."

"I don't think that's it. What happened after I left?"

"Nothing. I got between you and him. Then the waitress came over. A couple of other people in the place started to gather. He took a second to check with the Irish guys, looked up, saw me and everybody else between him and you, so he just went out to his squad car and got on the radio. Maybe to get a line on you. I guess you're right. If he was legit, he would have gone after you."

"Thanks for stepping in. I might have pissed him off enough to shoot me if you hadn't gotten between us."

"It's tough for a cop to explain shooting a guy in the back. I just made it a little harder for him. So what the hell have we got here?"

"We got two scam artists who have the balls to face me down with my gun on the table, and are hooked in with the cops for protection."

"Did you get anything out of them?"

"They said they took my brother to an after-hours club, then left him when it looked like they couldn't get him drunk enough to fleece him."

"You believe them?"

"I don't think he was lying. And I don't think they're the ones who beat my brother."

"Why not?"

"No way they could have come through it without some damage. They might have been able to hit George from behind and beaten him when he was down, but I just didn't see that in them. And if they had done that to my brother they would never have come back to that bar and faced me down."

"I doubt the bartender told them it was you."

"Probably not. But when they saw me they didn't even try to leave."

Zitter shrugged. "And they didn't know you had me between them and the door. So now what?"

"Those two are long gone for now. The only thing I've got is finding the after-hours club they took him to. You know of any in that neighborhood?"

"No. Not really."

"Which is it? Not really or no?"

"I used to know a couple of places years back, but I'm sure they're gone now. Most of 'em don't stay in one place for too long. You know you can't just walk into one of those joints, much less ask a lot of questions."

"Can you find out where some of them are?"

"Probably. Not tonight. I'll have to make a few calls to people I know."

"What is it the cops have assigned to keep after these places?"

Zitter turned onto York Avenue and headed over to 65th to get on the FDR. "Used to be about five or six detectives had the assignment in each borough, along with other shit they had to do. They'd work out of an all-borough command somewhere. Then after the fire that killed all those people in that illegal club in the Bronx a while back, they hooked up building inspectors and fire marshals with the cops.

"But as far as I remember the cops still do the initial checking. If they find something, they call in the building inspectors and fire department. I don't know who's running that squad in Manhattan. I can find out."

"Do these places pay off the detectives to stay in business?"

"I don't know. I think most of 'em just keep moving around. If they were to pay off someone, it wouldn't be just the detectives. It'd be some inspector or deputy inspector. The higher-ups would make sure the squad steers clear of a particular place."

"Pull over a second, Sam."

"What are you going to do?"

"Start finding out where these clubs are."

"Hey listen, pal, those two cops aren't going to let you get away with what you pulled back there. I'd stay off the streets if I were you."

"Come on, Sam, pull over and let me out."

Zitter stopped the car at a curb and turned to Devlin. "Where are you going to look? There could be a half a dozen in Manhattan alone. More up in Harlem. A bunch out in Brooklyn."

"No, it would have been in Manhattan. I don't see my brother taking a long ride somewhere with those guys no matter how much fun he was having."

"Shit, they could have holed up in half a dozen regular bars. A lot of joints lock the doors and keep drinking for hours with a few of the regulars. Those guys must know bartenders who'd let 'em keep drinking after hours."

"No. They said it was an after-hours club. That bartender figured it that way, too."

"Meanwhile his ass is grass.

"Yeah, I hope his pals tear his head off."

"So," Zitter asked, "you determined to try and find some tonight?"

"Yeah. Why don't you call it a night and start checking for me in the morning?"

Zitter looked at his watch. It was an old Bulova with most of the chrome finish long worn off. It said the time was 11:40. "Not likely I'm going to find out anything tonight. I'll start in the morning. Don't get yourself killed."

"Thanks."

Devlin got out and slammed the door. Zitter leaned over the front seat and talked out the passenger window. "Maybe that cop is just a friend of those guys. He was Irish, too, you know."

Devlin leaned into the passenger side window and said, "No cop comes running that fast for a friend. That guy's on a payroll. I'll call you in the morning."

CHAPTER 15

Devlin walked into Jimmy Pappas's restaurant fifteen minutes later. The big Greek was working the bar with his son Peter. The place was called The Fish, located on Columbus Avenue between 88th and 89th, occupying a space in the midst of the gentrification that was finally making Jimmy Pappas rich.

When Devlin walked in, it was Thursday morning, just past midnight. It was barely two days since his night out with George, but with so many hours spent awake, it seemed as if it had been twice that long.

Jimmy Pappas was at the far end of the bar. His stomach looked bigger, his black mustache looked thicker, and the man's constant frown was more severe than Devlin remembered but other than that it was the same Jimmy Pappas. White shirt, black tie, and starched white apron tied above his generous belly.

Devlin walked to where Pappas was standing, thinking that he had never seen Jimmy Pappas anywhere else but behind a bar.

Pappas spotted him quickly, but his face remained expressionless. His eyes blinked as he tried to match Devlin's face with his name. Devlin put out his hand and said, "Jimmy, Jack Devlin."

Pappas threw his head back and grimaced because he had not been able to remember Devlin's name.

He took Devlin's hand without leaning forward off the back-bar. "I woulda had it in two more seconds. Jack Devlin. How are you?"

"Not so great, Jimmy. I'd like to talk to you."

Pappas frowned and asked, "How long has it been since I seen you?"

"A long time. I'm sorry to barge in on you, Jimmy, but I need a favor."

"I ain't seen you for what, fifteen, eighteen years and you come in asking me for a favor?'

"Yeah."

The big Greek pursed his lips. Fifteen years ago, Devlin had helped him stop a State Liquor Authority investigator from shaking down Pappas. Pappas remembered his help but still didn't like the notion of paying Devlin back.

"What kind of favor?"

"I need to know the locations of after-hours clubs in Manhattan. I haven't been around here for years. Restaurant and bar people know where they are. So I thought of you. I figured you might know."

Pappas asked, "What do you need to know about those places for?"

"It's a long story that you don't want to hear. Can you help me, Jimmy?"

Pappas pulled a Pall Mall out of his shirt pocket and lit it. Devlin waited.

Pappas wasn't sure he wanted to help. "I don't know where any of those places are now. It's been years since I went to one. You know they aren't meant to be found. You can't just get an address. You gotta know exactly where they are."

"Do any of your waiters or waitresses know?"

Pappas finally made his decision. "Yeah, my kid probably knows a few places." He leaned forward and pointed his finger at Devlin. I'm going to let him come over here and talk to you, but I don t want you asking him to take you or getting him involved. I owe you from years ago, but you are going to make trouble for someone at one of these places. I know it just by looking at you." Pappas took another deep drag out of his Pall Mall. "I know that look. I'm sorry you got problems, Jack, but don't involve my kid."

"I won't."

Pappas abruptly walked to the other end of the bar. Devlin watched him talk to his son for about a minute. The son nodded as his father spoke.

Peter came out from behind the bar and walked up to Devlin. He looked nothing at all like his father. Devlin thought that Jimmy Pappas's wife must be a beautiful woman.

The young man extended his hand. "Peter Pappas. Let's sit down over there."

They walked to a table in the back and sat down facing each other. "My father told me you want to know about after-hours clubs?"

Devlin said, "Yes."

Peter waited for Devlin to say more, but when he didn't, he started talking.

"Okay. Here's what I know. There's a place on Fifty-sixth between Second and Third called Eternity. It's on the uptown side of the block. About the middle. It's next to a parking garage. There's a blue door. That's the entrance. The club is up one flight of stairs. The place has two floors. Not anything exotic. They have some slot machines and one of those big wheels with dice on it like you see at the Italian festivals. The place is fairly safe, not too grungy, but kind of a rip-off. Five bucks for a beer. If you want to keep drinking after the regular bars close, the place is okay. It can get pretty wild in there sometimes.

"Another club I know about is over in Alphabet City. Avenue D, I think. Around Houston. I've never been there. Called Save the Tiger or something. I wouldn't go over there on a bet. Can't tell you much about it.

"Then there's an Irish bar called Deadwood way up on Broadway and 118th. Place is a regular bar, but it opens about one or two and stays open until noon or something. I was there once. You just walk in. No hassles. Nothing special, really, but you can drink all night in there. They actually have a liquor license. I don't know how the hell they stay open after four, but they do it.

"I also heard of a place in Chelsea, I think it's called Begin or something, but I've never been there. I know there's a bunch of clubs in Brooklyn, mostly in Bay Ridge. The ones in Brooklyn are mostly connected joints I think. Never been to any of them, either."

"So the ones you've been to are this Eternity place and the Irish bar uptown?"

"Yeah."

Devlin asked, "How can I get into Eternity?"

"Make up some bullshit. Tell the guy at the door you're a bartender just off work. He'll probably let you in. I guess you never know for sure. It's better to go with someone."

"What time do they open?"

"About three, but it doesn't really get busy until four or five. Some of the hardcore places don't open till four. Some start up about three."

"Okay, Peter, thanks. I appreciate your help."

"No problem."

Devlin stood up from the table to leave, but Peter stopped him. "Uh, sir."

Devlin sat down. "Yes?"

"Uh, at these places the bouncers check you over pretty good. They pat you down or run a metal detector over you, so, uh, don't have any kind of a weapon on you, you know?"

Devlin nodded. "Thanks."

As he walked out, he stopped at the bar and told Jimmy Pappas, "Thanks, Jimmy."

The Greek nodded and watched him leave, hoping he'd never see or hear from Jack Devlin again.

#

Susan had known Wexler was going to demand sex from her, but she just hadn't known when. He waited about two months, long enough for her to grow accustomed to the money and the apartment. Accustomed enough not to want to lose them.

After they closed the Starlight, Wexler always drove her home. One morning, when Randy stopped the Mercedes in front of her apartment building, Wexler simply said, "It's time we had sex."

He rode up in the elevator with her without a word. When they entered the apartment, he said, "Take me to your bedroom."

Once in the bedroom he told her, "Take off my clothes and fold them carefully, please."

He stood while she did this, so she had to get down on her knees to take off his underwear and socks. When her face was in front of his penis he told her, "Look at it. How many men have you seen with a cock this big?"

Susan looked and knew what he wanted to hear. "Not many, Robert. It's very big. Very big and nice. You have a very nice body." Susan was glad that Wexler did, in fact, have a fairly large cock and was in excellent shape for a man his age. It made it less ridiculous for her to comment.

"Touch it. Stroke me until I am hard."

Again, Susan did as she was told. It was obvious to her that just as he engineered the sexual atmosphere of the Starlight, he wanted to use sex as a means to control her.

"There's a condom in my pants pocket, get it and take me to your bathroom."

She found the condom and led Wexler into her bathroom.

"Turn on the shower and adjust it."

The room began to fill with a misty steam from the hot water.

"Now take off your clothes, slowly."

Susan wanted to make Wexler watch her every move. She stepped out of her heels, unzipped her skirt, and let it fall to the floor. She had on pantyhose over lace panties. She turned around and let Wexler watch her full round buttocks as she bent over and slid the pantyhose down her long legs.

She turned around and saw Wexler staring at her with total indulgence. She felt as if he could see every piece of her. She thought about a mole on her left hip, the scar on her knee, the tiny stretch marks on the sides of her full breasts. She tried to remember the last time she waxed her legs and pubic hair because she felt as if Wexler could see every stubble.

She knew Wexler enjoyed looking at her breasts, so she saved taking off her bra for last. She bent over and let him see her cleavage before she unhooked the bra.

Susan had always been proud of her body. Her skin was alabaster white. It had a natural sheen and richness to it. But the way Wexler stared at her without saying a word, she felt her body was slightly unclean.

When she was naked, Wexler told her to lift the lid of the toilet and sit. "Spread your legs."

She did.

"Wider."

She hesitated, and Wexler repeated his request with an extra edge in his voice. "Wider."

Defiantly she spread her legs as far apart as she could. Wexler stepped in between her parted knees and said, "Now suck me. Suck me very nicely and massage my ass while you do it."

Again, it was Susan's turn to be in control, so she took Wexler into her mouth and tried to make him squirm with pleasure. Wexler enjoyed himself but wouldn't allow her to make him come. He eased himself out of her mouth and told her, "Put the condom on me with your mouth, and then wet it down with your tongue."

She followed his instructions, and he told her, "Stand up, turn around and bend over the sink so your nipples are just touching the porcelain."

She did it.

"Now put one foot on the toilet."

When she was in position, Wexler entered her from behind, slowly and gently. With her back to him and the room filled with steam, Susan could imagine Wexler to be whomever she wanted, so she let herself relax and enjoy the feelings. Wexler increased the speed and depth of his thrusts. Susan wanted him to come quickly, so she squirmed and pushed her against Wexler and tried to squeeze his cock in her vagina. Susan started to grunt slightly, but Wexler didn't make a sound. She knew he was getting closer, so she began to moan and meet his thrusts. Wexler's hands grabbed her hips and pulled her into him. He rasped out, "Hold my balls while I come."

She reached between her legs and held him while he climaxed. She was glad when he came. She wanted to end the domineering sex, but Wexler had much more to demand of her. She had to attend to him. Take off the condom. Bring him into the shower and wash him all over. Then back out into the bedroom where she had to dress him.

Each subsequent session was very similar. He never took her to bed. It was always done in the bathroom. And he always found some way to degrade her just slightly. Not so much that she would rebel completely, for Wexler knew she had it in her, but just enough so he could bring her right up to the line without going over.

The last thing he told her was to wash his shorts and socks so that the next time he came over, he didn't have to go home in dirty underwear.

CHAPTER 16

By the time Devlin left the Greek's place, it was 1:15 A.M. Too early to start checking the after-hours clubs, too late to try to get some sleep first.

He was on Columbus and 81st Street. The night suddenly seemed a little fresher and cooler. Enough time had passed so that some of the day's heat had seeped out of the concrete. Devlin headed downtown. He had to walk. Get the kinks out. Let his arms swing loose, and his head clear. He doubted if any cops would be looking for him on the West Side.

Even though it was late, there were plenty of people on the streets. He passed a man in his fifties walking a small poodle. A knot of three men in their twenties came toward him. They were dressed casually. Jeans, shorts, polo shirts, and T-shirts. One had a Mets cap on his head with the bill cocked to the right. One carried an open bottle of Rolling Rock beer. Their loud voices disturbed Devlin's train of thought.

He kept walking, picking up the pace, stretching his muscles. He let his mind wander back over the last three days. He had buried a father and almost lost his brother. It had all happened so quickly. For years there was little contact with his family, then suddenly he was immersed in it, and just as suddenly he seemed to be fighting for his family's very existence. If he lost his brother, it would all be gone. Marilyn and the children would have no more connection to him. And he already knew that his brother would never be the same.

He might be permanently crippled. At the very least he'd have scars and pains that would last the rest of his life. And some part of George would have to resent his brother for leaving him alone that night.

Devlin stopped at a payphone and picked up the receiver to dial Gramercy Hospital's Intensive Care Unit, but instead of a dial tone, he got a mechanical clicking sound.

He set the receiver down and looked around for another bank of payphones. He saw three phones on the next block and started walking. About the middle of the block, a black man with torn brown pants, no shoes, and a filthy T-shirt stepped toward him holding out a cardboard coffee cup from a Greek diner.

Devlin still held the quarter he had pulled out to make the phone call. He dropped it into the decrepit cardboard cup. It didn't hit any other coins.

You couldn't walk the streets of New York for any amount of time without being stopped for money. Some of the people asking for money were crackheads, some were drunks, some were just home- less and desperate. Something had gone terribly wrong, thought Devlin, but it seemed that everyone had just learned to live with it. How did it happen? Could there be so many people who wanted to grab money and property and housing for themselves that thousands were turned out on the street to make way for them? Was the greed that strong? Did people really think they could get away with it?

And then he thought, someone decided they could get away with beating my brother half to death. Why not get away with renovating single-room-occupancy hotels for yuppie co-ops and throwing the people who used to live in them out on the street?

He reached the bank of three payphones. The first one had a dial tone, but a plate had been slid across the coin slot, and he couldn't deposit a quarter. The phone next to it worked, and he finally placed his call. The broken phones and homeless and thoughts of arrogance were enough to set his anger simmering again. He couldn't get rid of it. The anger just wouldn't leave him alone.

He got through to the nurse on duty in the ICU and tried to picture what she looked like through her voice. The head nurse he had talked to when he first visited was small and blond and hunched over. He didn't know then if she was hunched over because she didn't like her figure, was tired or was just worn down from the burden of deathly serious illness day after day.

The nurse put him on hold for about a minute. When she came back, she said, "Mr. Devlin's condition is stable. He did seem more responsive this afternoon. He is running a slight fever. It could be from the surgical intervention or from the IV lines. He's on a course of antibiotics for that. His lungs are clear. Cerebral swelling continues to decrease."

"Is he still on the respirator?"

"Yes, but I think the doctor will start weaning him tomorrow."

"What does that mean?"

"Gradually turn the machine down, and then disconnect him when he is breathing on his own."

The tone in her voice and the speed of her sentences told Devlin she had gone past the point where she wanted to answer any more questions.

"One more thing."

A curt, "Yes?"

"When they get him off the respirator, will they take that tube out of his mouth?"

"No. Not for a while. We have to keep him intubated until we're sure he doesn't need the respirator. We don't want to do it over again if he has to go back on. Also, it's easier to suction his lungs if they get congested."

"Thank you."

"Goodbye."

It seemed it was important for her to hang up first.

Devlin thought about calling Marilyn, but he knew it was too late. Then he decided to call his office at Pacific Rim in Los Angeles and get that over with. He punched in the number, preceded by 0, and when the tone came on, he punched in his credit card number.

He knew the answering service would pick up since it was past eleven in L.A.

A woman's voice said, "Pacific Rim."

Devlin said, "This is a message from Jack Devlin for Mr. Chow."

"Yes."

"Tell him I will be delayed in New York. My brother has had an accident. He is in the hospital. I will be using the company's apartment for a while longer. I'll be in touch tomorrow."

The woman said, "We'll give him the message."

Devlin said thanks, hung up the phone and continued walking, picking up his pace.

During daytime hours, he would start to gather information on the after-hours clubs—Zitter, David Freedman, maybe put Pacific Rim on it. For now, he would check out Peter Pappas's lead.

Then it hit him. He stopped and stabbed at his left armpit. He had to get rid of his gun. They were going to check for weapons at these clubs. There was no way he was going to get in with his .45.

He was just passing 72nd Street and Central Park West. He could have caught a cab and gone back to SoHo to Pacific Rim's loft to stash the gun, clean up, change clothes, eat. But instead, he stopped at yet another payphone, dialed 411 and got the number for D. Austen on 63rd Street.

He dialed the number and let it ring three times. He thought about how she would sound when she woke up and grimaced, but he let the phone ring a fourth and then a fifth time.

There was no hello. She answered with, "Who is this?"

"Daryl. I'm sorry. It's me, Jack. I need to come over."

There was a moment of silence. Then she asked, "Why?"

"I need a place to stash my gun."

"What? Are you trying to be funny at two in the morning?"

"Look. I want to see you. I need a place to be for a little while. Tell me yes or no."

Pause. Then, "Yes. The doormen leave at midnight. Ring me from the lobby." Then he heard her hang up.

He replaced the receiver and hailed a cab. For a moment, he thought about jogging through the park to clear his head and dissipate some of his anger. But he didn't want to sweat up his clothes. He had nothing clean to change into.

When he arrived at Daryl's apartment building, he found her buzzer in the lobby and pushed it once. She rang him in.

She was standing in the doorway waiting for him when he stepped out of the elevator. She had on a short silk robe styled like a kimono. It was white, and there were wispy lines of pink lilacs printed on it. She was barefoot, her long legs looked smooth and inviting. She stood with one foot on top of the other.

Her hair was down, and she had a look on her face that could have meant she was mad. He didn't know if she was going to smile as he approached, or if she was going to stay mad.

Devlin walked straight at her waiting to see which it would be. He figured he could walk right back out and take that cab downtown if he had to. He didn't want more trouble than he already had.

When he reached her, she asked him, "Are you all right?"

"Yes."

She put her hand flat on Devlin's chest and asked him, "You're not coming up here for some quick fuck, are you? Because if you are, you can leave now."

"No. I'm not. I wanted to see you. And I need another favor."

She put her hand down, and Devlin realized she had been blocking his entrance. She turned, and he followed her into the apartment.

From behind he could tell there was nothing on under the silk robe and despite what he said the desire to make love to her felt almost overwhelming.

Daryl walked into the kitchen and with her back to him asked, "Do you want coffee?"

"Yes."

Devlin didn't want to sit and watch her make coffee, so he turned into the bathroom while she went into the kitchen.

He emptied his bladder, washed his face and dried off with a clean towel. He pressed a blob of toothpaste on his finger, put it into his mouth, then cupped water into his mouth. He swirled it all around and spit it out. Dried off again and went into the kitchen.

The cups with instant coffee in them sat on the table. The water was ready. Daryl filled the cups.

They sat at the small table sipping the coffee for a moment and then Daryl said, "Talk to me."

"We found my brother."

Her eyes opened wide, and she asked, "Where?"

"In the hospital. Somebody beat the shit out of him. He's in a coma."

"Oh God, Jack, is he going to be all right?"

"I won't know for a few days. The doctor said there's a chance there won't be any permanent damage, but he looks like hell right now. They had to do an operation to relieve the swelling in his head."

"Oh my God. What happened?"

"Nobody knows. But I'm going to find out."

"How?"

"Track down what happened to him starting from that bar where I left him."

"God, I feel terrible. We run off and leave your brother alone, and he almost gets killed."

"It wasn't your fault. It was mine."

"Bullshit. It was my fault, too. I feel responsible. It was me in that bar with the come-hither look on my stupid face."

"You couldn't have known what was going to happen."

"Why don't you leave this to the cops? I mean, why put yourself in danger?"

"Do you really think the cops are going to do anything about it?"

Daryl looked at Devlin over the rim of her coffee cup. "And you can?"

Devlin leaned toward her. "I guess I'll find out, won't I?"

"Are you crazy?"

"Why? Because I want to do something about it? What's crazy is that if I don't, nobody else will."

"I don't believe that."

"You don't? I'll tell you what I don't believe. I don't believe the cops will ever find out who did it. And if they got lucky and did find out, I don't believe they'd ever get enough evidence so a D.A. could make a case out of it. And even if the cops did find the bastards and a D.A. did have enough evidence to prosecute I don't believe there's a goddamn judge in this city who can make anyone serve hard time for it."

"So *you* have to be the justice system?"

Devlin's voice rose in anger. "Tell me another way. You really think that just because little school kids put their hands on their hearts and recite the Pledge of Allegiance this country can provide liberty and justice for all? How about justice for one? For my brother?"

"I know what you're saying, but what good does it do if you end up ... "

Devlin finished her sentence. "End up like my brother?"

"Yes. Now tell me you don't believe that can happen."

"It can happen. But not without a lot of others going down, too." Devlin sat back in the chair and pulled in his anger. "Look, I don't want to yell at you about it. There's no point in arguing. I just can't let something like this pass."

Daryl stood up and emptied her coffee into the sink. "This is insane. How did I get involved in this?"

"You aren't involved. You shouldn't be involved. I shouldn't be here except I just wanted to be around somebody who's ..."

"Who's what?"

The challenge in her voice stopped his answer. She asked again, "Who's what?"

"I don't know. Maybe just someone who isn't a part of all the shit that goes on out there."

Daryl turned to him and said, "Christ, I don't even know you." She shook her head. "How did I let myself get involved in this? Because you're so goddamn handsome? Because you have such a good body? Because my boyfriend left me? It's crazy. I have no idea who you really are."

Devlin stood up and took off his linen jacket. She saw the sweat stains under his arms as he unstrapped his shoulder harness and took off the holster with the big .45-caliber Caspian semi-automatic.

"Of course you do. You've got your eyes and your instincts. You know me enough to know I'm right. I've been on the right side against bad guys for twenty years. New York City cop, Army military police, Secret Service, and now a private company run by a man who knows what's right and doesn't mind fighting for it. That's me. The guy you slept with in your bed; the guy you followed back into that bar; the guy you let in here tonight at two o'clock in the morning. You know me, and you know goddamn well I won't sit next to my brother in that goddamn hospital and do nothing."

Devlin had wrapped the holster rig around his gun and set it between them on the kitchen table.

"You're right not to want to get involved. I shouldn't be here. But I wanted to see you, and you said yes, so I'm here. If you want me to leave, or you want to get back to sleep, tell me to get the hell out and go back to bed."

Daryl said, "Okay. It's okay. I'm glad you came over. It's just all so fucking weird I don't know what to say. This whole mess around you makes me sad, and yes it makes me angry. And yes, I'd like to just strangle whoever hurt your brother. But I'm worried about you. And I could get to be crazy about you very easily. So tell me what you want to do with that ugly gun of yours, and for God's sake the one thing I forbid you to do is to make me another one of the things you worry about. I couldn't stand that. I trust you now. I don't know why, but I do. So you do what you have to do, and I'll understand."

"Okay."

"If something comes out on the other side of this mess, then we'll worry about what's right."

"Thank you."

"You're welcome."

Devlin stood up. "Thank you again. If you don't mind, while I'm here I'd like to clean up a little before I go back out there."

"Of course."

He picked up the gun and holster and walked to the cabinet above her refrigerator. He took the gun out of the holster and slipped out the ammunition clip, put the gun back into the holster and wrapped the shoulder straps around the holster and the ammunition clip. He reached over the refrigerator and opened the cabinet. It was a place for things that were rarely used—a coffee urn, a box of tableware, a crocheted table cloth. He placed the gun behind everything and closed the cabinet.

"Try to forget that's up there."

He showered, shaved with her Lady Bic again, used her towel, her deodorant, and her hairbrush. He dressed back into his dirty clothes with a slight shudder.

When he came out of the bathroom, Daryl was buried under her blanket in the chilled, air-conditioned bedroom. He bent over and told her he was leaving. She reached up and stroked his face and mumbled, "Be careful."

He walked out of the apartment feeling better than when he'd walked in.

CHAPTER 17

The place was right where Peter Pappas said it would be. But the door wasn't blue anymore. It was dead black with a blot of silver graffiti that looked like the letters VXR. The door was metal-clad and set back about six inches into a wooden frame. It looked as if it hadn't been opened in years. There was a knob, but Devlin didn't even bother turning it. He looked around the door frame and spotted a buzzer on the right side.

He pressed the buzzer and heard a tinny ring somewhere inside. It seemed to be ringing in emptiness. Suddenly the door popped open, and Devlin had to step back. A small man with a beat-up face and a tweed cap stood in the doorway. He wore a knit shirt and khaki pants.

Devlin spoke first. "You open?"

The doorman leaned out the doorway and looked up and down the block and said, "Who are you?"

"Bartender. A guy I work with told me about the place."

He kept looking up and down the street and said, "You tend bar, huh? Where do you tend bar? Who's your friend?"

"Monday, Wednesday, Friday at Doyle's Pub. Saturday down in the Village. What's the problem?"

He looked at Devlin and said, "No problem. No problem. Step in. Step in."

He opened the door wide enough for Devlin to enter a small foyer at the bottom of a stairwell that went straight up one flight to another doorway. Devlin started to walk up the stairs, and the doorman held his shoulder gently and said, "Hang on a second. I'm upstairs. Let me send down the downstairs guy."

The man in the tweed cap went up the stairs two at a time and disappeared inside the club. A young man big enough to have to stoop under the doorway at the top of the stairs appeared. He had a sullen look on his face and stringy brown hair that came down to his shoulders. He wore an army fatigue jacket, blue jeans, and boots. He shook the hair out of his face and started down the stairs. He seemed to fill the stairwell.

"Hey," he said. Devlin stepped back to make room for him in the foyer. "Stand still."

The big bouncer's voice sounded as if his vocal cords had been worked over with rough sandpaper. Devlin would have bet that voice came from a punch that cracked the bouncer's windpipe.

Devlin spread apart his linen sport jacket while the giant patted him down.

He smiled a quick grimace at Devlin and said, "You're clean, aren't you?"

Devlin said, "Yeah, except for some sweat. Hot night."

He started just below Devlin's armpits and ran his hands all the way down the length of Devlin's body. Then up and down both legs. He stood up straight and placed his big hand flat on Devlin's chest, then around and up and down his back.

He knew exactly what he was doing. He took his time to feel what was under his hands. When he was done, he told Devlin, "Ten bucks cover charge."

Devlin pulled out a ten, and the bouncer took a stack of tickets out of his army fatigue jacket. He handed one to Devlin and said, "Give the ticket to the guy at the top."

As Devlin walked upstairs, the big man sat down on the stairs and waited for the next ring of the bell.

The guy in the tweed cap smiled and took Devlin's ticket and motioned him into the club. The club looked like an old bar that had been decorated for a party about two years ago and left that way. Dingy streamers hung from the ceiling, and strings of tiny lights framed a dirty mirror behind a wooden bar which Devlin faced as he entered.

The room extended to Devlin's left for about twenty feet and continued left around a corner for about another ten feet. Just around the corner, there was a stairway that to led another floor. At the bottom of the L-shaped room were the electronic slot machines and the big dice wheel that Peter Pappas had described.

There were only about a dozen people in the club. Apparently, three-thirty in the morning was early for the place.

Devlin took a seat at the bar. The bartender looked to be about thirty. He had thick black hair that was blow-dried and styled. He wore a shirt that looked like black silk and black slacks. Devlin stepped up, and the bartender asked right way, "What can I get for you?" He sounded almost as Irish as Brian at O'Callahan's. Devlin was also sure the doorman in the tweed cap who had let him in was Irish.

Devlin said, "Jameson and water."

The bartender reached for the bottle without looking. The bartender filled a plastic cup with ice and poured in the whiskey and water. Devlin put a twenty on the bar and got back fifteen dollars.

He sat at the bar and looked over the club through the mirror he was facing. The ceiling was low; the furniture mismatched and cheap; the lighting haphazard. It was too dim to make out very many details.

There was loud music blaring from speakers that were hanging on the walls. It was a strange place. More than a bar, less than a what? A club? A casino? It was a strange hybrid put together to give people somewhere to go after legitimate bars and clubs closed.

It felt as if he were at a party that hadn't quite started yet. There was a furtive, insistent energy flowing through the place as if the people there were waiting for something.

A couple of stools to Devlin's left, an attractive woman sat at the bar. She had long dark hair, brushed straight back. She wore a full-length trench coat despite the hot weather outside. She smoked cigarettes and huddled with the bartender in conversation.

There were two black ladies who seemed to move steadily around the club. Devlin couldn't be sure if they were hustling drinks or sex or what. Devlin took a swallow of his whiskey and watched as the bartender came out from behind the bar and headed for the ladies' bathroom near the club entrance.

The dark-haired woman got off her bar stool and followed him, carrying a large black purse. Devlin saw she was heavier than he would have guessed from her face.

She went into the ladies' room. In a few minutes, the bartender came out carrying a small brown paper bag. It looked like a lunch bag. He folded it tightly at the top and stuck it on a shelf behind the bar. The woman came out a minute later, took her seat, and waited for the next transaction.

Devlin got up, picked up his drink, and began circulating. Nobody was playing the slot machines or big wheel. He walked over to the stairway that led upstairs. He climbed up to the second floor and entered a large room with couches and chairs and a few tables scattered around. To the right, off the big room, was a small side room. Somebody was either passed out or sleeping on a couch.

Another exchange of money and small packages was going on in the big room. A black guy in a long black leather coat was doing the transaction with a blond guy who looked like a biker—T-shirt, tattoos, jeans, and long hair. Devlin hadn't seen anyone snorting or smoking whatever was being sold, but everything was so out in the open, he doubted anyone would have cared.

Devlin walked to the end of the room and sat on one of the couches. He put his drink on the table and tried to blend into the shadows. The bell downstairs rang more frequently, and each time it did the noise and music seemed to increase.

Before ten minutes had passed the black dealer came over and sat next to Devlin on the couch.

"How're you doin', man?"

"Okay."

"Okay? Okay good, man. You lookin' for something, I got coke, I got smoke, I got crank, I got 'hides. What do you need?"

Devlin reached forward and took a swallow of his Irish whiskey. "I'm looking for someone who was supposed to meet me here. A big guy."

"Lotsa big guys come in here, man. Fucking Eye-talian stallions come in here, they be like in a King Kong contest."

"No, this was an Irish guy. But dressed normal. In a business suit. A regular guy. I can't remember if he was supposed to meet me tonight or last night or what. You up here regularly?"

"Yeah. All the time, man. 'Bout this time. You need shit, you find me here most every night."

"You didn't see anybody who looked like I'm describing tonight, or in the last couple of nights?"

"I don't fuckin' know. Shit, I'm not no surveillance team here. You want some coke? What do you want?"

"Not tonight. Thanks." Devlin stood up.

"Snort some of this shit you be ready for a night and a day."

"Some other time."

Devlin walked downstairs. He finished the whiskey before he made it back to the bar. He ordered another and sat down.

One of the black girls who had been circulating around the club sat next to him. She wore a black skirt and a tight-fitting spandex tube top that flattened her breasts and showed the outline of her nipples. She had dark, dusky skin. Devlin remembered a black cop once telling him that you could tell which blacks were junkies because their skin had a dull, ashy look.

She was almost pretty; she was almost sexy. Devlin figured that at four A.M. *almost* would be good enough for a lot of guys.

She smiled at him and said, "Buy me a drink?"

"What're you drinking?"

"Seven and seven."

Devlin called the bartender and said, "Seven and seven."

The bartender knew the drink before Devlin asked.

While she waited for it she asked, "Are you alone?"

"Yeah."

"You want to have these drinks upstairs? Get more comfortable."

"I want to ask you something first," Devlin said.

"What?"

"Were you in here night before last?"

"Yeah."

"Did you see a big guy in a business suit, dark hair, about six-six, heavyset. Probably walked in with two Irish guys."

"Was the big guy white?"

"Yes."

"No, I didn't see no white guy in a business suit that big. I was here until 'bout six in the morning. I don't remember him." The drinks came. The girl leaned closer to Devlin and put a hand on his thigh and said, "Come on, you big enough for me. I'll make you feel real comfortable upstairs."

"How much do you charge?"

"That's the second question, huh?"

"Yeah."

"Forty dollars. Give you a nice handjob, blowjob. I'll make you come good."

Devlin reached into his pocket and pulled out a twenty. "Tell you what. Here's twenty. Save ourselves the trip. You just relax, and we'll let it go at that."

"Aw, come on. You sweet. Just gimme another twenty and we can have some fun."

"No thanks, really."

She stroked his thigh some more and said, "Come on, baby, you already paid me half. Gimme another twenty and I'll get you all the way there."

"Not tonight, honey."

Devlin slid off his stool and walked to the other end of the bar. He got the attention of the bartender, who was still in conversation with the dark-haired lady. He broke off the conversation and came over to Devlin. Devlin said, "How you doing? Can I ask you—were you tending bar here night before last?"

"Every night, pal. Last night, night before last, every night."

"Do you remember me from that night?"

The bartender looked closely at Devlin and said, "No. Should I?"

"I'm not sure," Devlin said. "It was one of those crazy nights. I was with my brother and two Irish guys. We were playing darts at a bar on Second Avenue. It got to be late, and we went to a couple of clubs. It was too late for regular bars. Had to go to after-hours clubs."

"You think you came here?"

"I don't know. My brother is a big guy. About six-six, over two-fifty. Dressed in a business suit. The other guys were smaller. Big smiles. Lot of teeth. Real friendly. One guy's name was Sean. I don't remember the other one's name."

"I don't know who the fuck you're talking about, and I don't much care. I get nervous when people come in here asking me questions."

"Sorry. Just trying to fill in some gaps. Are there any other after-hours clubs in this neighborhood?"

"Why don't you get the fuck out of here and go look for them."

Devlin felt his short fuse burning. He finished his drink and put it down on the bar. "So long, pal. Thanks for the hospitality."

"Don't mention it."

Two more guys were coming up the stairs as Devlin was leaving. The doorman made him wait until they were up the stairs and in the club before he let Devlin out onto the stairs. At the foot of the stairs, the big bouncer stood up from his seat and waited for Devlin. When he reached the bottom, Devlin asked the bouncer, "I was supposed to meet a guy here tonight, but he never showed. Big guy about your size. Probably in a business suit."

The sandpaper voice asked him, "So?"

"Yeah, the funny thing is, I can't remember now if he said Thursday or Tuesday. You see anybody like that night before last?"

"No. You leavin'?"

"Yeah. Thanks."

The bouncer opened the door, checked the street, and then opened it just wide enough for Devlin to squeeze out.

The street was quiet, almost serene, but the whiskey was energizing him. He breathed out heavily through his nose and tasted the liquor again. He felt like spitting out the alcohol, but it was too late for that, and he welcomed the edges being softened. He walked west to Third Avenue and waited for a cab to appear.

The ride up to Broadway and 118th Street didn't take long. The cab driver blasted up the empty streets at 50 miles per hour, which seemed blazingly fast in Manhattan.

The driver had a scraggly beard and dreadlocks, stuffed under a huge knit cap of black, green, and red yarn. Reggae music pumped out of a portable cassette player propped on the front seat. There were plenty of Rastafarians in New York, but this one was white, and his hack license said his name was Mark Rubenstein. Devlin wondered how many Jewish Rastas there were in the world.

The bar Peter Pappas had told him about wasn't on Broadway. It was about four doors west, on 118th Street. It was called Deadwood. The front window was painted black except for a small square area filled by a neon Lite Beer sign. There was no way to see inside the place, or tell if it was open. Devlin tried the wooden front door, but it was locked. There was no buzzer anywhere in sight, so he knocked twice.

The door immediately popped open. A young guy almost Devlin's size wearing a black T-shirt with a Mercedes Benz logo on it stepped out and looked at Devlin.

"We're closed."

Devlin smelled the Scotch on his breath and looked into rheumy, drunken eyes. "Come on, I just got off work. I need a nightcap."

"Where you work?"

"Terry's on Sixty-eighth. Bartender."

"Who you work with?"

"Nobody. I do the bar by myself. It ain't that big a place."

"Okay, fuck it. Come on in."

The frisk this time wasn't as professional, but it would have certainly turned up a gun.

Devlin stepped into a million Irish bars. It had that smell that would never ever leave. Beer, soaked into wooden floors where it rotted and grew and brewed into a sweet-sour smell that mixed with years of cigar and cigarette smoke, cheap hair oil, and sweat.

The bartender stood motionless. He had thin, dirty gray hair plastered back, tired eyes and the expected bulbous nose with the tiny network of broken veins.

He tended his bar for four alcoholics sitting stooped over their eternal nightcaps. Beer, vodka, gin. They drank the cheapest versions of the liquor.

At the far end of the bar were three young men. Maybe cab drivers. They were drinking long-necked bottles of Budweiser and shots of dark whiskey.

This was a place to keep feeding the drunk until the next move was a pissed-in bed or oblivion. This was the low end, but somehow very comforting and engaging.

It was like a womb that insulated the drinkers in their own world. No loud music. No loud voices or laughter. No dishes clanking or young actress waitresses trying to attract attention or move too quickly.

Many years ago in Queens, Devlin's father had worked in a hardware store. His brother, Devlin's Uncle Wayne, had owned a bar in their old neighborhood. His father would occasionally stop in for a drink after work. Once Devlin had been sent to the bar by his mother to check and see if his dad was with Wayne.

Devlin remembered walking into the place. Wayne was behind the bar with his foot propped up on the sink. There were several older men nursing drinks. Wayne's wife, Ruth, was coming out of the kitchen with hamburgers for a couple at one of the tables. It seemed smoky and comfortable and warm in there with the colorful neon beer signs and dim overhead lights.

Devlin's father looked too neat and composed to be in the place, but perfectly happy to be having a beer with his brother. Devlin remembered how neat his father's hair looked, and how calm he seemed in the bar.

Maybe if his father had drunk for fifty more years, he would have ended up in a place like this.

Devlin took a seat and the bartender came to him quickly. He inclined his head and turned an ear to Devlin.

"Give me a shot of Jack Daniel's and a short draft."

Without a word, the bartender nodded and went about his business.

The liquor was served on cardboard coasters. The shot glass was small. Just as well. Devlin was getting tired of resisting the booze. He drank down the grainy bourbon that stung his tongue and throat for a moment before he swallowed the cold beer. The combination seemed perfect. Suddenly, a wave of sorrow passed through him. Suddenly Devlin missed his father. He wished his father and brother and he were all sitting in his Uncle Wayne's bar. And in ten or fifteen minutes his worried mother would come in looking for them all, and she'd scold them, then laugh and be very happy that her men were together enjoying a drink. Maybe even enjoying a little too much to drink.

Devlin muttered a quiet curse and stood up. He bent his head and ran his hand across his face. He forced it all out of his mind.

The bartender stepped forward, and Devlin nodded. The small

shot glass was filled with amber liquid again, and Devlin downed it with the beer. It tasted just as sweet and reassuring.

He knew if his brother had ever been here, he would have left unharmed.

Devlin left the whole twenty-dollar bill on the bar this time.

He got out before it was too late. But he fought the lure of the booze all the way back to the loft in SoHo. The sun was coming up on another steamy New York morning. His body ached for sleep, but he didn't relish giving in to it now. He didn't look forward to meeting the demons that were ready to arise.

CHAPTER 18

Devlin fought the dreams until almost one in the afternoon. The cold dead face of his father. His brother's mouth twisted by the tape. The sickening sounds of fists against flesh, bones cracking, a neurosurgeon's drill buzzing into a skull. In his nightmares, he even smelled the nauseating alcohol scent of the hospital.

When he finally woke up dry-mouthed and achy, he felt as if he needed to wash out his brain.

He was disoriented. His days were turning into nights, and his life seemed stuck in some kind of twilight world.

He showered, shaved, and ate yogurt, orange juice, and toast. His mind seemed clear enough to work, so he sat down at the phone and started in. The first call was to Marilyn. He asked the right questions, wanting to hear acceptance and forgiveness in her voice more than he wanted to hear answers. Answers were all he got. George was the same. Marilyn was all right. The kids were okay. Rote answers that spoke volumes.

He checked in again with Pacific Rim. There were no messages, but he knew William Chow would be thinking about a response to his message.

Finally, he called Zitter. A woman answered with an extremely appealing voice. She put him through, and when Zitter came on the conversation was short.

"Devlin, are you okay?"

"Yeah."

"I've got information for you, but I don't want to discuss it over the phone. We'd better meet."

"Where and when?"

"Meet me at a place called the Corner Bistro. It's near my office. Eighth Avenue and Thirteenth. A few steps back from Eighth where it crosses West Fourth."

"I know where it is."

"Good. How about eight? I've still got quite a bit to do around here."

"Fine."

"Goodbye."

Devlin hung up and cursed out loud. The thought of crooked cops making trouble for him was infuriating. He checked his watch. It was almost five. He decided he had to beat some of the sluggish, dangerous lethargy that was creeping into him.

He knew a club that charged a day rate for nonmembers, and by 5:45 P.M. he was on the treadmill starting out slow and easy. The health club was on top of a condo on the west side of Greenwich Village. It was a small club, most of it devoted to racquetball courts downstairs, but there was enough equipment for what Devlin needed to do.

He was running at a good clip by six. When the machine said, he had done five miles he felt most of the booze and inaction had been sweated out of him.

By 6:33 he was attacking the Nautilus machines and weights. The club was beginning to get crowded, but no one dared get in Devlin's way. Devlin was too big and intense-looking. He didn't use the machines, he attacked them. All the machines had to fight back with was weight, and Devlin was doing a good job of handling all of it.

Devlin knew that when you don't work out for a while, not too long, just a few extra days, you usually come back much stronger than if you were working out regularly. This was one of those days. Devlin was working at the top of his strength. No one in that club had seen anybody work the Nautilus machines at such high settings, much less done it themselves. The frames rattled, the pulleys and wires screeched. Devlin wore a fixed stare. His breathing came in grunts under the strain. He walked from one machine to the next carrying a thick white towel so he could mop the sweat that rolled down his face and arms, and wipe off the places where his skin touched the machines.

With each set his muscles bulged fuller and fuller with blood— coming apart under the force that they exerted, splitting into millions of micro-tears that would eventually heal and make the muscles stronger and harder.

After each set on the machines, Devlin used free weights to push his muscles further. The rest between sets was short. Just enough to gain strength to push through the next eight or ten or twelve repetitions.

The other men in the workout room looked at Devlin furtively. The women who usually worked out with an aloofness that kept men away let themselves look at Devlin openly, if only for brief snatches. Devlin ignored them all and kept banging away until he was done. Afterward, he stood in the shower carefully soaping down and trying to let the heat seep out of his body and allow the blood to stop racing.

He knew he might have overdone the workout. But it had helped clear out the cobwebs and dissipate some of his anger. He was calmer now. More methodical. He had blown off some of the pressure that could make him dangerously reckless.

When he left the fitness center, it was five minutes to eight. The bar where Zitter was meeting him was about a fifteen-minute walk uptown.

He could have hailed a cab, but Devlin walked the distance slowly and easily, letting his body finally settle down. If the cops wanted to find him, they'd have to pick him out of the other people strolling through the warm summer night on the Village streets.

By the time he got to the bar, he had cooled off enough to stop sweating. Zitter was sitting in the back. It was an old Village place that had been there for years. Cool air conditioning greeted Devlin as he walked in. There was a bar area in front and an eating area in the back. Everything was old and dark and wooden.

Zitter was at a table nursing a mug of beer while he looked over some typewritten sheets. Devlin sat down opposite him and dropped his gym bag hold his sweat-soaked workout clothes on the chair next to him. Today Zitter was wearing a tan blazer with a green polo shirt and tan pants.

Devlin smiled.

Zitter asked, "What are you smilin' at?"

"Your clothes."

"What about 'em?"

"They match. They actually match."

"So what?"

"I was beginning to think you were color-blind."

"Don't fuckin' tell anyone, but I am color-blind."

"Really?"

"Yeah, really."

"How'd you pass your police physical? Didn't they show you that card with all the colored spots and a number sort of mixed in there?"

"Yeah, that's when I found out."

"So how'd you pass?"

"Ah, hell, I just said what the guy in front of me on the line said. Nobody was paying much attention, but I was shocked as hell that I didn't see any numbers on those cards."

"Well, I guess it didn't make much difference."

"Naw. My wife always set out my clothes for me. Have to do it myself since she passed away. Guess I usually fuck up. No one seems to mind."

"When did she pass away, Sam?"

"Two years ago. Colon cancer that got into her liver. Took her two years to die from it. Wasn't too bad until about the last two or three months."

"Sorry."

"Yeah. Me, too." Zitter finished his beer and said, "Enough of that. We got more immediate problems."

"What do you mean?"

"Your pal Freedman called me. That cop put a fucking bulletin out on you. It was in every precinct this morning. Full description. Said you assaulted a police officer while in performance of his duties."

"Let them arrest me and try to make it stick. No Assistant D.A. is going to arraign me on that. The cop doesn't have a scratch on him."

That ain't the point. If he or any other cops in on this thing spot you, they got a report in the file to cover their ass if they decide to shoot you or rough you up."

"I can't let it stop me. Did you find out anything about these after-hours clubs?"

"Yeah. A fucking quagmire. You know, you get a lead, you ask some people about these places—before you know it, everything turns weird. I got ahold of a few guys I know, but the stories are half-assed. They're usually so fucked up from drinking or snorting or whatever they do to stay up all night that when they get there, they hardly remember where they've been. Guy says, 'Yeah, well, there's one in Chelsea.' You ask him where? He says, 'Shit, I don't know. I think like Twenty-eighth Street, around Eighth.' That don't cut it. These places aren't meant to be found. You got to know exactly where they are."

"So did you get past that?"

"You know it ain't easy to come up with this shit in a few hours."

"I know, Sam. I know it isn't."

"I got four places that I think you can find based on the information I have."

Zitter handed him the typed sheet he had been reading when Devlin walked in. It was on Zitter's office stationery. The letterhead bore the name and New York address of his Intrepid Investigations, plus the addresses of branch offices in Los Angeles, London, and Mexico. The typeface was a rather ornate script. It was nothing like Devlin imagined the letterhead would be.

The names and addresses of the clubs were typed neatly. One club had no name, just the title Social Club, on 84th Street on the East Side. One was midtown on 38th Street. It was called Club 38. The third listing was for a club called Begin on Eighth Avenue in Chelsea. The last one was Starlight on lower Broadway.

Neither of the two places Devlin had visited that morning were on the list.

"How many others do you think are in Manhattan?"

"I'd say three or four at the most. I mean real after-hours clubs. They're hard to keep track of. Took a hell of a lot of phone calls to get these."

Zitter continued, "There are a couple of old neighborhood dives that I left off the list. A little Italian luncheonette on Sullivan Street that's been known to stay open. A couple of bars that lock their doors at four A.M. and pretend they're only letting in friends. One place for punk kids in Alphabet City. The ones I've listed are the real thing. I'm figuring if those guys wanted to take your brother someplace they wouldn't bring him to a shithole."

"I agree."

"As for getting into these places, I can't guarantee it. They might be suspicious of you. I don't really have any names you can mention. Also, don't try to bring in any weapons. Most places either frisk you or run a metal detector over you."

"Right."

"How'd you make out last night? Find any places?"

"Yeah. One on Fifty-third, East Side, another one way uptown on the West Side."

"Any luck?"

"Lucky to have found them I guess and cross them off the list.

"No trace of him at either place?"

"No. The only connection was that they both seemed to be run by Irish."

"Really?"

"Yeah."

"Interesting."

"Don't know if it means anything. I'm sure my brother wasn't at either place with those guys."

Zitter pointed a thumb at his list. "I can't say you'll find anything in these places either."

"Right now, it's all I've got. Except for the McKay brothers' connection to the cops. Got any ideas about that?"

Zitter shook his head, "Nope. Not any more than I told you last night. Maybe I could look into this cop, Donovan."

"Do it. If you find out what those brothers have got going with the cops, maybe we can find out what happened to my brother."

"Maybe."

Devlin asked, "Who do you know who can help you?"

"You heard of the Sons of Erin?"

"Those guys?"

"Why not? We're talkin' about Irish cops."

Devlin said, "They tried to recruit me when I was just out of the Academy."

"You didn't bite?"

"No way."

"Why not?"

"I didn't need to be anybody else's son. Who do you know in there?"

"The grand vizier or whatever the hell they call their whip. Think he'll talk to an old Jew ex-cop?"

"Why not?"

"Yeah, bullshit why not. Fucking old-line Irish cops are the worst. But I know Patrick Kelly from the old days, and he owes me."

"Good." Devlin pulled an envelope out of the side pocket on his gym bag. "The meter's still running, so here's another thousand on retainer. Let me know when it's used up."

Zitter looked inside the envelope and counted ten hundred-dollar bills. Where the fuck do you get all these hundreds? Makes me feel like I'm working for a crook."

Devlin didn't answer.

"All right. None of my business."

"Ever hear of Grand Cayman?"

"Yeah."

"They do two things down there. Scuba dive and hide cash. I did a job down there and came out with my pay in cash. It's all earned, Sam."

"I said you didn't have to answer."

"I know that. Let me know if you need more."

"I will, thanks." Zitter picked up a menu. "You gonna eat?"

"What do they have here?"

"The usual bar shit—hamburgers, chili, BLTs."

"I'll pass. You go ahead. Put it on the expense account." Devlin stood up to leave.

"Where're you goin'?"

"To see my brother."

Before Devlin could go, Zitter said, "As long as I'm settling all my worries, let me ask you one other thing."

"What?"

"You find these guys who did your brother, you find out it was no accident or anything, what're you going to do?"

"I don't know."

"That's the wrong answer."

Devlin looked at Zitter for a moment and then said, "Okay. If I find them, I'm going to immediately turn them over to the proper authorities. You can quote me on that. You asked your client, and that's what he told you."

"That's better," said Zitter.

"I'll be in touch."

Devlin dropped off his gym bag at the loft, ate a fresh turkey sandwich he had picked up at a deli, and changed into dark slacks, a black polo shirt, and a gray silk and linen sport coat flecked with dark threads weaving through the silk and linen.

He walked to the back room in the loft where he had interrogated the bartender from O'Callahan's. There was a small closet along the back wall. The door was two-inch fire-treated wood, clad in a metal sheath. A large lock was in the center of the door. It controlled a ratchet system that sent four steel rods into the top, bottom, and sides of the door frame. An Israeli had invented the door lock, and it was the only one that could keep out a determined New York burglar. Even if the door frame was bent with hydraulic pumps, the steel rods would hold the door on.

Of course, most thieves would avoid the entire mechanism and punch through the wall, so this closet was a cinder-block box covered with steel sheets and sheet rock.

Behind the door was Pacific Rim's New York arsenal. The weaponry ranged from aerosol canisters of powerful Cap-Stun spray to high-powered automatic rifles.

Devlin ignored everything except a long canvas bag propped against the corner.

He pulled out the bag and untied the top. Inside was an assortment of hardwood staffs used as fighting sticks by Aikido masters. The staffs ranged in size from just under six feet to a little under six inches. Devlin picked out the six-inch stick.

He gripped it in his right hand. The diameter was about two inches. Both ends of the stick were cut blunt. It looked like a plain wooden dowel that was a little thicker than one might expect. In Devlin's hand, it was a deadly weapon.

He gripped it, rolled it in his palm, flipped it over. Devlin could use it as an extension of his arm, his fist, or his hand. It could punch, poke or simply give his fist a solid foundation for punching.

Devlin decided to hide it in the open. He slipped the fighting stick into the outside breast pocket of his sport jacket.

He checked the time. It was 9:30 P.M. The Intensive Care Unit would still be open for business.

CHAPTER 19

While Devlin was on his way to visit his brother, Sam Zitter was entering an apartment building in the Riverdale section of the Bronx. It was an unusual building—fifteen stories high, built out of glazed, blue brick you could pick out amid the drab grays of the city from miles away. It was shaped like a soft U and sat overlooking the Spuyten Duyvil curve of the Harlem River.

Mrs. Kelly opened the door for Sam. This is no Irish Colleen, thought Zitter. She had platinum blond hair and wore a white silk blouse with pearls and a flared red skirt. She looked like a saleswoman at Bloomingdale's trying to hide her age under too much makeup.

Mrs. Kelly spoke softly. "You're Detective Zitter?"

"Yes, ma'am."

"Right this way. Patrick is waiting for you in his study."

Zitter followed her down a narrow corridor to Kelly's study. The apartment was on the top floor of the building, and the room Zitter walked into had a beautiful view of the glittering buildings across the river in Washington Heights.

The room itself looked like the business office of a local politician. Behind Kelly was a set of French windows. That left three walls available to commemorate the veteran cop.

The wall opposite his desk was dominated by a laminated wooden plaque that bore the seal of the New York City Police Department's Sons of Erin—the fraternal organization of Irish New York cops.

The rest of that wall was covered with smaller plaques from various police forces and organizations.

Another wall bore Kelly's diplomas from the City College of New York and John Jay College. The third wall had pictures—family pictures, photos of Kelly at various police functions, pictures of Kelly with obscure political figures or other officers of the Sons of Erin. The prize on this wall was a signed photograph of Kelly with Ed Koch, taken in a Chinese restaurant.

Kelly sat at a large wooden desk in a worn-out executive chair that creaked every time he moved. Patrick Kelly looked like a priest instead of a cop. He had full head of white hair. He was short and stout, but he was quick in his movements. The eyes, unfortunately, killed the saintly image. They were small and hard. Pig's eyes. Shrewd little pig's eyes.

For a guy who never made it past Deputy Inspector, Zitter thought this so-called study decorated with two-bit memorabilia was all a bit much.

Kelly stood up quickly and came around his big desk to shake Zitter's hand. "How are you, Sammy me boy? Sit down, sit down. How can I help you?"

Zitter took a seat on the other side of the desk, and Kelly creaked into his chair.

Well, Patrick, as you can imagine with me schlepping up here at ten o'clock at night, I've got a problem."

"And what's that?"

"One of my clients has run into some difficulty with a cop by the name of Donovan. Works out of the one-nine."

"What kind of difficulty?"

"A relative of my client was severely beaten three days ago. We managed to find two of the people who were with him around the time of the beating. Two Irish guys who go by the names of Sean and William McKay. These two apparently run some sort of hustle in cahoots with various bartenders."

"What kind of hustle?"

"Bartender spots some well-heeled customer who's drinking too much. Puts these guys on him. They join the party. Hustle the guy at darts. They end up ripping him off, either by taking his money outright or beating them at darts."

"What does Officer Donovan have to do with this?"

"We're not sure. That's why I'm here. My client found these two hustlers in an Irish bar. He confronted them. One of the two went to the bathroom and called the cops. Officer Donovan showed up."

"Your client confronted them?"

"He's that kind of a person."

"And where were you?"

"At the scene."

"So the cops came, so what?"

"This particular cop didn't show up to investigate. He showed up to pull the McKay boys out of a tight situation. No questions asked. No arrest. No attempt to detain my client, even though he insulted the cop pretty good."

"Who's this client of yours?"

"A man upset by what happened to his brother."

"I see. You you think there might be some sort of collusion going on between these two brothers and the coppers?"

"Yeah."

"What do you know about these McKay fellas?"

"Not much, but they look a lot rougher around the edges than I thought they would."

"How so?"

"You still ask questions pretty good, don't you, Patrick?

Kelly sat up and smiled. "I guess I do at that. Nothing can beat those years of hardcore experience, hey?"

"Guess not."

"Who do you think they are?"

"These McKay guys?"

"Yes," said Kelly.

"Who knows? I could make a few guesses, but what good would it do?"

"Hmm. But you know these McKay guys are crooks?"

"Yeah. That we know."

"Well, it wouldn't be the first time coppers were mixed up with crooks. I hope this Donovan isn't one of ours."

"Can you find out?"

Suddenly Kelly stopped talking and looked at Zitter straight on. "You know, it used to be that 'one of ours' was any cop. Not like that anymore, is it, Sam?"

"Not for a long time."

"Not since that godawful Knapp Commission, I'd say. It's every man for himself out there. No more code of silence. No more loyalty."

"Not much."

"Well, that's what old guys like me and the Sons are fighting for."

"Right."

"Keep the old values alive in this day and age, Sam. Keep 'em alive, at least until we can get the hell out."

"That's the plan, huh?"

"Why? You think it's ever going back to the way it used to be?"

"When cops took pride in their job? When cops would tell the outside world go fuck yourself if they tried to break us down? No way, Sam. Those days are gone. You see who they're making into top brass these days? P.R. flacks. Has-beens. Women. The goddamn commissioner isn't even from the force, Sam. All we can do is keep a few neighborhoods and our own lads protected and let the rest go to hell."

"That's it?"

"I'm afraid so, Sam. Hate to say it, but I'm afraid so. Anyhow, I'll look into this thing with Officer Donovan. I know some good boys in the one-nine. We'll check him out. You know who else is on his squad?"

"No. I haven't snooped around yet. The only angle is the cop being

Irish, and it made me think of you. I just figured you might have a way to see what's up with the guy."

"Say no more. I'll do what I can."

"Thanks, I'd appreciate it."

"Think nothing of it. Someday I'll be out there with you, and you'll help me."

"How much longer you going to hang in?"

"Well, I did my twenty a little over two years ago, but still have two kids in college. One's at B.U., the other at American University. Can't afford to go on the half-pension just yet."

"Where are you working now?"

"Out of the big place, One Police in Manhattan."

"What have they got you doing?"

"Easy stuff. Administrative. Looking after a few special detective squads. That sort of thing."

"Well, as long as you're safe and sound. That's the main thing."

"Safe and sound," said Kelly, "that's the ticket, all right."

Zitter stood up and said, "I'll be on my way."

Kelly walked him to the door. They shook hands again. It felt to Zitter like he had been dismissed. He knew Kelly would come up with something for him. He had a feeling it was going to be something he didn't expect.

CHAPTER 20

Devlin had seen many kinds of damage done to people, but he had never seen someone have a stroke right in front of him.

When he first walked up to his brother's bed, he expected to see improvement, but George was worse. His skin looked beyond pale. It was a sickly gray. They had tried to shave him, but couldn't get to the stubble around the respirator tube sticking out of the left corner of his mouth. Now there were ugly short hairs around his upper and lower lip.

But it wasn't just the pallor and ungainly facial hair. His brother was diminishing. They had been feeding him nothing but fluids for over three days. He must have lost at least fifteen pounds. The tone was going from his muscle. There was too much *aliveness* gone from him.

And then it happened. It started with a rasping choke. George's eyes opened wide revealing a dead, startled stare. Then his body arched and collapsed all at once. He began trembling slightly. The right side of his face slowly collapsed, and the entire right side of George's body seemed to deflate.

Devlin yelled for the nurse. A small Filipino woman came running from the nurses' station. Devlin stepped aside to let her get close to George's bedside. She peeled back his eyelid and felt for his pulse. She quickly checked the respiratory rate and the IV lines, then she turned and half-ran back to the nurses' station, telling Devlin as she passed him, "I'll get the doctor."

Devlin looked at his brother and muttered, "Oh shit, George, come on, goddammit. Don't do this. Don't do this."

It was over so fast. Within seconds, half of George seemed to be gone.

A young doctor appeared and strode quickly toward George's bed. He told Devlin, "Please wait outside."

Devlin turned and walked slowly to the ICU waiting room. The doctor came in to see him fifteen minutes later. He was about twenty-five years old. He wore a white coat and looked as if he hadn't slept well in weeks. Devlin stood up and approached him, but before he could ask a question, the young doctor held up his hand and started speaking.

"Look, I'm sorry. This is my week on duty, and it's been miserable. I've had about ten hours sleep in the last sixty hours. I don't have any energy for bedside manners."

"Forget the bedside manners. Just tell me what happened."

The doctor stopped and looked at Devlin carefully for the first time, then he started talking quickly. "Okay, your brother had a stroke. It's not uncommon in cases like his. It could be a transient thing. Transient ischemic attack, or it could be something more serious."

"But you can't tell now?"

"No, I can't. If you pressed me, I'd say it was serious. He's paralyzed on most of his right side as far as I can tell. A lot could clear up spontaneously. This is probably a small clot, some residue from the surgery or trauma that broke loose and lodged somewhere in his brain. It could get absorbed, it could flow through. That's often what happens in these cases."

"Give me best case, worst case."

"Best case it goes away. Worst case it doesn't. What kind of a question is that?"

Devlin yelled, "I don't know! What the hell is happening to my brother?"

"Look, take it easy. It's a mess right now. In a week, it could be a thousand percent better. He's on a drug, Heparin, to keep his blood thin so this sort of thing doesn't happen. When his doctor finds out what happened, he may adjust the dosage. Right now, your brother is comfortable. There's nothing more we can do."

"Okay, okay. I didn't mean to yell. I just can't . . . I don't know. Thanks, doctor." Devlin turned and walked out clenching and unclenching his hands in frustration and anger.

When he hit the street, he checked his watch. Not quite eleven o'clock. Whatever tension the workout had relieved was back. Watching his brother lose half his face like that had shocked him to the core.

It was too early to check out the after-hours clubs Zitter had found, and Devlin suddenly felt ravenous. The workout and tension left him feeling drained. He needed fuel for the night's work, so he walked west to an Italian restaurant on Irving Place. He spent a long time with his meal and had two cappuccinos and it was still only half-past midnight.

He sat in three bars, spending over an hour in each, slowly drinking one shot of Jameson in each with a cup of coffee. Not nearly enough to make him drunk, but enough to calm him a bit.

He kept thinking and worrying about George. He kept clenching his teeth thinking about who could have done that to him.

He thought about wanting to be at Daryl's instead of in a bar. Thinking how unlike him it was to leave his gun with a woman he hardly knew. In between brooding he talked to the bartenders in a friendly way, carefully bringing up the topic of after-hours clubs with each of them. One bartender knew about clubs in Brooklyn, one fell into Zitter's category of people who were too drunk to remember where he had been, and the third bartender wouldn't tell him anything.

By the time he was done, it was almost four A.M., and Devlin had developed a nice tight caffeine edge with enough whiskey to soften it.

The deeper he let himself go into the Irish whiskey and bars, the closer he felt to his brother and father, and the more he missed them, and the more he wanted to smash whoever had crippled his brother and taken him so far away.

A strange and violent mood bubbled under the caffeine and whiskey, and it left very little tolerance for the bouncers at the first club on Zitter's list.

He had picked the club on the East Side at 88ᵗʰ Street since it was the one closest to the bar where he'd left his brother.

The place didn't look very hospitable as Devlin approached it from across the street. The building looked as if it had some sort of storage area or garage on the bottom floor with small commercial offices on the three floors above it. The entire bottom part of the building was solid brick except for a single door on the right corner covered by graffiti.

There were three bouncers standing outside the darkened door. One bouncer was black, bald, and enjoying how bad he looked. He had on dark glasses and a long black coat that seemed to be made out of parachute silk. The second bouncer was also black. He stood behind his bald partner. He wore a Sergio Tacchini warm-up suit and a baseball cap turned sideways. The cap had JEFFY D written on it in large block letters formed out of mirrored glass. The third bouncer looked Italian. He wore black jeans and a black T-shirt.

All three were well over six feet tall. None weighed less than 230 pounds, most of it muscle made from weight-lifting. The three spent a lot of energy glowering and trying to intimidate whoever came near the entrance.

Devlin watched them from across the street. During the fifteen minutes he waited, everyone who approached the club was black. The bald bouncer would nod them in, and then one of the other two bouncers would open the door and walk them in.

Devlin quickly decided he wasn't going to get into the club by walking up and acting friendly. And he wasn't going to get anywhere if he walked up and tried to cripple the bouncers.

He waited patiently until he saw three people emerge from a cab down the street. He moved quickly to intercept them before they approached the entrance. There were two women and a man, all three black. The man had on red pants and a maroon double-breasted jacket with wide shoulders and what looked like leopard-skin lapels. He had soft curly hair that tumbled down the back of his neck. The hair was heavily oiled. The women both wore off-the-shoulder dresses which were tight sheaths that ended just about mid-thigh.

One girl had a petite figure, the other was big and buxom and full-hipped.

Devlin asked the man, "Are you going to the club up the street?"

The man looked Devlin over before he answered, "Why do you ask?"

"I'd like to go in with you if you don't mind. I don't think I can get in otherwise."

The man smiled unexpectedly. It was a dazzling white smile and said, "You know goddamn well you can't get in that club. You don't belong in there, my friend."

Before Devlin could say another word, the big woman grabbed his arm and announced, "You all come along with me, honey. Ricky, I am taking this big man in myself." She looked at Devlin and said, "What do you say to that, sugar?"

"Thank you very much."

She laughed, Ricky laughed, and all four of them proceeded up the block.

When they arrived at the door, the bald bouncer stepped aside and motioned for the Italian to open the door. Devlin stepped into a small hallway and immediately felt a surge of hot fetid air pushed into him by blasting speakers pounding out a bass so heavy he could feel the vibrations in his chest. Devlin could feel more than see the sweating dancing mass in front of him.

Devlin heard the door shut behind him and turned to see the bald bouncer making his way toward him past Ricky and the petite woman. Devlin slipped the wooden fighting stick from his breast pocket. He knew immediately the big black was coming for him.

The large woman edged away from Devlin as soon as the bouncer closed in.

The man stood right in front of Devlin, putting his face inches away. He stared hard at Devlin through his dark glasses. Devlin didn't step back. They were the same height, but Devlin figured the bouncer outweighed him by at least twenty pounds. He also figured the bouncer's dark glasses had prevented him from seeing Devlin slide the fighting stick into his hand.

The bouncer put his face closer to Devlin's, and Devlin felt the adrenaline start pulsing through his system. The black spoke quietly to him. "You pretty slick aren't you, white boy?"

Devlin answered calmly, "You mean hooking up with these people?"

"Yeah. That's what I mean. You think I didn't see you hanging out across the street? Huh?"

"I wasn't sure. But I was sure you weren't going to let me in alone."

"You got that right, boy."

Devlin held his jacket open and said, "I'm not here to cause trouble. A friend of mine told me about the place. Just like to check it out."

"First we check you out."

The bouncer started frisking Devlin with hands big enough to cover whole sections of his body. Devlin willed his heart to slow down under the adrenaline rush. When the bouncer felt under Devlin's armpits, he smiled and said, "Sweatin' a little bit tonight aren't we, boy?"

In a rush Devlin imagined the satisfaction of cracking open the top of the bald gleaming head with one crunching downward blow of the hard, wooden stick. Did this man try to humiliate his brother, too? Did his drunken brother become angry and push him away, push him and his huge hands off his body? His brother was taller and bigger than this man, but he was drunk that night, and George was certainly no fighter. He wouldn't have much of a chance against this one, backed up by two more like him. Did his brother come into this black den and get beaten to the point where his brain swelled inside his skull?

Maybe it was animal instinct, but suddenly the bouncer stopped frisking for weapons and badges and stepped back from Devlin and smiled. "You be cool, big man. Just remember me next time. You say hello to me or ask for big bad Eddie, and you get in. You might not stay for very long, but you get in."

Devlin answered, "Okay, friend," and exhaled slowly as the anger subsided in him.

Ricky pushed past Devlin and guided both women ahead of him. They disappeared into the throng on the other side. It seemed none of them wanted anything to do with Devlin if the bouncers were going to give him a hard time.

Devlin followed them into the club, but let them walk away. In front of him was a large square space approximately fifty feet by fifty feet. It was nothing more than the raw ground floor of a warehouse. The walls were bare brick. Exposed pipes, ductwork, and electrical BX cable ran along the walls.

In the middle of the open area, there were two rows of square cement pillars spaced about fifteen feet apart.

Large reflector lamps in metal holders were clamped to the pillars and various pipework in the ceilings. Above the bright pools of light, it was dark and indistinct, but Devlin estimated the ceiling was at least twenty feet high.

There were almost a hundred people dancing to insistent rap music.

At the far end of the room a D.J. was set up on a small stage, slapping records onto turntables, dancing, rapping into his microphone and working the crowd. The music was so loud it hurt Devlin's ears. The music bore into him like punches. He hated it.

On the wall to his right, Devlin saw a long bar. People were standing two and three deep, but Devlin wanted a drink before he left this crazy place that he already knew his brother and the two Irishmen would never have gotten into.

He walked to the end of the bar and was quickly noticed by the bartender and just as quickly ignored. Devlin looked for any other whites in the place and saw a few women on the dance floor but no men.

As he waited for a chance to get the bartender's attention, he felt a tug on his left arm. He turned and saw the big black woman he had come in with.

"What you drinkin', honey?" she yelled above the music.

"Jack Daniel's on ice," he yelled back.

She reached over and took the twenty-dollar bill that was in his hand and pushed him back from the bar.

She yelled out a piercing holler, "Alex! Alexxx!"

The bartender saw her, came over and leaned toward her to get her order. Devlin watched as she got the drinks and the change.

She walked up to him, handed him a wet plastic cup of whiskey and ice and stuffed his change in his side pocket. She took his free hand and started tugging him to follow her into the dark area beyond the lights of the dance floor.

Devlin followed, very uncomfortable that he was being pulled along by this woman, and more uncomfortable that he hadn't seen her come up on his left. Christ, he thought, I must be more out of it than I realized.

She quickly led him to a steel staircase that ran up the wall opposite the bar. She yelled back, "Come on, honey," and started up the narrow stairs. Devlin followed her, watching her big round ass swaying in front of his face.

The top of the stairs led to a mezzanine that surrounded the dance floor on three sides. All along the mezzanine were tables, couches, chairs. In the dim light, Devlin could make out various couples and groups. He smelled the sweet tang of marijuana in the air and the acrid stench of crack cocaine.

She led him back to a far corner and pulled him down onto a low couch that was just big enough for the two of them. As she sat down, her dress slid all the way up to just below her crotch. Devlin's drink sloshed over and wet his knee and hand. She took a big drink from her plastic glass, and Devlin did the same from his. The kick of the bourbon felt good.

Without warning, she grabbed Devlin by the back of the head and pulled his mouth onto hers. Her lips were so full and so soft they felt unreal. She ground a kiss into his mouth and plunged a big wet tongue past his teeth. She separated quickly and licked a cold drop of bourbon off Devlin's chin.

"My name is Marlene, and I wanna know what a big white honkie like you is doing in this place." She spoke in such a loud, boisterous voice that Devlin had no trouble hearing her over the music. She seemed to stretch out and toy with every third word.

Devlin smiled and said, "I come here all the time."

"Stop bullshittin' me, boy. Tell me what you're doin' here, and tell me if you gonna buy me some nice cocaine and then take me home and fuck my big black pussy."

"I don't have time for women who are so shy."

She let out a whoop of laughter and slapped Devlin's shoulder. "Lord, ain't it the truth! Don't mind me, honey, I'm just feelin' good. I'm glad you got past that evil of bald-headed motherfucker at the door. What'd he say his name was?"

"Eddie. Big bad Eddie."

"Big bad bullshit. You looked like you was about to go for him back there. I felt the air crackle back there, boy! I got a feelin' you could've taught that motherfucker a lesson."

"Not tonight."

"Why not tonight?"

"Don't have the energy."

She shifted on the couch, slid her legs up under her so she was kneeling back on her calves and faced Devlin. "Come on now, talk to me. What you doin' here?"

Devlin decided he might as well find out if Marlene could help him. "Three nights ago, my brother was out with two other guys. They went to some after-hours club, I'm not sure which one. Somebody beat my brother pretty bad. I'm trying to find out who."

"Who your brother say did it?"

"He didn't say. He's in a coma."

"So how you know it was in a club?"

"The guys he was with told me."

"They didn't tell you which club?"

"No."

"They not your friends, huh?"

"No."

"All those guys white?"

"Yeah."

"They didn't come in here."

"Doesn't seem like it."

"They might let a white couple in or one guy with some black folks like they let you in, but they ain't going to let no three white guys walk in."

"I guess not."

"No way. They wouldn't be dumb enough to start with the bouncers, would they?"

"I don't think so."

"Sounds like you better look elsewhere, honey."

"I guess so."

"You gonna leave a big, fine woman like me behind while you go off on some wild goose chase?"

"Hate to do it."

She slipped her hand along the inside of Devlin's thigh until she grabbed a handful of his cock and balls. For a moment, Devlin imagined her grabbing him in a vise grip and paralyzing him with pain. She felt the tension sweep through him. She leaned toward him and purred in his ear, "Take it easy, honey. You just let me say good-bye my own way."

Her hand gently stroked and prodded and Devlin felt himself quickly getting hard. She was half on top of him, pushing her lush breasts into his chest. She started kissing him and licking at the base of his neck. She lifted herself off him and whispered, "Finish your drink, honey."

She pushed her hand against his shoulder and propped herself back far enough to down the rest of her drink. As she arched back to swallow, her large breasts strained against the fabric of her tight sheath of a dress. She had large nipples, and they were fiercely erect.

Devlin finished his drink just before she plastered her mouth on his. Before he knew it, she slid a chunk of ice into his mouth, and before he could even swallow it, she had pulled open his pants and zipped open his fly. With one hand, she pushed down the elastic of his briefs and deftly flipped his erect cock into the open. In an instant, Devlin felt his cock submerged into the soft wetness of her mouth, the inside still cold from the ice.

He soon wished he hadn't let her do it. The band of his under-wear pushed uncomfortably against the base of his cock, she was supporting half of her considerable weight on his hip, and he was sure someone was watching this spectacle even though the mezza-nine was mostly dark.

But Christ, he thought, this woman's mouth and tongue are unreal.

Before the mixture of pleasure and pain became unbearable, he grunted, "Marlene, not here. Come on. Give me a break."

She slid her mouth slowly all the way up his erect cock and came off him with a kissing smack. "Oooh weeee, honey. I just wanted to see if all you white boys had little bitty dicks."

She watched as Devlin folded himself back into his pants.

"Damn, honey, that thing just about glows in the dark here, don't it?"

"It's the only thing in this place that's white."

She laughed and turned sideways against Devlin and laughed. "Sheeeiit, honey, you got nothing to be ashamed of there."

She grabbed his arm and pulled it around her and placed his hand on her right breast. Then she carefully placed his index finger on her nipple and moved it slowly back and forth.

"You know, Whitey, you and I could have some nice fun tonight."

"I couldn't handle you."

"Yes, you could. I'm just a pussycat. But you have to run around to nasty after-hours clubs."

"You know of any other clubs?"

"I know a couple of 'em up in Harlem. Some real wild places. But I don't know any others in Manhattan."

"Uh-huh."

She slid his hand deep into her cleavage. Her skin was soft and slick with a sheen of sweat. It must have been 110 degrees where they were sitting.

"Christ, I can't think straight with you."

"You still think you want to give up these big titties just aching for you, honey?"

Devlin pulled his hand out and sat up straight. "Yes! You'll kill me. I gotta get out of here."

She sat up and pulled down her skirt. "Well, I guess I ain't getting no white meat tonight."

"Sorry. How about a raincheck?"

"I don't plan for no rainy days, angel. You miss me, you miss out on the best." She turned and moved to within an inch from his face. He smelled her perfume and the tang of gin on her breath. She spoke so softly he could barely hear her above the distant thrumming music. "Sweetheart, for the rest of yo' life, you gonna have to imagine what it would a been like to spend the night with Marlene."

And then she was gone. A big, lusty woman sashaying into the darkness.

Devlin quickly felt his pockets, just to make sure his money and keys were still there. Then he laughed in the darkness.

CHAPTER 21

The call came for Wexler while Devlin was fighting off Marlene. Wexler was sitting at his usual spot at the end of the bar when the bartender handed him the cordless phone.

"Wexler."

"McKay, here."

"Yes?"

"I called to let you know there may be some repercussions from our little visit the other night."

"Refresh my memory."

"You recall William and I brought a mark to the club. Big fellow, quite jovial until he discovered most of the money was missing from his wallet."

"Yes, now I remember. Joe and Eddie had to escort him out. I wish you wouldn't sully my place with your petty con games."

"We needed a place to take a gentleman. Couldn't take him to one of those low-class dives of yours, could we?"

"What is it you want?"

"I'd say your boys were a little too enthusiastic in their jobs. Apparently, they did quite a bit of damage, and now the boyo's brother is trying to find out who did what to whom."

"His brother? Who is his brother?"

"Name is Devlin. Haven't found out much about him, but his excellency is working on it. Whoever this Devlin is, he had the guts to track us down, stick a gun in our faces and bust our noses before we could get rid of him."

"What are you talking about?"

"Listen carefully and then I'm hanging up. I'll go through this once. Joe and Eddie put the hurt to a guy we brought to your club. The man's brother is out to find who did it. He also hired a detective to help him. He tracked down Billy and me to O'Callahan's and stuck a gun in our face. He already knew we had taken his brother to an after-hours club, but we didn't tell him it was your place."

Wexler interrupted. "What has this got to do with me?"

"Listen, and I'll tell you. Billy called one of Kelly's cops, a guy named Donovan, who got us out of O'Callahan's. This crazy man Devlin almost went after Donovan, too. He's nuts. Anyhow, the detective he hired knows Kelly from the old days. The detective asked Kelly for help on connecting Donovan to us. Kelly tipped Donovan, Donovan tipped us, I'm tipping you. If this fucking Devlin shows up at your place, you'd best be ready. Okay? That's it."

"Good God. You expect me to follow that?"

"I have no expectations. You've been duly warned."

"Well, what does he look like?"

"He's big. Six-four. Six-five. Dark hair. Healthy-looking bastard and pretty damn intense, I'll tell you. Got a little scar in his right eyebrow, and he knows a bit about knockin' people around. He fancies himself a tough guy."

"Wonderful. That's exactly what I need. More macho trash."

"Best keep him out."

"Best you all just disappear. Goodbye."

Wexler sat and fumed. Stupid, ugly, and unnecessary. He wondered if Joe and Eddie were becoming more trouble than they were worth. He signaled to the bartender. "Call Bernard downstairs and tell him to come up for a moment."

When the big downstairs doorman appeared, Wexler motioned him to sit next to him at the bar.

"Yes, sir?"

"Sometime in the next couple of days, perhaps even tonight, a man may appear trying to enter the club. Most likely alone. He's big, six-four, dark hair, a scar running through his right eyebrow."

"Yes, sir."

"Don't let him walk in easily, but don't refuse him."

"Okay."

"And when you send him up on the elevator, call Joe and Eddie and tell them he's coming."

"Not before he gets on?"

"No. I don't want him to see you make the call."

"What do you want me to call him so they know who I'm talking about?"

"Call him Mr. Smith."

"Mr. Smith. Got it. That's it?"

"Yes. On your way downstairs send Joe and Eddie in here."

Benny left and a moment later the two hulks walked up to the bar with their usual half-crazed grins. Like two stupid bulldogs wanting to be petted.

Wexler didn't tell them to sit. He felt like hitting them on the side of their heads with a club, but they would probably take it as a sign of affection.

"Listen to me."

"Yes, sir," they both said.

"Tonight, maybe tomorrow or the next day, Benny will call you from downstairs and say a Mr. Smith is coming up."

"Mr. Smith," they both said.

"Right. Mr. Smith. When he tells you that, I want you to inform Susan and me that Mr. Smith is coming up. Then I want both of you to go into the kitchen, and stay there until I come and get you."

Joe asked, "We stay there even if there's trouble?"

"You stay there until I come get you or send someone in for you."

Eddie asked, "What are we going to do with the guy?"

"I'll tell you. But I don't want him to see you two when he walks in. Go back to work."

"Yes, sir."

As they walked back to the club foyer, Joe turned to Eddie and mimicked Wexler. "'I don't want him to see you when he walks in.' Fuck him."

"Yeah," said Joe, "fuck him twice, the little faggot."

The last one Wexler gave instructions to was Susan. He watched as she approached him. She was wearing a simple dress that wrapped around and buttoned at the waist. Perhaps thousands of women had worn that style of dress for office or social occasions. But on Susan, it looked like a dress designed to emphasize a woman's figure. The material crossing in front of her chest separated and emphasized her full breasts. The skirt wrapping around her legs gave the promise that the slit along the side might part enough to glimpse more of her long, shapely legs.

It was six-fifteen in the morning, and Susan had drunk enough alcohol that she walked with a controlled sway. Somehow the fact that she was turning into a lush, that her exquisite face was loosening ever so slightly, puffing ever so imperceptibly day by day—somehow her gradual dissolution made her more appealing to Wexler.

Suddenly he became excited. He decided that tonight he would take Susan to her apartment and fuck her. But how to humiliate her just a little bit more, he wondered. Perhaps make her kneel on the bare floor in front of him. No bath mat or towel under her knees. He imagined seeing the square marks of the tile floor etched into her knees.

Susan approached and stood next to him at the bar.

"Sit, my dear."

She did, without a word.

"Today, maybe tomorrow or the next day, Joe or Eddie will tell you a Mr. Smith is coming in. I don't want him to see those two, so when he comes in you greet him. Check him with the metal detector and send him into the club. Don't do anything special. Just be there instead of Joe or Eddie when he comes in."

"A Mr. Smith?"

"Yes."

"Fine."

As she walked back to her table near the front of the club, she felt a shiver run down her back. His eyes, she thought. His mean eyes had that look. A feeling of dread hit. And then all she could see was the warm amber liquid waiting for her in the large brandy snifter that was always kept full for her. All her attention shifted to the sweet bite of the Grand Marnier. Even as she lifted the glass, Susan knew that the more she drank, the less it hurt, and the less she could do to get Robert Wexler out of her life.

CHAPTER 22

The bouncer in the purple Tacchini warm-up suit popped open the door for Devlin, and he stepped out of the heat, smoke, noise, and darkness into the cool half-light of a Manhattan dawn.

Devlin spit the taste of Marlene's gin out of his mouth and thought about her saliva drying on his cock. He was tired, sweaty, and slightly drunk. And that made him vulnerable. He was roaming in a netherworld that sane people had nothing to do with, and yet he knew he wasn't going to stop.

The gray dawn settled over Devlin as he walked west toward Third Avenue. He took out the neatly typed sheet of paper Zitter had given him in the old Village bar. The orange glow from the high-intensity streetlights and the slowly brightening sky made it easy to read the page. There were two clubs left on the list. Devlin was afraid he might fall asleep in the cab if he rode all the way downtown, so he picked the club in Chelsea.

The address was on Eighth Avenue near 28th Street. In parentheses, next to the address was written *Ask for Billy.*

He got out of the cab on Eighth and 27th Street and started walking uptown. It was 5:45 A.M. and the traffic was already building up on Eighth Avenue. Devlin could see mail trucks lined up on 33rd Street near the main post office. New York was waking up for work.

The building at the address Zitter gave him was a five-story townhouse. A flight of stone steps ran up to a lobby lit with a fluorescent light that made the walls look a ghostly greenish white. No lights shone from any window in the building.

Devlin checked the address again. It didn't look at all like any kind of gathering place could be in this building, but the number matched.

He walked up and tested the lobby entrance door. It was open. He entered the small vestibule and looked around. To his right was a set of double-glass doors covered on the inside by thick red curtains.

The telltale bell was in plain view. He rang it and after a moment the curtains behind the glass doors parted slightly, but the doors didn't open. He gave the bell a quick ring and after about ten seconds the curtains parted and a face peered at him from inside.

The face belonged to a short, balding man who looked like every neighborhood bartender Devlin had ever seen. He lifted his chin at Devlin asking him a silent question, Devlin leaned toward the spot where the two doors joined and said, "I'm a friend of Billy's."

The face disappeared behind the curtain, locks clicked, and the door popped open.

The man looked up at Devlin and said, "Okay. Come in. My doorman never saw you before so he didn't open up."

Behind the small bartender was a smiling twenty-year-old who looked about as threatening as the Pillsbury Dough Boy. He was chubby and had an idiot's grin on his face.

The bartender told him, "Billy ain't here. He should be in later." Then he walked back to his post behind the bar.

Devlin had figured "Billy" was just a password. He wondered what he was going to do if "Billy" walked in. He should have asked Zitter about this place. If he had, he probably would have crossed it off his list. One look told him there was no way the McKay brothers would be regulars here.

The club was one large rectangular room with a butcher-block bar on one side. It was immaculately clean, decorated with posters of Frank Sinatra, Angie Dickinson, and Marilyn Monroe. And it was filled with wise guys. Big men with big stomachs, gold chains, and pinky rings. Everybody seemed to know everybody else. They laughed loudly and shouted names like Fat Tony, Louie, and Big Ed.

At the far end of the room, a blackjack table was set up. Five men were hunched over the table placing bets with chips and waiting for a dealer with thick glasses in dark frames to deal the game out of a boot.

Devlin didn't belong. The question was how to get out without attracting attention. He was probably the only one in the place without a gun.

Devlin felt as though at least two guys were already checking him out, wondering who he was. He gave it no more than ten minutes before someone would start questioning why he was there. He didn't want to think about all the mobster tonnage in the place deciding to kick his ass and throw him out.

He walked over to the glass doors. The doorman with the idiot smile jumped up quickly from his table and unlocked them.

"See ya," he said.

Devlin said, "Thanks." He was out before anyone noticed his fast exit. Outside it was full daylight. The shock of having night disappear so suddenly didn't help clear up the confusion that spiraled in Devlin's mind. It was taking too much time and energy to find out nothing. He didn't feel he was anywhere near knowing what happened to his brother.

There was one more club on Zitter's list. He was going to try it before he quit.

He hailed a cab on Seventh Avenue. Devlin told the driver, "Head downtown, will you?"

"Where to?"

Devlin took out Zitter's list and looked at the address for the Starlight. "460 Broadway."

"You got it."

The driver had him there in seven minutes. Devlin got out of the cab feeling as if he might have to spend the rest of his life skulking around after-hours clubs. He wanted a shower, his mouth was dry from the booze he was drinking, and he needed sleep.

The building looked like every other commercial loft building on lower Broadway, except this one had *not* been renovated. He peered inside. In the back of the lobby, he saw a very big black man sitting on a stool behind a podium. Devlin checked his watch. It was nearly seven in the morning. Too early for a commercial building's doorman to be on duty, but not too late for an after-hours club to be open.

He walked straight to the desk. The booze and the frustration eliminated any hesitation. He asked the big man, "What floor is the Starlight Club on?"

Bernie stood up and came from behind his desk without a word. He wore a dark, brown suit and a white shirt with a silk tie that had an interesting pattern made up of brown, gray, and black.

He was big enough so that he could look down at Devlin, and arrogant enough to look down and somehow still have his chin lifted in the air. The black man was telling Devlin he was rude, and he had yet to say a word.

He stared at Devlin a few seconds. Devlin waited it out. Finally, he told Devlin, "There'a no club in this building."

Devlin said quietly, "Yes, there is. My friends have been here, and they highly recommended it. I know you can't let everyone in, but I'd like to see the club if at all possible."

"What friends you talkin' bout?"

"A couple of bartenders I know on the West Side."

Bernie stared at him some more and said, "This is a private club."

"I'm sure it's worth the membership fee."

"The fee is fifty dollars."

Devlin took out a hundred-dollar bill and handed it to Bernie who said, "I don't have change."

Devlin smiled and said, "Keep it."

"Thank you." Bernie reached into the pocket of his suit jacket and took out a business card. It was printed on red card stock with the name STARLIGHT printed in white against the red background.

"Here's your membership card. If I'm not here, this will get you in."

Devlin said, "Thanks. If you're here, you'll remember me?"

"I remember faces."

"That's good. That's very convenient."

"Open your jacket, friend."

Devlin spread apart his jacket knowing the fighting stick was in the outside breast pocket. He held the jacket wide while Bernie quickly patted him down, then said, "Follow me."

He led Devlin to the elevator. Devlin waited while Bernie leaned inside and unlocked the button for the sixth floor, pressed it, then locked it again. He held the door for Devlin and told him, "Sixth floor. Knock once on the door and wait."

Devlin stepped into the elevator.

As the elevator door closed, Bernie picked up the phone behind his podium and called upstairs. Joe answered, and Bernie said, "Mr. Smith is on the way up. Don't forget to tell Mr. Wexler."

Joe and Eddie immediately walked back into the club, telling Susan as they passed to take their place outside. They reported to Wexler and disappeared into the kitchen. She was looking out the peephole when Devlin walked up and knocked. She quickly opened the door so she could get a better look at Devlin.

He was big, but not hulking. The way his clothes hung on him, she could tell he was muscular. The clothes were expensive: silk, fine cotton, nice shoes. She liked his face, too. Handsome, but weathered and a little beaten. He had the dreamy look of a tired drunk, which she also liked.

Devlin inclined his head, smiled, and asked, "May I come in?"

Susan thought his manner was rather charming. She forced herself to stop looking at him and said, "Yes. Of course."

She was holding a small metal detector and felt foolish standing there with it, but did her job. She carefully ran it all around his body. When she bent down to run the metal detector over his lower body, the alcohol made her grab Devlin's shoulder to steady herself. It felt as if she were leaning against the side of a tree.

Devlin resisted the urge to reach out and support her. She looked too beautiful and elegant to be anywhere near the places he had been in the past two nights. He stood still, enjoying the weight of her against him. He concentrated on the feel of her hand against his shoulder. While she was busy with the metal detector, he looked at her full, lush body and at her breasts straining against the light summer dress.

He said to her, "It's usually an unpleasant male bouncer who does this instead of a beautiful woman."

"Well," said Susan as she slowly ran the wand of the detector up between Devlin's legs, "I could find an unpleasant bouncer for you if you'd like."

"No thanks."

Susan pictured running the metal detector gently up into Devlin's crotch. She straightened up and pulled back into herself. She knew Wexler could easily be standing behind her watching. She cleared her throat and asked, "Would you like a table or do you prefer to just sit at the bar?"

"A table please." Suddenly he felt ravenous. "Do you serve food?"

"Just hors d'oeuvres, but they're very good." Susan turned to lead him into the club. "Come with me."

Devlin followed her through the front room, past the game room area, and into the main room. The club was about half full, but there was plenty of energy and movement in each section. By the back-gammon tables, someone must have made a winning point because there were yells and cheers. The place had the air of furtiveness and abandon that the other clubs had, but this one was not for drunks or young black hipsters or punks or Mafiosi. This club was for people with money. It was much more plush and comfortable than any of the other clubs. A woman as beautiful as the hostess that greeted him didn't seem out of place at all.

She sat Devlin at his table and said, "I'll send the waiter by for your order. What can I get you to drink?"

"Champagne. Very cold if that's possible."

"Certainly."

Devlin watched her from behind, Wexler watched from in front. He was at his usual position near the end of the bar. Both enjoyed their respective views, but Wexler's gaze quickly shifted to Devlin, and within seconds Devlin felt Wexler's eyes boring into him.

The moment their eyes locked, Devlin knew three things: the man staring at him was in charge of this club. He had been expecting him. And he was mean as a rat.

He quickly ran down the possibilities. Unlike the other clubs he had been to, if the McKays had taken his brother here, George would have walked in without hesitation. Would the McKays figure he would search out after-hours clubs? Yes. Could they have alerted the man sitting at the bar? Yes.

Wexler broke off the staring contest and returned to his notebook lying open on the bar. Susan stood at the middle of the bar waiting for Devlin's champagne. The bartender put a split of Mumm on a tray with a champagne glass. Susan felt the bottle to make sure it was cold, then turned and brought the drink to Devlin's table.

As she uncorked the small bottle of champagne Devlin said to her, "I'd like you to tell me something about this club."

"What would you like to know?"

Devlin watched the champagne fizz into the frosted glass and said, "Where are the bouncers?"

Susan stopped pouring and placed the bottle next to the glass. When she heard Devlin's question, a cold chill hit her just below the sternum. She looked at the mysterious "Mr. Smith." Whoever he was, he certainly wasn't a typical guest. She didn't answer for a few seconds.

Maybe it was the liquor she had been drinking all night or her fear and loathing of Wexler, or maybe it was simply the way Devlin looked at her. Maybe it was all those things that triggered her rebellious nature. She made the decision that she knew was going to change things one way or the other, forever. She told Devlin, "They're out of sight in the kitchen."

"Why is that?"

"The owner doesn't want you to see them."

"How does he know about me?"

"I don't know."

Devlin could see Susan's nerves were strung tight. He didn't want to force her to talk out in the open. "Thank you. I think we should talk more."

And then Susan plunged in all the way. "Not here. Call me. 555-1427."

"Got it. By the way, what's your name?"

"Susan."

She turned and walked away from him as fast as she could without appearing as terrified as she suddenly felt. She knew Wexler was watching, and she wanted to look back at him, but she was afraid he would see her face. She placed the serving tray on the bar and walked straight to her table near the entrance. She sat down and took a long swallow of the Grand Marnier. Good Christ, she thought, what the hell have I done now?

CHAPTER 23

Devlin didn't look at Susan or talk to her again. He finished his champagne, walked to the bathroom, relieved himself, washed his hands and face, came back, and sat at the bar. He sat at the corner of the bar so that Wexler, seated on the other side of the corner, was almost facing him. He asked the bartender for a glass of orange juice and club soda.

Wexler kept writing in his notebook, but Devlin had violated his space. He felt Devlin's presence. He felt Devlin staring at him. And he was furious. How dare the victim of his trap sit here and defy him like this.

Finally, he looked up from his notebook and returned Devlin's stare, daring him to say something. Devlin took the dare without hesitation. He leaned over the corner of the bar, extended his hand, and said, "I'm Jack Devlin. You look like the owner of this place."

Wexler didn't take Devlin's hand, but he did answer, "Yes. I am."

Devlin pushed him, "And your name?"

"Wexler. Robert Wexler."

"Well, then, that's good. It's going to be easier now that I know your name."

"What's going to be easier?"

"Finding out about you, Mr. Wexler."

"Oh really? And what would you like to know about me?"

"If you're the one responsible."

"For what?"

"Mr. Wexler, have you ever had any trouble in here? Disgruntled members or guests? People who for some reason get upset and have to be dealt with?"

"Occasionally."

"Occasionally. Any recent occasions?"

"I don't discuss my business with strangers."

"Well, I thought I just introduced myself."

"I don't care what you thought. I don't think about people like you at all." Wexler closed his notebook, placed it in his breast pocket, and stood up.

Devlin swiveled off his bar stool, took a step to the corner of the bar and blocked Wexler's way. Wexler was so surprised that Devlin had dared to block his way that for a moment he didn't move. And in the next second Devlin's arrogance caused such fury in Wexler that he actually saw black dots float in front of his eyes. Wexler forced himself to stay in control. Neither man said anything for a moment, and then Wexler managed to smile and say, "You're standing in my way. I suggest you don't do that."

Devlin already knew he had found the right place. And it was obvious this wasn't the right moment to do anything about it, but he couldn't let Wexler off without at least a veiled threat. "Just one question, before you go. Are you here regularly or just occasionally? I'd like to know where to find you if I need to."

Wexler stepped around Devlin without another word, and Devlin didn't try to stop him. Wexler walked straight into the kitchen. Joe and Eddie were standing at Wong's work table stuffing their mouths with hors d'oeuvres they'd made the Vietnamese chef prepare for them. One look at Wexler and they stopped putting food in their mouths.

Wexler talked without really looking at them. He told them, "There is a man sitting at the bar. Joe, you go down by the back stairs and get your car. Eddie, when I tell you, walk out of here, take a close look at that man, then go downstairs and meet Joe. Look at him closely so you'll know him when he leaves."

Joe said, "The famous Mr. Smith, huh?"

"Yes. Don't say anything more, just listen and do what I tell you. Follow him when he leaves. Before he gets wherever he's going, I want you to stop him."

"Stop him?" Joe asked.

Wexler continued, "Yes. Take him someplace where you won't be interrupted, and I want you to do three things. Give him a message from me—tell him no one ever comes into my club and dares to confront me in a threatening manner. Then teach him a lesson in respect. After that, make him tell you everything he knows about this place and about me and who gave him that information. Do you understand?"

"Yes, sir," they both answered.

"You can do anything you want to him, but don't kill him. I want him to survive to enjoy the memory of his insufferable arrogance."

Neither one of the behemoths said a word. They didn't want Wexler to change his orders. Unleashing them like this was too good to believe. For a moment neither of them could move. Then Wexler barked, "Go!" and they both moved at once.

Joe headed for the back stairs, and Eddie walked quickly out to the main room. He passed the bar area and stared at Devlin for a moment, then quickly walked out the front door. Devlin watched the menacing giant out of the corner of his eye, happy that he had flushed the prey into the open, but quickly wondering what the hell he was going to do about it. He was tired and slow with alcohol. And his only weapon was the small fighting stick.

But it didn't matter. He was in. He had the right place and at least some of the people responsible for hurting his brother. All he had to do now was survive the next few minutes.

Devlin assumed whatever was going to happen would take place out on the street. He finished his orange juice and soda, slid off his bar stool, and made his way out to the elevator.

He passed Susan but gave no indication he saw her. It seemed as though he waited a long time for the elevator. Perhaps the big guy in the lobby was keeping him up there until Wexler's man was ready out on the street.

As Devlin came out of the elevator, the doorman put out a hand and slammed it hard against Devlin's chest to stop him. In a split-second, Devlin twisted his right shoulder into Bernie's arm, snatched the fighting stick from his breast pocket, and pivoted in the opposite direction, jamming the end of the fighting stick into the tender space just below the doorman's nose. Bernie bellowed in rage as his two front teeth cracked at the roots. Both hands went to his face to try to hold back the pain. Devlin's momentum had turned him sideways to Bernie, but he quickly turned back, slammed both hands into the black man's chest, and shoved him into the wall behind them. Devlin savagely kicked the doorman's feet out from under him, and he went down hard on his tailbone. Bernie's head pitched forward. Before he could raise it, Devlin grabbed the man's lower lip between his right forefinger and thumb and rammed his head back hard against the wall with his left hand. He snarled at the doorman, "You remember faces, right?"

Bernie grabbed Devlin's wrist to hold him so he couldn't tear his lip off. Tears of pain gathered in his eyes. He could only grunt in reply.

"Three nights ago, that bouncer who just left took a big man out of this club. Right?"

Bernie nodded yes.

"The big guy who came out just before me. Right?"

Again, Bernie nodded.

"Did you help beat the man up? Why'd you do it? What happened?"

Bernie shook his head no and tried to hold up two fingers. Devlin let up on his grip slightly so the doorman could talk, but it was a mistake. The pain and the rage made the man into a formidable foe. Devlin was straddling him as he sat against the wall, and Bernie somehow worked up enough leverage to kick his shin up into Devlin's groin. Devlin should have blocked the kick before it started, but he was too slow from the booze. He only managed to half-block the kick. It didn't find the mark between his legs, but it did find a target on the side of Devlin's right knee. The pain was instant and debilitating. Devlin's knee crumbled under him, and he almost fell to the floor.

Still sitting, big Bernie swung a wild roundhouse blow with his right hand and caught Devlin on the left side of his head. He knocked Devlin away from him, but Bernie paid the price because Devlin kept most of his grip on Bernie's lip. The skin at the right corner of his mouth split apart, tearing a gash in his cheek almost three inches long.

Devlin was down on one knee, dazed.

Insane with pain, Bernie scrambled to get on his feet before Devlin did. Devlin had just enough time to stand before Bernie dropped into a crouch and charged at him with the intention of slamming him into the wall.

He looked like a huge defensive lineman lunging at Devlin, but instead of trying to block his attack, Devlin stepped to one side, grabbed the back of Bernie's suit jacket, and shoved him in the same direction he was charging.

Bernie crashed into the reception podium and wall with so much force he broke his left wrist trying to block his impact, shattered his cheekbone, and cracked three vertebrae in his neck before he slid down the wall in an unconscious heap.

Devlin staggered back two steps. His left ear rang from Bernie's blow. His right knee throbbed with pain. He tested his knee and found that it supported his weight and moved normally. The fighting stick was still in his right hand. He slid it back into his pocket and flexed his hand. The hand was hard to open and close, but nothing was damaged. He took a deep breath and felt a wave of exhaustion wash over him as the adrenaline began to burn off. He didn't think he could fight off another one of these beasts. Devlin had to get by the big bouncer he saw leave, but he really wasn't sure he could do it now.

The bouncer had to be waiting outside. Luckily not too close to the entrance, or he would have been on him by now.

Devlin walked toward the doorway to the lobby but kept back out of sight from the street. Traffic on Broadway was quickly building into the morning rush hour. The entrance to the building was near the corner, and as traffic stopped for the red light down the block, cars were backing up in front of the building. There were plenty of cabs on the street cruising to pick up passengers on their way to work.

Devlin waited and watched carefully. When an empty taxi stopped in front of the building, he quickly dashed out and got into the back seat. Eddie and Joe, parked across the street in a Lincoln Town Car, almost missed seeing Devlin make his move.

Joe grabbed Eddie's arm excitedly and asked, "That's him, right? The guy who got in the cab. That's him, isn't it?"

Eddie pushed off Joe's iron grip and told him, "Yes! Goddammit!" Joe turned the ignition key so hard that he bent it. He kept turning until the starter motor began to scream and grind against the revving engine. He managed to bull his way into traffic just in time to make the same green light that Devlin's cab breezed through.

In the cab, Devlin tried to spot Eddie on the street, but saw nothing. He did hear horns honking behind him and turned to see the big Lincoln bolting into traffic. He could make out two men in the car, both of whom seemed big enough to be the bouncer he had seen leave the club ahead of him. The thought of *two* men that size after him made Devlin wish he had his .45.

He told the cab driver, "Go around to Houston and go west to Bedford. Then turn right and go up Hudson."

The cab driver was a feisty old black guy with a leather newsboy cap stuck back on his gray head. He told Devlin, "I need an address, brother. I can't be takin' directions from you for every turn."

Devlin told him, "I'm going to Port Authority on Eighth Avenue."

Devlin slumped down in his seat. He pictured them ramming the cab, forcing them into a curb, and pulling him out onto the street to beat him into a bloody, broken mess.

Devlin knew without looking back that the Town Car was

following them onto the narrow Village streets. But he turned to make sure, and sure enough the car was right behind them. Too close to pretend anything else.

Devlin was glad he had confronted Wexler in the club. He had learned long ago that nothing much happened in any investigation unless you kicked the nest until the roaches streamed out. When they did, the smart thing was to be ready with a plan to face the onslaught.

He had done the right thing at the wrong time. He had been stupid. He had nothing to use against the two monsters breathing down his neck. No gun, no backup. He wasn't leading them into a trap. He wasn't able to finish them off himself.

The cab stopped at a red light at Hudson and Bank streets, near the small park where he had met David Freedman at the start of this mess. He found himself tensed up in the backseat of the cab, almost certain that before the light changed the door to the cab would be wrenched open, and the two bouncers would be on him. He had to do something. The hell if he'd sit here waiting.

He leaned forward and told the cab driver, "Bear to the right. Go back down Bleecker."

The cab driver turned and yelled at him, "Damn it, this ain't a fuckin' tour bus. Tell me where you want to go or get the fuck out."

Devlin slammed his hand against the Lucite barrier that separated him from the driver. "Shut the hell up and do what I tell you!" He shoved a fifty-dollar bill through the small slot in the barrier and yelled, "Drive."

The cab driver was immediately cowed. This was no white businessman on the way to work who would take his bullshit. He turned down Bleecker and stopped at the light at 11th Street.

Devlin had come up with an escape plan, but ran out of time. Joe stopped the Lincoln right behind the taxi. Before the light changed, Joe and Eddie came out of their car and stormed after the cab. Joe headed for the cab's rear right door, Eddie for the left door. They wanted to trap Devlin in the backseat.

Devlin saw them coming. He locked the right-side door. And then just as Eddie came abreast of the left-side door, Devlin turned and braced his feet against it. When Eddie grabbed the handle of the unblocked door, Devlin shoved the door at him with all the strength he had in his legs.

The door slammed into Eddie. He tried to block it with crossed arms, but Devlin had shoved the door with such force it knocked Eddie back two yards and off his feet. As the big man went down, Devlin scrambled out of the open door. He was out on the street. He had prevented them from trapping him in the cab and was ready to run south, but Joe was already hustling around the front of the cab to stop Devlin.

Incredibly, the cab driver suddenly became involved.

He yelled at Joe, "Get the fuck away from my cab, motherfucker!" and actually stepped on the gas—aiming the cab into Joe, forcing Joe to jump out of the way, giving Devlin took the opportunity to do something he had never done – he ran away from a fight. He sprinted around the back of the cab, crossed the street, and kept on running.

His plan had been to have the cab driver take him to the 6th Precinct police station on 10th Street, figuring he'd rather risk getting arrested by the police than crippled by Joe and Eddie. But the bouncers had attacked two short blocks too soon. If he could outrun them, he had a chance.

Devlin had a half-block head start. Joe had stopped to kick a huge dent into the side of the fleeing cab. Eddie had taken a couple of seconds to get up off the sidewalk, but both were now running full blast after Devlin.

Eddie was faster. By the time Devlin reached Perry Street, he could hear Eddie's feet slamming into the sidewalk behind him. Devlin could almost feel the huge hand about to grab his collar and wrench him off his feet. He had to do something before they were both on top of him, but how could he survive if he stopped to fight them?

Just before Tenth Street, he made a desperate move. He grabbed a small tree to stop his forward momentum, swung completely around the tree and threw a roundhouse kick directly into Eddie's chest.

The timing was perfect. Unfortunately, Eddie was so big he absorbed the blow and still had enough strength to grab Devlin's leg. If he hadn't held on to the tree, Devlin would have been dragged down as Eddie crumpled to his knees. Devlin barely kept his balance and managed to pull his leg out of Eddie's grip, just as Joe arrived. Joe lunged for Devlin's head, and he would have torn it off if Devlin hadn't landed on his two feet and managed to duck. But the big man was faster than Devlin imagined. Joe stopped his forward motion and twisted an elbow that slammed Devlin so hard in the chest that it broke his grip on the tree and knocked him back into the street.

Devlin landed hard on his ass. Joe was on him instantly, but not before Devlin raised his foot and caught him in the chest.

Joe's weight crushed down on his leg, but Devlin was too smart to try to hold him off. He pivoted under the weight and managed to push Joe off to the side. Joe went down hard, Devlin scrambled to his feet, but before he was even fully upright Eddie grabbed him from behind, enveloping him in a bear hug, shoving Devlin forward into the side of a car.

The impact of their bodies dented the car door and the window shattered in a shower of blue pellets. The car's alarm went off, filling the air with a wailing siren.

Devlin had prepared himself for the impact. He forced out his air and tensed his body at just the right moment. Despite being slammed into the car, he was able to stay conscious. He was still trapped in the bear hug, but he retaliated by smashing the back of his head into Eddie's face. Once, twice. He felt the bones in Eddie's nose and face crunch and Eddie's teeth cut into his scalp. Three times and still the big man would not release his grip. Eddie's face was bloody from the pounding, but he still held on. Mustering his enormous strength, he lifted Devlin off his feet, preparing to throw him down to the concrete. But Devlin had one last effort. As he was lifted off the ground, he quickly brought his knees to his chest, managed to get his feet against the side of the car, and pushed back with all the strength left in both his legs.

It was enough to send Eddie reeling backward, off-balance. Both men crashed into Joe, who had been angling to get a punch into Devlin. Over 700 pounds of flesh and bones fell into the middle of Bleecker Street.

Eddie's bear hug snapped, and with his last bit of strength Devlin lurched to his feet, turned the corner, and reeled west on Tenth in a staggering, stumbling run.

The big bouncers were still not beaten. They were up and running in seconds. But as soon as they reached Tenths Street, they saw Devlin's goal. The police precinct was in plain sight up the street. Traffic had stopped on Bleecker, a crowd was gathering, a car alarm was screaming. Cops should have already appeared on the scene. Devlin was too close to the precinct entrance. Joe and Eddie, seething with frustration, turned and ran for their car.

Devlin never looked behind him. He ran toward the precinct. He felt blood running down the back of his neck. When he was almost abreast of the entrance, he slowed to a walk. Only then did he dare to look behind to see if he was still being pursued. The bouncers were gone.

Without Joe and Eddie chasing him, there was no reason to go into the police station, particularly with Donovan's bulletin hanging over him, and the back of his head streaming blood.

He kept going straight to Hudson Street, hailed another cab and got in before the cabby could see the blood that was soon going to cover his backseat.

"Sixty-third and Third," he told the cab driver. Devlin didn't want to head downtown to the loft because it meant going back in the direction of the Starlight Club. What he did want was his gun, his bleeding stopped, and a place to gather his strength and plot assault on his enemies. Now he knew who they were.

CHAPTER 24

Daryl was just about to get up and start dressing when the doorman rang her from the lobby. It didn't surprise her that it was Devlin, but what he looked like when he walked in shocked her. The back of his silk sport coat and shirt were wet with blood. His bruises and scrapes were beginning to redden and swell.

She gasped, "My God, what happened to you?"

"Take it easy. It's worse than it looks."

"Who did this to you?"

"Most likely the same guys who got my brother."

"Who? What happened?"

Devlin put his hand on Daryl's shoulder and told her, "Hang on a second. Help me get this bleeding stopped, and I'll tell you."

Daryl forced herself to hold off on her questions and followed Devlin into the bathroom. He peeled off his blood-soaked coat and shirt. Even the back of his pants was stained with his blood. He took his pants off, revealing a red crescent of blood at the top of his briefs.

"Are you still bleeding?"

"I don't know. Take a look and tell me how big the cut is on the back of my head. It's probably not that big. Head wounds bleed a lot."

"Oh, God."

"Come on. Take a look."

Daryl squinted as she went behind Devlin. He stood facing the mirror over the sink and told her, "Go on, spread apart my hair and tell me how big the cut is."

She did as he told her and said, "Ugh. It looks like about two inches long."

Devlin held his thumb and forefinger two inches apart and said, "It's that big?"

"No. Not quite."

"Okay. Good. We can close it up without stitches. Is it still bleeding?"

"No, it's sort of oozing."

"Okay. Got a scissors?"

"Yes."

"Cut away my hair. Don't poke around, just cut it as short as you can. Try not to give me too big a bald spot. Then shave around it so I can get enough bare skin to squeeze it shut with some tape."

Daryl started to work. At first, it made her queasy, but she soon found herself so absorbed in the effort that the sight of the jagged wound didn't nauseate her. When she had enough hair stripped away, Devlin made her pour hydrogen peroxide over the gash. While she did that he cut two butterfly bandages out of adhesive tape, showed her how to squeeze the cut together, and hold it in place with the tape. She did the best she could with it, then covered everything with a large Band-Aid.

Devlin turned and said, "You're better than some doctors I know."

"You sure you don't need stitches?"

"I haven't got time to get them. When are you leaving for work?"

"In about an hour. What happened to you?"

"Let me take a shower, and I'll tell you as much as I can before you go."

Devlin stood in the shower carefully checking over the damage. His right ear was puffy and sore, and the corner of his jaw ached from Bernie's blow. The knee that blocked the kick was a little stiff but all right. Getting slammed into the car had bruised all his knuckles, his left elbow, and his left hip.

Those men had had ungodly strength. And they seemed to be

able to take so much pain it seemed impossible to stop them with anything less than a bullet. Probably two.

He was hurt, but nothing was broken. Devlin knew he had been lucky to survive.

By the time he was done carefully washing his hair and showering off the dirt and sweat and blood from the long night, Daryl was dressed and ready for work.

Devlin came out naked, holding a towel. He covered a pillow on her bed with the towel and sat on the edge of the bed. All he wanted to do was lie down and sleep away some of the pain and exhaustion, but he said to her, "Is it okay if I sleep here for a while?"

"Of course."

"I found the people who hurt my brother."

"Who are they?"

"Bouncers in an after-hours club downtown. But I'm pretty sure they wouldn't do anything on their own. The guy who runs the place must have put them on my brother."

"And they tried to hurt you?"

"Yes."

"How did they know you were looking for them? You didn't go after them, did you?"

"No, I'm not that stupid. They were waiting for me."

"Why? How'd they know?"

"I'm not a hundred percent sure, yet."

"Jack, you've got to just go to the police and stop this thing before you get killed."

"It's not that simple."

"How do you expect me to get involved in something like this? You come in here beat-up and bloody. You've got that damn gun stuck in my kitchen. I can't do this, Jack. This is crazy."

"Look, I came back to get the gun and get out of here. I'm sorry you got involved, but you are and there's nothing I can do. Just don't throw me out until I get a chance to get myself together here."

"Oh Christ, I'm not throwing you out. I want to help you, but I've never done anything like this in my life."

Devlin leaned back on the bed. He was too bruised to discuss any of it anymore. "So what? You have anything better to do?"

Daryl stared at his lean, exquisite body, at his tired face and exhausted eyes. She knew she was going to do whatever he asked.

"Anything is better than this," she said.

"Maybe."

"Are you going to be all right?"

"Yes. Go to work. I just need some rest."

"You sure?"

"I'm sure. What time will you be back?"

"About six."

"Good. Six is perfect. I'll either be here, or I'll call you at six. Stop worrying."

Daryl said, "We'd better talk when I get back."

"Okay."

"I put your underwear, shirt, and pants in the washer. You'll have to put them in the dryer. I don't know what to do about your jacket."

Devlin mumbled, "Thanks."

She turned and walked out of the bedroom, then turned back to say something, but Devlin was already asleep. One foot was on the floor. She walked back, lifted his leg back on the bed and covered him with the top sheet.

She turned down the air conditioning so he wouldn't be too cold and closed the door quietly.

#

Joe drove slowly back to the club. Eddie sat on the passenger side holding his handkerchief to his bloody, pulpy nose. He didn't care about the blood or the pain, but he was furious knowing that his right eye would probably swell shut from the blows to his cheekbone, and both eyes would be black for a week.

He said to Joe, "That's one dead motherfucker, my friend."

"One dead, sorry-ass motherfucker," said Joe.

"Should have followed that fuck right into the cops and beat him to death before their fucking eyes."

"They wouldn't have let us, Eddie."

"Ten fuckin' cops will have to shoot my ass to stop me next time."

"The cocksucker had some balls, though, huh?"

"His fucking balls are going to be in his mouth."

Joe said, "You know what I hate more than that guy gettin' away?"

"What?"

"I hate that we gotta tell that fuck Wexler he got away."

"Fuck Wexler!" yelled Eddie.

It was 10:30 A.M. by the time they walked into the club. It was almost empty. Wexler was still sitting in his usual spot, livid over what had happened to Bernie. He looked at Joe and Eddie and knew immediately that they had failed. He had never seen either of them with so much as a scratch on them, and now they both looked beaten. Eddie's face and nose were already swelling horribly.

Before Wexler could say anything, Joe said, "We didn't give him the beating we wanted to."

Bareky controlling his anger, Wexler asked, "Why?"

"He's pretty cute. He hid in the lobby of the building until an empty cab stopped. He jumped in the cab before we could get to him. We had to run his cab off the road and jump him on the street. He had some fight in him. Before we could bust him up, the cops came. We had to get the hell away."

"You ran from the cops?"

"Yes, sir."

"Where?"

"Over near Bleecker and Tenth."

"How badly did you hurt him?"

Joe shrugged. "Not as bad as we wanted to. He was still moving."

"Did the cops arrest him?"

Joe shrugged again. "Fuck if I know."

Wexler was too disgusted with his bouncers to do anything but turn away and dismiss them with a wave of his hand. "Go."

Eddie headed for the kitchen, but Joe didn't budge.

"Mr. Wexler," he asked, "can you tell us where we can find him?"

Without looking at Joe, he said, "No. Get out."

Wexler picked up the cordless phone on the bar. He dialed Patrick Kelly's number.

The deputy inspector answered crisply. "Kelly speaking."

"Wexler here."

"Yes. What can I do for you?"

"I'm having a problem with that man McKay spoke to me about."

"I told McKay to warn you."

"He did. The man's name is Devlin. He is proving to be more difficult than we anticipated."

"You were warned."

"Are you going to say that to me again?"

"Sometimes I'm not sure you hear things, Robert."

"No lectures, please. The man's name is Devlin. There's a possibility he was arrested this morning by police in the Sixth Precinct. If so, I'd like you to follow up on it."

"A possibility?"

"Yes. I'm not sure. He might have gotten away."

"I'll look into it."

"If he's still free I need him taken care of. I need to know everything I can about him, and I need your advice and assistance in getting rid of him. He is turning out to be quite a nuisance."

"Is that so?"

"Yes. That's so. If he's simply out for revenge because of his brother, that's one thing. But if he's working for someone to take down our operation, that's another matter entirely."

"What makes you say that?"

"He roughs up your McKay brothers. Faces down the cop they

call in. Comes into my club, cripples my doorman, and manages to fight off Joe and Eddie. I'd say something is going on here that's a much bigger problem than it should be."

"Perhaps."

"Yes. Perhaps. But one thing there's no perhaps about—my problems are your problems. There's too much at stake here to let this go any further."

"All right. I agree. I'll see to it."

"Please keep me informed."

"Goodbye."

Wexler turned off the phone and stared into space. His gaze wandered to where Susan was sitting at her front table. His eyes narrowed as he planned something to absorb the black anger he could once again feel rising in the back of his head.

CHAPTER 25

Pain woke Devlin from a fitful sleep. His mind told him to stay in bed and not move. But his throbbing head and aching body told him to get up and do something about it.

He slowly swung his feet to the floor and surveyed the damage. All four knuckles of his left hand were bruised and swollen from banging into the car. Three knuckles on his right hand had similar scrapes. An ugly bruise was forming on his left elbow and his left hip. His right knee was stiff from blocking the doorman's kick. Everywhere his body hit the car he hurt. He knew more painful spots would emerge over the next couple of days. You never felt a fight until long after it was over.

He went into the bathroom and took out a bottle of Nuprin from Daryl's medicine chest. He poured out four caplets, 1,000 milligrams, and walked to the kitchen. It was more than the label said to take, but it still wouldn't be enough.

When he got to the kitchen, he opened her refrigerator and took out a bottle of club soda which he used to wash down the pain medicine and cut down his thirst.

He saw his bloody jacket hanging over a chair and remembered he had to change his clothes from the washer to the dryer.

He found a small washer/dryer unit in a closet next to the kitchen and made the switch, setting the timer for one hour.

He yearned for a few hours more sleep, but he had too much to do. He looked at the digital clock numbers on Daryl's microwave oven. It was 2:56. Sleep would have to wait.

He sat down naked at Daryl's kitchen table, picked up her phone, and dialed the Pacific Rim loft in SoHo. The answering machine came on. He punched in the right code numbers and listened to the stream of messages. Zitter had called three times, Marilyn twice. William Chow, the head of Pacific Rim, left one very clear message: "Call me now."

Devlin had been expecting the call. He dialed the L.A. number of Pacific Rim using his credit card, spoke briefly to the receptionist, and was immediately put through to Chow, who asked in his soft, strangely soothing voice, "Tell me what has transpired since our last contact."

Chow already knew about Devlin's father. Devlin told him everything that had happened since the funeral, quickly and succinctly.

Chow listened without interruption, then said, "Revenge is a luxury."

Devlin heard Chow clicking the computer keyboard in the background.

Devlin answered, "Revenge or not, it's past deciding now."

"You can simply get on a plane. I need you now for an assignment."

"I can't leave my brother."

"You're not with your brother."

"Close enough."

"I need you in Oahu, Hawaii."

"When?"

"As soon as possible."

"I need three or four days at the most."

Chow said nothing for about thirty seconds. Devlin could hear the occasional click of the keyboard. He knew Chow was instructing the computers at Pacific Rim to perform some task for him. Was he calling up airline flight schedules? Looking up doctors' names in his database for Devlin's brother? Devlin could only guess. He sat without saying anything.

Chow's voice came back. He said, "Interesting."

"What?" asked Devlin.

"I put the name Robert Wexler into our computer. We have a file on him."

"What does it say?"

"His name comes up from a case we had about a year ago involving Nakamura Electronics. Their U.S. office is in Mahwah, New Jersey."

"Nakamura?"

"Yes," Chow continued, "some executives from the main office in Osaka who were visiting the New Jersey headquarters had a problem at a property owned by Mr. Wexler."

"What kind of problem?"

"Attempted blackmail by a prostitute."

"A night on the town in Manhattan?"

"Yes."

"Did Pacific Rim solve the problem for them?"

"Partially. It might be worth investing some effort in this Robert Wexler. Let me think about this. Where can I reach you?"

Devlin gave him Daryl's phone number, and Chow hung up. Devlin called the hospital and found that George's condition was stable. Next, he called Marilyn. She seemed somewhat more willing to talk to him. He ate some food, finished drying his clothes. The phone rang exactly one hour after Chow had hung up.

Without introduction, Chow told him, "I'm faxing some information on Wexler to the loft. It may be of help. What do you intend to do?"

"Find out as much as I can about him and his operation and take him down."

"Excellent. What do you need from us to help?"

"I need good, fast skip tracers to help uncover information, and I need your contacts to find a fighter—hand-to-hand combat. I need a backup to help me."

The computer keys clicked in the background and Chow told Devlin, "I will contact a man for you in New York named Ozawa. Give me a few minutes and then phone him." Chow recited a phone number and address. "If I haven't spoken to him by the time you reach him, give him my name, explain what you want, and tell him to bill me.

"As for skip tracers, there is an excellent resource in New York. Use them. It will be faster than trying to work it through at this end. The agency name is William Parker Investigations. Use Pacific Rim as a referral."

"Thank you."

"Contact me in three days. I'll have the Hawaii briefing set up by then."

"Right."

Devlin was on the phone for the next hour. By the time he was done, he had an appointment with Ozawa for nine o'clock that night, and a meeting with William Parker for nine the next morning.

By then it was five o'clock. Devlin's next move was to call the woman from the Starlight Club at six, but first he dialed Zitter's number. Zitter answered his own phone. "Intrepid Investigations."

"Sam, it's Devlin."

"Are you all right?"

"Yeah."

"I've been trying to reach you at that number you gave me, and the beeper. I get a machine at one and nothing on the other."

"I got the machine's message. I forgot to take your beeper."

"Shit. I was worried. I fucked up. Inadvertently, but I fucked up."

"How?"

"One of those clubs on my list knew you were coming."

"That's right."

"Sorry. A weird fucking coincidence."

"What do you mean? I figured it was the McKays."

"No. I think the word came from higher up."

"Who?"

"Patrick Kelly."

"Who's that, your connection in the Sons of Erin?"

"Yeah. I remember him as an arrogant little bastard, but when I asked him what he was doing for the Department, I expected to hear a big spiel. Instead, he skimmed over it. Wouldn't tell me anything specific."

"So?"

"So it made me wonder, what the fuck was this guy doing? I called a few people I know at One Police."

"And?"

"I found out among other things that the fucking shanty Irish bastard is in charge of the social club squads."

"The detectives who are supposed to shut them down?"

"Yep."

"And this guy Kelly is in charge of them?"

"Among other things."

"Sounds like they have the fox in charge of the chicken coop."

"It figures, don't it? Who the fuck would invest money in a good after-hours joint if he wasn't wired in with the cops?"

"Too much risk otherwise."

"Exactly. So what happened to you? Which place knew you were coming?"

"The last place on your list. I walked in, and there was no muscle in sight. When I got out, they jumped me."

"You didn't shoot anybody, did you?"

"Didn't have my gun. Can't get into those places armed."

"Yeah, right. Are you okay?"

"I managed to get away without too much damage. So this guy Kelly provides protection for some of these after-hours joints? How's is work?"

"My guess is he just directs his detectives elsewhere. Makes 'em concentrate on the ethnic clubs and punk places. There's plenty of joints to put heat on besides the ones he's protecting. And let's say someone finds out about one of Kelly's places? It's still got to go through him. If a complaint comes in, he tips them off, they shut down until the heat blows over, and everyone goes on about their merry fucking way."

"Perfect."

"Who knows, Kelly probably owns a couple of these clubs. You said you found one place run by Irish guys? Kelly probably has some clique inside that fucking Sons of Erin running the places. That cop Donovan you ran into. Punks like him."

"Where do those McKay brothers fit in?"

"Who knows? He's got to have some guys outside the force, too. Goddamn little Irish mafia being run by a deputy inspector."

"The same story over and over again, Sam. Guys with money and power who think they can do whatever the hell they want."

"Like beat the shit out of your brother."

"Yeah."

"You find out what happened to him?"

"Not exactly. He ran into some sort of trouble, and the bouncers took him out. Maybe those McKay guys got his cash and left him holding a bill with no money. He probably got pissed and made a ruckus. If it was the guys who came after me, he's lucky he's alive."

"Shit. What are you gonna do? You can't go up against these guys."

"Yeah? Watch me."

"You're crazy."

"Here's what I want you to do. By nine o'clock tomorrow, I want you to have as much information on Kelly as you can get. His birth date, home address, license number of his car, social security number, bank, anything you can find out."

"Aw, come on. You think you can get the goods on this guy? For what?"

"For whatever it's worth. Will you do it?"

"I'm getting too old for this shit."

"No you're not. Where can I reach you about eight-thirty tomorrow morning?"

"I'll be here."

"Good. I'm counting on you, Sam."

"All right."

"Hey, Sam?"

"What?"

"Until I tell you different, don't talk to anybody else, don't roust anybody."

"Look, Devlin, I'm sorry I tipped the bad guys on you. It happens. Maybe I knew somewhere without knowing it that Kelly was a skunk. I know you can't take any chances, but don't worry about me. I'm on your side."

"All right."

"And what the hell, you and I both know the only way to shake this shit loose is to put your head on the table and see who tries to cut it off."

"Yeah, but I almost lost mine this morning."

"I know. I know. You're right. Be careful. And don't tell me anything that you're afraid will bounce back on you."

"I'll call you in the morning."

Devlin hung up the phone, walked to the clothes dryer, and took out his clothes. They were warm from the dryer. Most of the blood was gone, but the pants looked like hell. They were wrinkled and shrunk from the heat. They were too short and too tight on him, which didn't help ease the pain that still wracked his hip and knee.

As he dressed, he tried to sort out his next moves. There wasn't room for any mistakes.

He walked back into the kitchen, opened the cabinet where his gun was stashed behind the blender and other junk. He strapped the holster on even though he knew he couldn't cover it up with the bloody jacket hanging on the back of the chair.

He heard the front door open. Daryl walked into the kitchen looking uncomfortable and disheveled from the heat outside.

The digital numbers on the microwave clock said 5:46. Almost time to call the woman from the club. He had her phone number and her name—Susan. Now all he needed was to convince Daryl to make the call.

CHAPTER 26

Susan Furlong sat staring at her phone. She knew the phone was going to ring at six, but she still didn't know what she was going to say.

She did know she never again wanted to live through the two hours she had spent with Wexler after they left the club that morning. Worse, she had finally abandoned the belief that she could do about it. For the first time in her life, Susan thought about killing herself.

When Wexler told Susan that morning he was coming up to the apartment with her, it didn't surprise her. He seemed to have an unerring sense of when she least wanted him around.

It had started like all the other times—stripping off his clothes, praising his body, telling him how big and full his penis was. But this time, when he led her to the bathroom, he was fully erect. The cruelty he was planning for her was exciting him.

As usual, she had to strip down to her panties and bra, but this time when he told her to kneel in front of him he made her do it on the bare, tile floor. At first, it was uncomfortable. Then it became painful. She continued to perform fellatio on him but sat back on her calves to take some of the weight off her knees. It only made the tiles dig in at a different spot.

She took her mouth away from him and reached for the bath mat that was folded over the tub.

Wexler quickly grabbed her hair and jerked her head toward him. The pain of her hair being pulled was immediate and intense.

"Did I tell you to stop?"

"This floor is hurting my knees."

"So what. Suck me until you're told to stop."

He forced her head into position, and this time he placed his right foot on her left thigh. He pressed his weight down on her until it felt as if the floor tiles were cutting through her skin.

All the while he pushed her head back and forth. She couldn't keep the tears from oozing out of her eyes. She thought he might climax soon, and it would be over, but he pulled her away from him and slapped her hard across the face.

"If you want to cry, I'll give you something to cry about. Stand up."

She was trembling now. The more frightened and hurt she became, the more Wexler liked it.

Wexler tormented her for over an hour. There was no blood. No permanent damage or injury. Just a slow, steady accretion of indignities and pain. Twice Susan tried to edge toward the medicine chest so she could grab the scissors on the bottom shelf and stab him but stopped herself. Wexler was too strong and too quick. She kept thinking of Wexler's pen jutting out of that waiter's eye.

When Susan was so numb with shame and loathing that Wexler could hardly detect any resistance or fight left in her, he finally allowed himself an orgasm.

But even when the humiliating sex was over, Wexler wasn't done. After they had showered and he was dressed, he told her to sit on the edge of the bed.

He said to her, "You didn't much like that, did you?"

"No."

"Then I want to ask you something."

Susan didn't respond.

"I want to ask you, what you are going to do about it?"

Susan looked up and said nothing.

Wexler bent over and took her face in his hand and said, "You're not going to do anything about it. You can't do anything about it. You have no money, no friends, no power, no strength. You have nothing."

Still, Susan didn't respond.

"You think that miserable pittance of eight thousand dollars you have squirreled away can do you any good?"

The question seared into her brain. How did he know? As if he could read her thoughts he said, "I know about your little savings account at Irving Trust, and your safe deposit box at Chemical Bank. I can take that away from you in minutes. I can fix it so it'll take you years to get to it, if ever. I know what you do, where you go, who you talk to."

He stuck his face an inch from hers. She could smell an acrid odor as he talked. "I know where your mother lives; I know about your poor pathetic mongoloid sister; I know about your other sister living with her dull husband in Roslyn, Long Island. I know more about you than you know about yourself."

Susan was reeling. Her hands started to shake from the combination of fear and hatred that burned inside her.

Wexler stood up straight, let go of her chin and stepped back from her. "I own you, and the minute I get tired of you, I'll throw you back in the garbage heap. So don't bore me with your childish pouting. Be ready for tonight at the usual time. And get to like it. I prefer cheerful people in my presence."

He had turned and left her sitting there. She had simply fallen back into the bed, curled her legs up into a fetal position and stayed that way for hours in a state of paralysis rather than sleep. But by six o'clock she was awake and staring at the phone with a kind of exhausted intensity. Instinctively, she knew that Wexler's behavior was connected to the mysterious Mr. Smith. Something he had done enraged Wexler, and she had become the target. She knew that she had never hated anyone as much as she hated Robert Wexler. He threatened her life, her family, Ceece, everything. What she didn't know was how to stop him.

At five after six the phone rang and startled her so much she twitched violently. On the third ring, she managed to lift the receiver and say, "Hello?"

A woman's voice asked, "Hello, is this Susan?"

"Yes?" She didn't recognize the voice. "Who's this?"

"I'm not sure if you remember me. My name is Margie. We met at the after-hours club where you work. I was with a tall guy, dark, pretty good-looking. Maybe you don't remember his name. You met him in your club the one time."

"No, I don't really—"

"I know it's strange for me to be calling you at *six o'clock* out of the blue like this, but I really would like to talk to you."

Even in Susan's dulled state the meaning of the call became clear to her.

"Oh yes," said Susan, "I remember you. I'd like to talk to you, too."

"Good. Are you busy tonight? Maybe we could meet for a drink."

"All right," said Susan, "when and where?"

"Say about an hour. Do you know that restaurant, Mulholland Drive?"

"On Sixty-third and Third?"

"Yes. That's the one."

"Okay. I'll see you there at seven."

"Fine."

Susan hung up the phone. At the other end, Daryl hung up and looked at Devlin. "It sounds like she got it."

"Good. Thanks."

"You really think her phone might be tapped?"

"I can't take the chance."

"Now what?"

"You've got to meet her."

"Why?"

"I can't let her be seen with me until I know it's safe."

"What about me?"

"You'll just be a friend meeting her for a drink. If she's being followed or there's any problem, you leave, and it ends."

Daryl looked at Devlin without saying anything for a couple of seconds. "I guess it beats staying home and watching the news."

CHAPTER 27

As soon as Daryl agreed to the meeting, Devlin picked up the phone and began making the necessary arrangements. Next, he had to take care of his shrunken pants and ruined jacket. He needed pants to cover himself and a jacket to cover his gun. From now on, he wasn't going anywhere without his custom Caspian.

Devlin asked Daryl, "What's the closest department store, Bloomingdale's?"

"Yes, but I hate that store."

"You don't have to shop. Just wait for me outside."

"And do what?"

Devlin handed her his holstered .45. "Hold this until I come out."

"What do I do, strap this on somewhere? Christ, it weighs a ton."

"Put it in a shopping bag."

Daryl found a small bag from Grace's Market, and they left. She walked next to him as they headed down Third Avenue. Devlin's shrunken, wrinkled pants made him look like a bum, and she was carrying a huge loaded gun, and none of it seemed to make a bit of difference to Devlin. No explanations, no concessions to appearance. He moved, she followed.

Devlin left her waiting outside Bloomingdale's and emerged twenty minutes later wearing tan slacks and an unconstructed light cotton sport jacket.

Daryl looked at him and said, "You're one of those guys that everything looks good on."

"If it's a forty-six long."

"Slacks are already hemmed?"

"Thirty-four, thirty-six. Polo. Their stuff fits me."

"So now what?"

Devlin gently took her elbow and led her back uptown. "Let me explain as we walk."

Devlin carefully told Daryl his plans as they headed back toward Mulholland Drive Restaurant. They approached a car service sedan double-parked at 61st Street and Third. There was a small sign in the side window that read, "Mr. D."

Devlin stopped and said, "Here's where we split up. Give me the shopping bag."

Daryl handed it to him.

"I'll be following you in this car. Don't worry, nothing will happen to you. Nobody but the woman will get close to you."

"Tell me what she looks like again."

"She's about your height, dark hair, her name is Susan."

"Good figure?"

"Yeah."

"Attractive?"

"Yes."

"Sure *you* don't want to meet her?"

"I'm sure. Tell her what I told you, and try to get her to come to the Marriott. I'll meet you there. If I don't join you at the bar within fifteen minutes after you arrive, get the hell out. Don't worry. I'll cover your exit."

Daryl nodded and turned up Third Avenue. Devlin got into the sedan and asked the driver his name. The driver turned around and said, "Mike Trey, sir."

The driver was black, about twenty-five, dressed in a blue blazer, gray slacks, and red-striped tie. He gave Devlin the immediate impression that he was a savvy kid. Devlin asked him, "Have you ever driven for Pacific Rim?"

"No, sir."

"Well, it might be a little unusual. Just do what I tell you."

The driver turned back to the wheel and said, "Yes, sir."

Devlin took off his coat and strapped on his gun, never taking his eyes off the street.

He told the driver, "Pull up a couple of blocks and see if you can park across the street from that Mulholland Drive place."

"No problem."

The driver expertly eased out into traffic, drifted across three lanes to the other side of the avenue, and pulled into an open spot next to a fire hydrant.

Devlin told him, "Okay, just shut it down and relax."

"No problem."

Devlin carefully watched the street. Five minutes later, he saw Susan approach the corner on the west side of Third Avenue. He watched her walk into the bar and very carefully scanned the street to see if she was being followed. He didn't spot anyone.

When Susan entered the restaurant, she looked around quickly, then walked toward the bar that ran along the wall to her right. She stopped and scanned the people sitting at the bar.

The only woman at the bar was Daryl, sitting alone. The two women's eyes met at almost the same moment. Daryl stood up from her bar stool and took a step toward Susan. Susan walked straight for her.

Susan was dressed in blue slacks and a white silk blouse that had black buttons and three large pleats on either side. She was wearing her dark hair loose. From where she stood, she looked beautiful. But as she approached Daryl the tension in her face cramped her features.

Daryl put out her hand and said, "I'm Daryl Austen, you must be Susan."

Susan shook her hand and said, "Yes. Could you please tell me what's going on?"

"Well, I'll try. Sit down and have a drink and I'll tell you as much as I can."

Susan craved the day's first jolt of alcohol and ordered a Bloody Mary. Before the drink came, Susan asked, "Did I get it right that you were calling for the man I met last night?"

"Yes. He felt it was better that I call you instead of him."

"He's right. I think my phone is tapped."

"He seems to know what to do in these situations."

"What situations?"

"Well, I guess he should explain all that to you."

"Who is he? Who are you?"

"He'll explain that. I'm just a friend of his."

"Why didn't he come here himself?"

"I guess he wanted to make sure you weren't followed."

Susan's drink came, and she took a long swallow from it, relishing the tang of the spicy tomato juice and vodka.

Daryl told her, "We're going to meet him at another place."

"I'm in no mood to play games."

Daryl looked at her almost finishing the Bloody Mary and said, "I don't think it's a game."

"Do you have anything more to tell me?"

"No."

Susan finished her Bloody Mary. "Well then, there's no point in staying here is there? Let's go meet your friend."

Before Daryl had a chance to say another word, Susan stood up, put a twenty-dollar bill on the bar and started for the door. Just before she pushed the door open, Susan turned to Daryl and asked, "By the way, what's your friend's name?"

Daryl hesitated, she wasn't sure if Devlin wanted his name known to this woman, but she was sure Susan wouldn't tolerate any evasions.

"His name is Jack Devlin."

Susan thought for a moment, shook her head, and said, "It doesn't mean a thing to me."

Daryl thought to herself, it soon will.

#

At One Police Plaza, Deputy Inspector Patrick Kelly was waiting for the computer run on the name Jack Devlin. He had assigned the task to an administrative assistant named Harold Feldmeir, who always had a somewhat surprised look on his face.

Feldmeir walked into Kelly's office, handed him the folder and said, "This fellow Devlin used to be a cop."

"Really?"

"Class of Seventy-two, New York Police Academy. Didn't last long. No criminal record. It's all in there. Computer pulls up a lot of records on him in Washington. I got some files modemed in from Army and Secret Service records, but I'm sure there's a lot more. I can't access all of it without clearances, and I can't get that until regular working hours. There should be enough in there to perk your interest."

"I'm sure there is, son. I'm sure there is. Let me get to it."

"Yes, sir." Feldmeir left Kelly to his reading.

#

Devlin watched the two women emerge from the restaurant. They made quite a pair. Daryl dressed in her perfect-fitting jeans, brown boots, and a light cotton pullover was tall, blond, trim with sharp features. Susan matched her in height but looked older, more sophisticated, more voluptuous. While Daryl's clothes were casual but flattering, Susan's were expensive and flattering. If Daryl was striking, Susan was beautiful.

Devlin asked his driver, "See those two women?"

"The minute they hit the street, man."

"Right. We're going to follow them. They're going to get a cab, so just hang back a few cars and follow whatever cab they get into."

"You got it, boss."

As soon as the women hailed a cab, the driver was ready to pull out after them. Devlin had to tell him, "No, not yet. Hang back a bit. Wait until I tell you."

"I don't want to lose them."

"Relax."

Devlin wanted to make sure he could spot anyone else following Susan and Daryl. As the cab pulled away, he didn't see any other car enter traffic. He waited a few moments just to be sure, then said, "Okay, go ahead."

Mike the driver bent over the wheel, concentrating on maneuvering through the traffic so he could keep the cab in sight.

The cab turned west on 66th. Devlin knew it would head through Central Park and probably make its way west to Broadway, then south to the hotel which was at 46th Street.

Devlin leaned forward and told the driver, "Look, don't worry about following them anymore. Just cut through the park, then head downtown to the Marriott Hotel on Broadway and Forty-sixth."

"Okay."

When they pulled up to the hotel, Devlin spotted Susan and Daryl just entering the hotel's revolving door.

The Marriott had been designed so that the hotel's lobby was not on the ground floor. It was located eight floors up. All that was on the ground floor entrance were a bellhop's desk, escalators leading upstairs, and a core of elevators. One floor up was a Broadway theater. Above that were meeting rooms and ballrooms. The hotel's main desk was in the eighth-floor lobby along with several restaurants, shops, and bars.

Devlin told the driver to wait for him on 46th Street and entered the hotel. He hadn't seen anyone following the women, but he had to make sure.

The two women proceeded to the area on the ground floor where the elevators arrived. Devlin saw them waiting, walked past the core of elevators and sprinted up the escalator that would take him to the theater lobby one flight up. There he continued up successive escalators to the eighth floor. As he anticipated, the crowd waiting for elevators on the ground floor prevented Susan and Daryl from getting to the eighth floor before he did.

When Daryl entered the lounge where Devlin told her to take Susan, she soon realized why he had chosen it. The entire seating area of the room revolved slowly around a circular bar set in the middle.

There was a balcony above the lounge that completely encircled it. Devlin sat in the balcony out of sight. While the women sat at the bar, he could watch everyone in the lounge revolve into view. If it appeared that anyone was observing the women, he would call off the meeting.

In one revolution of ten minutes, Devlin was convinced no one had followed the women. He descended the staircase and sat on the bar stool next to Susan.

She turned. He extended his hand and said, "I'm Jack Devlin."

Susan shook his hand, taking in the bruises on his face and knuckles and said, "It looks like you ran into Wexler's men."

"Yes."

"I'm surprised you're still walking."

"I was lucky."

"You were. So, what is this all about? I take it you have some problem with Robert Wexler."

"You're right. But if you don't mind, I'd prefer not to discuss it here. I have a suite reserved upstairs. I think it would be more private and more comfortable if we discussed it there."

"Look, maybe using your friend and this roundabout way of getting to meet with you was necessary, but I'm not going into any hotel room with you. If you want to talk to me, you'd better do it right here."

Devlin watched her drain her drink and motion for another. She was drinking straight vodka on ice.

Devlin said, "All right. Let me explain."

He told her about leaving his brother at O'Callahan's. He told her about the McKay brothers taking George to an after-hours club. He described George and asked her if she had seen him at the Starlight. She said, "Yes."

He said, "Do you know what happened to him?"

"Not really. He was in there a few nights before you showed up. Joe and Eddie escorted him out."

"Why?"

"I think the guys he came in with left and stuck him with the bill. He tried to pay with a credit card. We don't take credit cards. I guess he was upset about the whole thing, and he started yelling. Wexler called in the muscle, and they took him out."

"My brother ended up in a hospital beaten half to death and with a skull fracture so bad they had to operate on him. Are you telling me they did that because my brother complained about paying his bill with a credit card?"

For a moment, Susan said nothing. She closed her eyes and quietly said, "God, those two are animals."

"Why would they do that?"

Susan turned and looked at Devlin. "Why? *Why?* Because that's what they do. Your brother probably fought back so they took him off somewhere and beat the shit out of him because they like to, and because they know they can get away with it. That's why."

For a moment, nobody said anything. Devlin stared straight ahead with such a terrible look on his face that Daryl was afraid to speak. Susan finished her drink.

Finally, Susan asked, "What do you want from me?"

"I want you to help me."

"Do what?"

"Make sure Wexler and his crew never do anything like that to anybody, ever again."

"And how am I supposed to do that?"

"Start by telling me everything you know about Wexler."

"How is that going to do anything?"

"It will."

"Look, Mr. Devlin, I might hate Wexler and his people even more than you, but you have no idea what you're getting involved in."

"That's why I need your help."

"Even if I try to help you, what difference will it make? Who are you? What can you do about them? If I help you, I'd be risking more than you can imagine."

"What's your risk?"

"My job, my apartment, my savings, my safety. More than I care to discuss."

"Wexler is giving you all that?"

"Yes."

"And what does he get?"

"He gets me."

Devlin quietly told her, "I'm not trying to threaten or coerce you, Susan. Please believe that. But I'm telling you right now – Wexler is going down. There won't be any job or anything else he can give you or anything he can take away from you when I'm done. I'm giving you a chance to get out while you can."

"Are you serious? You think you can take on Wexler?"

"Yes."

"Why should I believe you?"

Devlin calmly asked, "What options do you have if you *don't* believe me?"

Susan took another swallow of her cold vodka and tried to sort out everything that was happening. She looked at her watch. She had a little more than an hour before Wexler would arrive at her apartment. If she did nothing or helped Wexler, she'd still be under his control. If she helped Devlin . . .?

"If I help you, what do I get out of it?"

"You get out from under someone that you admit is dangerous to you and that you hate. I'll give you a place to stay that's safe.

And when this is all over, I'll give you ten thousand dollars to stake you to a new start."

"And I'm supposed to trust you can do all that?"

"Got anybody else you can trust to do it?"

Susan knew she wanted to believe this man, but that didn't mean she could. She gave her head one quick shake and asked Devlin, "What exactly do you want me to do? I mean right now. How does all this happen?"

"Right now, all you have to do is move into this hotel tonight. The room isn't in any name Wexler knows. I made sure no one followed you here. You'll be safe. I'll get whatever you need from your apartment. Give me whatever information you can on Wexler. That's all you have to do. Just walk away from it right now—the apartment, the club, all of it. Walk away, help me, and start over free of Wexler."

"And that's all you want from me?"

"Probably. There could be more, but I don't know what it would be. If there's anything else you have to do, we can decide when the time comes. You don't have to commit to any more than what I just described."

"It's too fast. Too crazy. I don't know what I'm getting into."

"It's the best offer you're going to get. You either stay here and end it now, or go back to Wexler. There isn't anything more I can tell you or guarantee you. It's your decision. Help me and you'll never regret it.

"I'm going over to the reservations desk to get the keys to the suite. I'm sorry it's so sudden, but you have to decide by the time I get back."

Devlin left the two women at the bar. Daryl wanted to say something but didn't know the right words. Susan ordered another drink. She looked at Daryl and said, "Maybe if I drink enough it won't matter what I do."

Daryl blurted out, "I think you should do what he says."

"Why?"

"Whoever this man Wexler is, if you know he was the one who almost killed Devlin's brother, and if he is hurting you—someone should stop him. If decent people can do that, they should."

"Is that what you're trying to do?"

"I guess I am."

"What do you know about Devlin?"

"He used to be a cop. He works for a private security company. He seems to have a lot of connections. And he's got big goddamn gun under his jacket."

Susan frowned, stared at her drink, and took another sip, but didn't say anything.

Devlin returned and laid a plastic room card key on the bar. He said, "That card opens a suite on the thirty-fourth floor. Pick it up, go to room Thirty-four seventeen, and you've got a chance to start over. Leave it and walk out of here, you know what you'll be going back to."

Susan stared at the plastic card. Daryl watched Susan. Devlin turned away from both of them and looked straight ahead. Susan looked at her watch. She had forty-five minutes before Wexler showed up at her apartment.

She stared at the card key and thought about the sound of Wexler's key turning in the lock on her apartment door. She could hear that sound. She knew she hated that sound so much it made her teeth grind. She didn't want to hear that key in her door. Not in forty-five minutes, not ever again. She picked up the room card key and left the bar without a word. Devlin let her walk ahead a few paces, then he and Daryl followed her out.

CHAPTER 28

Deputy Inspector Kelly put the last piece of paper into the manila folder Feldmeir had given him. The folder held computer printouts, copies of police reports, intelligence reports, copies of Army records, and NYPD personnel reports. Kelly rubbed his eyes to ease the sting.

Kelly knew a lot more about Devlin than when he had started reading. He knew that Devlin had graduated first in his class at the NYPD Academy, then had quit the force six months later, leaving behind several reports that his superiors had written to cover their asses rather than explain why.

From there it was into the Army where he was assigned to the military police. He did a tour in Vietnam, most of it spent in the bars of Saigon dealing with violent Army personnel. From the Army, he entered the Secret Service and apparently worked his way up the ladder until he was in charge of guarding Jimmy Carter during the last half of his presidency.

After Carter, Devlin's days in public service were over. He went to work for a security company called Pacific Rim based in Los Angeles. The company did a lot of work for Asian corporations with operations in the States.

It was a great deal of information, but none of it fully explained to Kelly why Jack Devlin had tracked down the McKay brothers who worked for him, threatened a police officer who was loyal to him, and walked into a very private after-hours club under his protection and threatened Robert Wexler.

What he had pieced together from the McKay brothers and his conversation with Sam Zitter indicated that Devlin was doing it because his brother had run into some trouble at the Starlight.

It seemed far-fetched, but so did any other reason for Devlin to be after Wexler. Was some Japanese conglomerate trying to take over his real estate interests? Was Devlin working for someone in a rival faction on the Irish side? Someone who was against Kelly's employing former IRA gunmen when they fled Ireland to hide in the States?

Kelly couldn't think of a reason good enough, but soon stopped trying. Devlin was dangerous. And for now, it didn't matter why Devlin was causing so much trouble. He had to be eliminated, and it had to be done quickly.

He decided to use a few detectives from his social club task force to track down Devlin, find out who or what had unleashed him, and then turn him over to Wexler's people for elimination.

\#

While Kelly was reading background on Devlin, Sam Zitter was getting ready to acquire his own batch of inside information on Kelly.

The difference in sources was significant. Kelly's came from typed reports and computer files. Zitter's would come from the garbage outside Kelly's apartment.

Zitter drove to Riverdale and parked a few blocks away from Patrick Kelly's apartment building. He stepped out of his car wearing green work clothes that made him look like a janitor. In his back pockets were a pair of extra-large yellow rubber gloves and a roll of heavy-duty plastic garbage bags.

He locked his car and walked to Kelly's address. It took him a few minutes to locate the building's garbage contained in two large metal Dumpsters at the back of the building. There were a few bags scattered around the Dumpsters, but most of the bags were stacked inside.

Zitter walked up to the first bin and exercised a right that had been guaranteed by the highest court in New York State. He searched somebody else's garbage and took it for his own. The law said that once garbage was put on a public street, searching that garbage was no longer an invasion of privacy.

It took a surprisingly short amount of time to locate Kelly's garbage amid the many bags stuffed in the Dumpsters. Zitter's technique was similar to the one used by scavengers who collect return deposit cans. With a penknife, he quickly slit open the plastic garbage bag, picked through it with his rubber-gloved fingers until he found an envelope or magazine with a name on it, then went on to the next bag. Unlike the can collectors, who slit the bags and left them that way, Zitter carefully placed the open bags into new bags. And unlike the can collectors, Zitter could barely tolerate the acrid smell of garbage, which had been fermenting for days in the hot weather.

Zitter worked as fast as he could. In thirty minutes the building's garbage was slit, picked through, and re-bagged. Zitter retrieved enough of Kelly's garbage to fill half of one large bag.

He walked back to his car carrying his treasure. Having the privacy of the back alley had made the job easier. It was always troublesome picking through garbage in plain view on a street in front of a house or apartment building.

The hardest work was yet to come: taking the garbage back to his office, pouring it out on a large worktable, and picking through the rotten, wet, messy parts until he found something useful.

Garbage was one of Zitter's best sources of reliable information. It was amazing how many people thought throwing something in a garbage bag meant getting rid of it. And it was more amazing how much a person's garbage revealed. People thought nothing of discarding bank statements, mortgage payment slips, credit card invoices, and telephone bills in garbage that could easily be searched by other people.

Zitter had used garbage to find everything from an ex-husband's hidden income to the real occupants of a rent-controlled apartment.

Except for the smell, Zitter loved picking through garbage.

#

As Zitter drove back to his office, Devlin, Susan, and Daryl entered a plush executive suite in the Marriott. The suite had two bedrooms separated by a large, well-furnished room. It had a couch with a coffee table in front of it, a round table with four chairs, a wet bar, TV, and two upholstered sitting chairs.

There were fresh flowers in the bedrooms, a bowl of fruit on the table in the center room, a bucket of ice, and a selection of soft drinks in the wet bar. There was no liquor in the suite.

Susan quickly surveyed her surroundings and announced, "I need liquor and cigarettes. I may have done a very foolish thing, and I'm not in the mood to do it sober."

Devlin took a seat on the couch and said, "You can order whatever you need from room service."

"Fine."

Susan immediately picked up the phone on the bar and dialed room service.

"I'd like a carton of Parliament cigarettes, a bottle of Absolut vodka, and a bottle of Grand Marnier sent to room 3417." She paused, listening to the other end. "Yes, send up some club soda. No, no hors d'oeuvres or food." She hung up the phone, turned to Devlin and said, "I hope you didn't expect me to stop drinking tonight."

"No, I didn't. I just thought I'd let you make the decision instead of me."

"Good. Now what?"

"Tell me what you need from your apartment."

"You've got about thirty minutes to get it before Wexler shows up there."

"So?"

"So I doubt if you want to run into him, that's all."

Devlin leaned toward Susan and said, "Do you think I give a damn if I run into that little weasel?"

"He can be very unpleasant."

"So can I. Don't worry about him anymore. Give me your keys and tell me what you need."

She handed Devlin a ring of keys. She told him what clothes she wanted and where her jewelry was hidden, and where he could find a small fireproof box that held her few important papers.

Devlin told her, "While I'm gone I'd like you to write down everything you know about Wexler. Where he lives. His phone number. License number of his cars, if you know them. Addresses of any buildings or property he owns. Names of his lawyers. Anything you can think of about him."

"I don't know much."

"You'd be surprised how much you can come up with once you start writing things down. Don't put any pressure on yourself, just write down what comes to mind. Take your time."

During all this Daryl sat quietly on the couch. Devlin headed toward the door. Daryl stood up and walked with him.

They stopped at the door and Daryl asked, "How long do you want me to stay here with her?"

"As long as you can. If she's in here alone and starts having second thoughts, she'll bolt. That would be the worst possible thing to happen right now. Just try and keep her company and reassure her."

"All right, if you think it's necessary. When are you coming back?"

"I'd say in a couple of hours."

"Then what?"

"I'm not sure yet."

"Are you going to stay here after you get back? Not that you wouldn't like spending the night with her."

"Hey, listen. This isn't about that."

"Sure. That would be a real hardship spending the night with her after she downs a few more glasses of vodka."

"Come on, Daryl."

"All right, all right. I'll stay the night, but really, that's it. I'm not used to babysitting grown women."

"I understand. Just for tonight. Tonight is the most important."

Daryl shrugged. "Go do what you have to do."

Devlin used the car service to get to Susan's apartment on the East Side at 65th and Second Avenue.

When Devlin walked into the apartment, he thought seriously about waiting for Wexler to arrive, but for what?

Rendering a beating would be simple. Beat Wexler exactly the way they had beaten his brother. He imagined doing it, and it felt ridiculous. He was through doing anything unplanned. And there was more to this now than Wexler. The NYPD Deputy Inspector who Zitter talked to had clearly gotten word to Wexler. He'd have to be dealt with, too. The sting of losing Susan would have to suffice as the first move against Wexler. And once Wexler discovered she was gone, the game would soon be heating up, and Devlin was far from ready.

Within ten minutes he had gathered everything he came for. He packed Susan's belongings into a suitcase, brought it down to Mike waiting in the car service sedan, and told him to take it to room 3417 at the Marriott.

Devlin checked his watch. He had only ten minutes until his appointment with Kaito Ozawa.

CHAPTER 29

Ozawa ran a private school for martial arts in TriBeCa. Very few people knew about Ozawa's dojo. It wasn't open to the public. It was the kind of resource Pacific Rim was able to provide. Devlin was glad that his problem had somehow coincided with William Chow's interests. Or perhaps, thought Devlin, Chow's story about the Nakamura executive in a whorehouse owned by Wexler was just Chow's contrivance to help him. He wouldn't put such a move past Chow. But it didn't really matter. Having the resources of Pacific Rim on his side was a major asset.

The dojo was in a small four-story building in the middle of a warehouse and loft neighborhood. Ozawa owned the entire building. On the ground floor was a garage big enough for several cars. Next to the garage door was a windowless steel door that led up a short flight of stairs to Ozawa's office and living quarters. There was a single buzzer near the door. No name, just the buzzer. Devlin rang it and waited for a return buzz to release the lock. Instead, it was opened by an elderly Japanese woman. The woman somehow managed to open the door and bow at the same time. She extended a hand and introduced herself as Mrs. Ozawa. She was small, even for a Japanese, but she had a beatific smile and a welcoming aura that made her presence seem large. Mrs. Ozawa wore a neat gray suit and a simple string of pearls. She seemed dressed to conduct business in a midtown office, even though it was past nine o'clock in a downtown loft neighborhood.

Devlin followed her up the stairs, where they entered a second door. The woman quietly led Devlin down a narrow hallway to Ozawa's office. She bowed slightly and motioned Devlin to enter. Ozawa sat behind a large desk made out of a solid slab of gray slate. The base of the desk was constructed out of two large steel girders painted in bright red acrylic. The girders were crossed and stacked one upon the other so they formed a huge red X.

Ozawa rose to offer Devlin his hand and looked exactly like the kind of man who should sit behind a desk made of steel and stone.

Devlin shook Ozawa's hand and felt the man's solid strength. Ozawa reminded Devlin of a small bull.

Devlin estimated Ozawa to be in his late fifties. He had a broad, ruggedly handsome face and a full head of salt-and-pepper hair, which was longer than one would expect on a man his age. He wore black slacks and a short black silk kimono.

Ozawa motioned for Devlin to sit and without any introduction told him, "I spoke with Mr. Chow. He explained what you need. I have a young man I think will be right for you. A true fighter. Exceptional. He has studied iaido under me, aikido, karate, and judo under other masters. He also knows good jujitsu."

"Sounds remarkable."

"Yes. Yes. Kind of obsessed, huh? But, yes, remarkable."

"Any knowledge of weapons?"

"Only sword."

"Iaido?"

"Hai. We believe all fighting derive from the sword. Maybe he knows about guns, but I don't think he ever touch one. Chow-san say no guns, no weapons."

"Not from our side. But I can't guarantee that some of the men we may be dealing with won't have guns."

"I understand. Okay. I introduce you to Mr. Pony?"

Ozawa led the way upstairs to the third floor, where his training area was located. It occupied the entire top floor of the narrow loft building. The dojo consisted of a bare wooden floor, polished to a slight sheen. The floor immediately impressed Devlin. It was made of solid white oak. Flawless strips without a single knot or bump, laid down so tightly that the entire floor looked like one seamless piece.

At the entrance to the dojo, there was a carpeted area with four folding chairs. At the far end was a small shrine. Kneeling in front of the shrine was the man Ozawa had selected. Upon seeing him from behind Devlin was struck by his size. For a man who fought without weapons, he seemed small. Especially when Devlin thought about the size of the men he would have to face. Men like the bouncers Robert Wexler had sent after him.

He wondered if this Mr. Pony had the bulk and body weight needed to go up against big men.

When they entered, the man stood and turned around. Devlin was surprised again, this time by how young he appeared.

Devlin and Ozawa both had shoes on, so they did not step on the dojo floor. They waited for the man to approach them, and Devlin was surprised a third time by the young man's ethnic origin. His features looked American Indian, but Devlin had never seen skin the color of James Pony's. It was a dark, coppery bronze. Darker and richer than any Native American. His hair was jet black. His cheekbones definitely looked American Indian, and his nose probably would have, too, except it had been broken too many times to retain the classic shape.

As the young fighter stood in front of them, some of Devlin's misgivings were dispelled by the quiet authority and strength the young man exuded. Even though he was only about five-ten, his physical presence was imposing. He had long arms, big bones, big hands, and he was packed with muscle. The kind of muscle that came from exercise and training. None of it was what Devlin considered to be the artificial muscle of body builders.

Pony stood in front of them in bare feet. He wore a pair of black jeans and a black T-shirt. No extra clothes, no extra flesh, no extra anything. Pony seemed to be totally without affectation.

Ozawa made the introductions. "Mr. Devlin, this is James Pony. James, Mr. Devlin."

They shook hands and appraised each other wordlessly. Devlin decided to get right to the point. "James, has Mr. Ozawa told you about the assignment?"

"Just that it would be hand-to-hand fighting in the real world. No dojos. Real fighting."

"How much fighting have you done?"

"You mean besides kumite and tournaments?"

"Yes."

"Not enough. I've done some work as a bodyguard. A little bit as a bouncer. I've done work for two detective agencies in the city. I've had to restrain people, handle a few problems, but never a fight on the outside with someone who had real training. Plenty of full contact in this dojo."

Devlin continued, "The men we are going up against are not exceptionally trained, but they are big, strong, usually mean, and certainly reckless. They can take a lot of punishment. In fact, an incredible amount of punishment. You'll need to take them out fast. Without hesitation. They are strong, and you will rarely be fighting just one. We might be in places where if you attack one, two or three or even more will swarm you.

"You can't afford to fight with them. You can't beat them down. You have to have the heft to go right at them and neutralize them fast. I'm sure you have great technique, but I'm not sure you have the size and strength to cripple big men quickly."

Pony stood silently for a moment, thinking. Then he said, "I'd be surprised if I couldn't do what you need."

"You don't have any doubts?"

"I can't say I have doubts. Especially against men who are not well trained. But, of course, I could be wrong."

Devlin nodded, carefully considering Pony's response, and continuing to look him over. Up close, Pony didn't look small. His shoulders and arms were very muscular. His legs seemed solid. But most of all, he stood before Devlin without ego or posture. He was contained. He kept within himself. He was calm and neutral but completely focused.

Devlin asked him, "Where are you from, James?"

"Long Island."

"You look Indian."

"My mother was Shinnecock. But my father was Portuguese. His ancestors were whalers."

"I see." Portuguese and Shinnecock Indian, thought Devlin. He'd never seen skin like Pony's before because he had never seen that mix. James Pony seemed to be one of a kind.

Devlin decided to trust Ozawa. Chow didn't make casual recommendations.

"All right, Mr. Pony, Mr. Ozawa, I'm sure it will be fine. It will probably be a day or two before we start. We'll talk more later." Ozawa bowed slightly and answered, "Hai. Mr. Pony's rate is five hundred dollars a day. If you want to train at dojo for any reason, fifty dollars an hour. Chow-san say we should bill Pacific Rim."

"Fine," said Devlin, "I'll be back tomorrow at noon, and let you know the schedule."

Devlin shook hands with both men, turned, and left the dojo. He found his way downstairs and out to the street unescorted.

CHAPTER 30

It was almost eleven by the time Devlin walked into the Marriott suite.

Susan was sitting alone on the couch nursing a large tumbler filled with club soda, ice, and vodka. She was so completely composed in her world of alcohol that she reminded Devlin of James Pony's self-contained aura.

The relaxed state of drunkenness Susan had attained seemed to make the age lines and tension in her face disappear. She had a strange air of serenity about her. There was no posturing or facial expression to distort her dark Mediterranean beauty. She was simply and completely *there*.

Devlin caught himself staring at her and forced himself to stop. He didn't have the time to fantasize about Susan.

He said hello to her and went into the small bedroom looking for Daryl. He wasn't surprised that the two women were not in the same room.

Daryl sat on one of the beds watching television. The volume was turned low. She was waiting for the eleven o'clock news to come on.

When Devlin entered, she turned off the television and waited for him to come over to her.

Devlin sat in a chair and put his feet on the bed. "Are you okay?"

Daryl shrugged.

Devlin asked, "So what's happened since I left?"

"Well, the vodka and ice queen accepted her clothes and things. Then she poured herself more vodka and sat at the desk to write something about that guy Wexler. When she started writing, I left her alone. I looked in on her about fifteen minutes ago, and she was about halfway through the bottle. I asked her how she was doing and she said fine. I think she just basically wants to sit and drink."

"Anesthesia."

"I didn't notice she was having surgery."

"Well, she's been cut off from her job, her apartment, her possessions, just about everything she has."

"She was drinking like a fish before you mentioned anything about leaving Wexler."

"Not feeling very charitable toward her, are you?"

"Nope."

"Why not?"

"Because I'm tired, and I'm jealous."

"What?"

"You heard me. I don't usually come out and admit things like that."

"Daryl, come on . . ."

"No, *you* come on. Have me fix your bloody head and carry your gun for you and babysit a lost, drunken woman, but don't act surprised or make me feel stupid when I tell you I'm jealous."

Devlin leaned forward and took Daryl's hand. "Daryl, I'm not interested in her. I'm interested in what she can do to help me get Wexler."

Daryl said quietly, "That woman is the kind who has men take care of her, Jack. You've taken her away from the man who is doing that, and you're going to be expected to take his place. She's going to want it all."

"She doesn't know what the hell she wants."

"Oh yes she does. I saw the way she looked at you when you walked into that bar downstairs."

Devlin stood up. "Listen, Daryl, I don't give a damn about what she wants. It's what I want that concerns me. I want information on

Wexler from her, and I'm going to get it."

"And what about what I want?"

"What do you want?"

Daryl thought about saying more, but simply said, "I don't know. I guess right now I just want to go to sleep."

"All right. I'll be back in the morning."

Devlin stood up and went out to the main room.

Susan watched him approach her.

"My turn?" she asked.

Her question made Devlin wonder if he was out of his mind to think these two women would hold up under this situation, but he had no choice but to keep at it. He smiled and said, "I guess so. How are you feeling?"

"Just about right, but it's early."

He wondered how much longer she was going to drink but didn't say anything about it. "I forgot, you're just starting your day."

"Pretty much. I'll be up all night, that's for sure."

"Were you able to write up anything for me?"

"I started to. It's over there. It might be better if you ask me questions."

Devlin walked over to the desk and picked up a piece of hotel stationery. Susan had written Wexler's name, his address, and phone number. Her handwriting was textbook perfect. Long, gracefully formed script. On the last line she had written, *Wexler is a pimp a pervert and a violent, disgusting bastard.* That was all.

He took the paper and the pen lying on the desk and walked back to the couch where Susan was ensconced. He sat next to her and said, "Well, we've got the basics down, let's try and fill in a few details."

He questioned her slowly and expertly for the next hour. He started from the time she and Wexler had first met and questioned her carefully and methodically.

Susan sipped her vodka and answered his questions. She spoke without emotion. At times, she stopped and waited for a thought or a memory to come back to her. Sometimes it did, sometimes she just shrugged and said, "I can't remember," or "I don't know."

During the pauses, Devlin found himself staring at her face. The perfect nose, the large, slightly almond-shaped eyes, the full lips—it was all right there for him to enjoy. Susan never tried to catch him staring. Most of the time she looked straight ahead, hardly moving, hardly ever looking at him.

When he was done, Devlin knew more about Robert Wexler than he had hoped. He knew about three buildings Wexler owned and one he had recently sold. He knew about four restaurants and clubs Wexler either owned or managed. He knew two of the cars he owned and even had the license plate number of the Mercedes. The more he gently probed, the more Susan remembered.

She recalled banks that Wexler had done business in. She remembered several credit cards he used. She knew the names of ten people who worked for him.

Each question and answer uncovered another layer. Another piece of information. Susan even thought she knew the name of his insurance company.

In a little over an hour, Devlin had more than enough to start the in-depth investigation he needed.

By the time they finished, it was almost one o'clock in the morning. Daryl was asleep. Devlin felt drained. Susan looked as if she was just about to start her evening.

He now had half the information he wanted. He called Zitter to see how he was progressing on getting similar information about Patrick Kelly.

Zitter answered the phone at his office on the first ring. "Intrepid."

Devlin asked, "Zitter?"

"Yeah. Sam the garbage man."

"You went garbage hunting, huh?"

"You knew I was when you asked for information."

"How'd you make out?"

"Not bad. I got about another half hour's work here, then I've had it. I'm past my bedtime already."

"What did you find?"

"Enough to get you started. A phone bill and an Amex statement. I got one canceled check, which leads me to believe there's probably more in that pile. Maybe a bank statement if I'm lucky."

"Good. Good."

"What time you need this stuff by?"

"Ten o'clock in the morning."

"All right, it's gettin' late. I'll look quickly through what I have left, then I'll write up the important stuff by hand. Anything that's readable, I'll just staple to the write-up. I'll leave it on my secretary's desk. Her name is Sylvia. She's in by nine for sure. I might not be. Just pick it up from her."

"Okay. Fine. Thanks, Sam."

"There's more here, but it requires a little more fucking time. Some letters, shit like that. You interested?"

"Not right now. Stick with anything financial. Can you keep whatever looks useful in case I want to go back over it?"

"Yeah. I'll give you what I have and save the rest."

"Thanks. I'll check with you in the morning."

"Late in the morning."

"Right."

"Good night."

Devlin hung up and sat at the hotel room desk for ten minutes carefully copying over his notes from the discussion with Susan. She sat on the couch, barely moving except for the steady sips she took from her vodka and soda.

When he finished, Devlin carefully folded his notes and put them in a hotel stationery envelope. Only after he tucked the envelope in his jacket pocket did Susan speak.

"We have a few more things to discuss, Mr. Devlin."

Devlin turned to face her. "Yes?"

"How long do you expect me to stay here?"

"Two or three nights at the most."

"Then what?"

"It depends."

"On what?"

"It depends on whether or not I've done what I want to do with Wexler."

"Are you going to kill him?"

Devlin didn't respond.

"Well, if you want to beat Wexler you're going to have to kill him, because he'll kill you the first chance he gets."

"Let me worry about that."

"If he kills you, it's *my* problem."

"I'll try not to cause you any problems."

"What kind of an answer is that?"

For the first time, Devlin noticed an edge in her voice. He told her, "Sorry if that sounded sarcastic. Wexler isn't going to kill me."

Susan glared at Devlin for a moment, then asked, "What about that money you spoke about?"

"I'll stand by our agreement."

"When do I get it?"

"How about tomorrow?"

"In cash?"

"Yes."

The glare was replaced by a skeptical look. "You're paying a lot for this."

"It isn't over yet. There could be more to deal with."

"What does that mean?"

"I'm not sure."

"What do you think you're buying with that ten thousand?"

"Your cooperation."

"You mean I have to do whatever you ask."

"This only has to do with Wexler."

"Well, I'm getting fucked by Wexler on command. Do I now have to spread my legs for you instead?"

Devlin saw that alcohol had fueled Susan's anger. She suddenly seemed on the verge of letting all her rage out at Devlin.

"No. It doesn't mean that. Whatever Wexler did to you, he did it, not me. You want to be angry at someone, be angry at him. Any other questions?"

"I just don't want to feel like I'm being bought and paid for and told when to sit and when to stand."

"That's not what I'm trying to do."

"What exactly are you trying to do? And why are you doing all this?"

Devlin leaned forward and patiently told her, "It's exactly what I said, but I'll say it again. It's not that hard to understand, Susan. Wexler almost killed my brother. He's probably crippled him for life. He tried to kill me. And I suspect he'll hurt you, too, the minute he can. Now, maybe most of the people walking around out there can let someone like Wexler get away with all that, but I can't. I *won't*. Do you understand what I'm saying? Am I making myself clear?"

Susan shrank back from him. "I still don't know why you think you can do anything to him. He's got connections, money, power, friends."

"What friends?"

"Cops."

"What cops?"

"I'm not sure. But someone high up. There's a cop who protects Wexler and the club."

"What else do you know?"

"All I know is Wexler is capable of horrible things, and he isn't worried about any repercussions. He acts like he's invincible."

"He's not. Believe me. The only one who can't be hurt is somebody who has nothing."

"I guess that's me."

"Not yet it isn't."

Susan put down her drink and stood up. Her white silk blouse and dark slacks hardly had a wrinkle. Standing up seemed to change her mood. There was a slight tremble in her voice. "Not yet, but pretty damn close."

She walked to the bar to get a cigarette. Her hand shook as she lit it. She angrily threw the match in an ashtray.

"Shit! I can't even light a cigarette without it showing. I'm sitting here trying to be tough, and I'm goddamn terrified. What the hell am I going to do? Tell me!"

Devlin stood up and went to her. He patiently told her, "You're going to stay here tonight. You'll sleep when you can. Tomorrow morning I'll be back, and we'll figure out that day. And the next and the next. One day at a time until it becomes very clear. Nobody knows you're here. In a couple of days, we'll move to another hotel. No one will find you if we're sensible and careful. You'll have plenty of time to figure things out.

"Maybe it will be a week. Maybe a month. But soon you'll know what to do. Soon Wexler will be out of your life. You'll get an apartment, a job. Whatever it takes. You've survived until now; you'll keep on surviving. Just hang in. Don't fall apart on me."

Susan exhaled the cigarette smoke in a long breath. "Okay."

"Good."

"You're not staying here tonight?"

"No. I've got to get clean clothes, do some things in the morning."

"So it's just me and the All-American girl?"

"She said she'd keep you company tonight."

"I guess it does feel better knowing someone else is here with me."

"I'm sure it does."

"So what's with you and the blond beauty?"

"We're friends."

"Just friends?"

Devlin didn't answer.

"Okay. That's your business. What time will you be back?"

"I'll be back about eleven-thirty, twelve."

"Do you think it's safe for me to go out for a walk?"

"Now?"

"When it gets daylight again."

"Put your hair up and wear sunglasses. Change your appearance a little."

"Oh, I intend to. By this time tomorrow, I'll be blonder than Miss America."

"Really?"

"Really. I've changed my name and looks enough to know it helps confuse whoever might be after you."

"What *is* your last name?"

"Right now, it's Furlong. But it's been Freund and Frisch and several others."

"Is your real name Susan?"

"Yes."

"And your real last name?"

"Ferlinghetti."

"Well, Susan Ferlinghetti, maybe it's time to change back to the real Susan. I'll see you in the morning."

Devlin walked toward the door. Susan stepped away from the bar and blocked his path. "Aren't you going to tuck me in for the night?" She stood right in front of him. She was close enough so that Devlin could smell her perfume and the tang of vodka and cigarettes on her breath. It was so easy for her to look alluring that even Devlin was surprised at how quickly she had set off a palpable sexual tension in the room. Devlin didn't make a move toward her.

She said, "Not tonight? Some other night then?"

"Susan, don't make it hard for me. Please."

"Hard to do what?"

"Resist you."

"Why would you want to do that?"

Devlin smiled at the relaxed way she asked him. "Just for tonight, Susan."

Susan moved a step closer. Her full breasts just touched Devlin's chest. She reached under his jacket and felt his waist and the small of his back. "No love handles on you, Mr. Devlin." Her right hand moved up until she gripped the leather holster holding the Caspian automatic. "Oh, what's this? Your big gun?"

Devlin gently held her wrist so she couldn't move her hand toward the gun.

She smiled slightly. "Ah. I finally got you to touch me."

She slowly drew her hand away from the holster and rested both hands against Devlin's chest for a moment. Then she gently pushed herself away from him. "You're not the only one who has to resist, you know."

"I'm not the one who's making it difficult."

"You're not? You send some beautiful young thing to do your bidding. You rescue me from a man who's making my life horrible. You set me up in a hotel suite, promise to give me money, and protect me. You play the big, handsome tough guy and you expect me to resist you?"

"Yeah."

Susan flipped her hair back and walked away from Devlin.

"All right. But I'm not going to do it sober."

She picked up her drink, sat on the couch and turned on the television. "Close the door to Miss America's room. I don't want to wake her up. Maybe there's a good movie on."

Devlin closed Daryl's door, said goodnight and left.

CHAPTER 31

When Wexler turned the key in Susan's lock, he sensed that something was wrong before he even opened the door. He wasn't surprised that Susan wasn't standing there ready to greet him. He closed the door behind him and stood quietly in the small foyer thinking carefully about all the past moments that seemed pertinent to the present.

He realized that he had weakened. The truth was, he had come to the apartment later than usual. He examined why. Partly because he wanted Susan to have a little extra time. That in itself confirmed a weakness. How could he possibly have changed his behavior toward someone who existed only to confirm that he owned something of value?

And that thought propelled his mind to a more troublesome realization. Wexler realized he didn't merely want to own Susan. He *wanted* Susan. She had a hold on him that he had refused to admit until that very moment, standing alone in the foyer. He wanted her. He desired her, and he wanted her to desire him.

The realization made him tremble slightly, because it came so soon after he knew that she was gone. He stood up straight and let the final reality descend on him. He had come late because he knew very well that she might not be here, and he had wanted to delay facing that fact as long as possible. He had known she was going to try to defy him the moment he saw her with Devlin at the club. He could feel the attraction between them across the room. That's why he had taken special care to humiliate her and frighten her into submission. But apparently, he had not succeeded.

And then suddenly Wexler smiled. He knew as sure as he was standing there that Devlin was connected to Susan's disappearance.

This man Devlin, whoever he was, had nicely raised the stakes beyond the simple brand of violence practiced by the Joes and Eddies of the world. Wexler believed that men like Joe and Eddie would always be the final recourse. In the end, someone had to be killed or beaten or terrorized into submission. But this time it appeared that the game up to the point where he finally killed Devlin was going to be interesting.

Wexler turned and left the apartment. He smiled as he rode the elevator down. He had a nice, warm, comfortable erection. This is going to be fun, he said to himself. And he immediately set his mind to work.

He got back into the Mercedes and told Randy to drive downtown. He picked up the cellular phone in his car and dialed Patrick Kelly's private home number.

Kelly answered on the second ring, "Yes?"

"Wexler here. I think we should have lunch tomorrow."

"Good idea."

"Shall we dine at some shanty Irish bar with steam tables or a decent restaurant?"

"I know you love the economy of a good Irish bar lunch," said Kelly, "but let's splurge."

"I'll see you at one o'clock at Aquavit. I presume you have some useful information on our friend Jack Devlin."

"That I do. I should have more by lunchtime."

"Splendid. See you then."

Wexler hung up the cellular phone. He checked his watch. Just after 9:20. Time for a leisurely dinner and the next phase of his plan.

Dinner was at Bouley's in TriBeCa. Wexler had decided he wanted a quiet place with muted lighting. He took out a small address book. In between forkfuls of nouvelle cuisine he wrote names and phone numbers on a sheet of paper.

He would eat a few coquilles Saint-Jacques, look at his list, sip his white Bordeaux, then carefully write down the name of a bouncer, the club where he worked, and a phone number.

He continued during his entree of saumon grille straight through to his dessert of tarte tatin.

By the time he finished, Wexler had selected ten names. He paid his bill in cash and returned to the Mercedes, where Randy sat patiently waiting. It was almost midnight. For the next two hours, Randy drove him to various clubs. Wexler found eight of the ten men on his list and spoke to them quietly while they stood at their posts. To each he said the same thing, "I'm looking for a man who has stolen valuables from me in quite a large amount. There is a good chance he may show up at your club. If you find him and bring him to me, the bounty is five thousand dollars. You can do anything you want to him except kill him."

To each of the bouncers, Wexler carefully described Devlin. He made sure they each remembered his description and Devlin's name.

The last bouncer he talked to was named Phil Messina. Messina received different instructions. He was simply told to report to the Starlight the following night.

Wexler planned to use Messina differently. The other bouncers Wexler talked to were violent and brutal. But Messina was in a class by himself.

Messina wasn't as big as most of the others. But his mere presence frightened people. It was the way Messina looked at you that was so disturbing. He would stare at you with deep-set eyes that lacked any sign of sympathy or human kindness. And he had thick lips that were usually formed into a weird, half-leering smile. Messina would stare and smile, and then suddenly strike out with such fierce brutality that he seemed inhuman. Joe and Eddie and the rest of his bouncers were bad. Messina was evil.

After recruiting his small army of thugs, Wexler arrived at the Starlight club a little later than usual, but he was pleased with himself. He decided he would even talk to Joe and Eddie. He took his place at the end of the bar and pictured all the men he had enlisted falling on Devlin. Of course, that wouldn't happen, but eventually one of them would find Devlin or Kelly's cops would find him. And then Wexler knew he would be able to inflict all the pain and humiliation the insolent, foolish man deserved. The thought of it comforted Wexler immensely.

CHAPTER 32

Even though it was past one o'clock in the morning, and he was bone tired from dealing with Susan, Devlin was determined to see his brother before he slept.

He took a cab downtown, dozed during the ride, and felt surprisingly refreshed when he arrived. His body was making the transition from being awake during the day to being awake all night.

The street outside the small hospital was quiet and peaceful. It seemed as if it belonged in another city. There was no traffic, no people. The late-night/early-morning air seemed fresh and cool.

Devlin walked through the hospital lobby, seeing only a security guard sipping a cup of coffee at the reception desk. He told the guard his brother was in the ICU. The guard made him sign the visitors' log and gave him a pass.

Devlin rode the elevator to the seventh floor. At the nurses' station, he stopped to ask about his brother. The nurse on duty was a Puerto Rican girl who looked too young and too small to be in charge of fighting off so much impending death.

She looked up from the chart she was working on when Devlin entered. She had beautiful cafe au lait skin and big brown eyes. The eyes were empty of sympathy. When he asked for his brother, she told him that George had been transferred to a regular medical ward. She told him his brother no longer needed to be in the Intensive Care Unit. He was off the life-support systems and stable.

"What about his stroke?"

"I don't know," she answered, looking back down at her chart, "you can speak to his doctor tomorrow."

"Can I see him tonight as long as I'm here?"

"Visiting hours are twelve to ten on the wards. Patients are sleeping there now."

Devlin turned to walk away. Then he realized that he hadn't asked where his brother was. "What room is he in now?"

"Sir, I don't know. They'll tell you at reception."

Devlin left before his anger welled up. He thought about calling Marilyn but knew it was too late for that.

He said to himself, the hell with it. At least George was out of the ICU. That was good news.

He took the elevator downstairs and walked out of the hospital thinking about his brother. He was frowning, picturing his brother alone, wondering if he were awake or asleep. Wondering if he were paralyzed or able to move. Devlin should have been more aware in the quiet night because he didn't see them until they had gotten out of their sedan across the street from the hospital entrance and approached him.

Devlin stopped a few feet from the sidewalk. It took him two seconds to make them as police detectives. One of them was about five-six, short and stocky. He wore a light green suit that badly needed cleaning and pressing. He had on a straw short-brimmed hat. He approached Devlin's right side. A younger man in a light-colored sport coat and dark slacks approached on Devlin's left. He was almost as tall as Devlin. His blond hair was cut short, military style. His white shirt was unbuttoned at the collar, and he wore no tie. The junior of the two detectives already had his hand under his jacket gripping the handle of his revolver.

The older detective stopped about five feet from Devlin. He calmly motioned for Devlin to stop. "Okay, Mr. Devlin. You're under arrest. Come quietly with us. We have a warrant for you."

Devlin knew he was lying. There was no evidence that would

make a judge in New York City issue a warrant for him. These had to be rogue cops connected to that deputy inspector.

Devlin looked to his right toward Second Avenue, to his left toward Third. At both ends of the street blue and white police cars blocked the intersection.

He turned to look at the hospital entrance behind him and saw the security guard ambling toward the doorway to see what was happening.

They'd boxed him in. Devlin knew if these cops got their hands on him he might not survive it. But how to get away without getting shot. He knew the younger cop would shoot after a quick warning. The .45 in the holster under his arm would be all they'd need to justify it.

He turned back toward the hospital and walked back toward the entrance.

The older cop yelled, "Hey, hold it!"

Devlin quickened his pace. It would be harder to shoot him if he kept his back to them. Bullets in the back were difficult to explain. The security guard stood outside the door watching. Devlin stared right into his eyes—forcing the man to be a witness.

In the next second, Devlin heard the two detectives running after him. He broke into a full run.

The hospital doorway was only about fifteen feet away, and Devlin knew he could get through the doors before the cops reached him.

The security guard wanted no part of Devlin. He stepped aside, and let him run past. The younger detective yelled, "Police. Stop, or we'll shoot."

Devlin pictured him drawing his gun. At the same instant, he heard the shot crack into the late-night air.

Devlin slammed through the glass double-doors with the detectives right behind him. He knew the uniformed cops out on the street would be calling in a 10-13 with a report of shots fired. Once they did that, every cop in the area would respond.

Devlin wondered if the cops in the patrol cars were smart enough to drive around and block the back of the hospital. But, of course, that didn't matter if the two behind him caught him.

As soon as Devlin made it through the entrance, he turned to his left and ran down a long linoleum-tiled corridor. His feet slipped on the waxy surface, but he opened a distance of about twenty feet between him and the pursuing detectives. And then he heard a sound that he identified immediately and just as immediately knew he shouldn't be hearing. It was the unmistakable sound of fists against flesh and bone.

He turned to see James Pony holding the taller, younger detective by the lapels of his cheap sport coat. Devlin had no idea where Pony had come from.

The shorter, heavyset detective rushed at Pony. While still holding the taller man, Pony snapped two fast, hard sidekicks into the older cop's chest and crotch.

Pony had somehow already disarmed the taller detective and was using his grip on the man to gain leverage for his kicks. The older detective collapsed to the floor, and Pony shifted to face the younger man. The cop grabbed at Pony's arms, but Pony smashed two quick Muay-Tai knee kicks into his ribs. What fascinated Devlin was that Pony was so quick and so fast on his feet that the kicks were delivered with both legs.

The tough-guy detective with a gun was already paralyzed with broken ribs, but Pony sensed the same bravado that Devlin did. He stepped back, released the man and in fractions of a second smashed first his left elbow and then his right into the defeated man's jaw. Devlin thought about the amount of wire the surgeons would use repairing a jaw fractured on both sides.

The attack had been brutal and effective, and had taken no more than ten seconds. No words. No extra movements. Just efficient work. Both detectives lay crumpled on the floor of the hospital lobby.

Without even looking in Devlin's direction, Pony drifted away from the scene in the opposite direction.

Devlin turned and ran. The resonance of Pony's attack reverberated and energized him.

He ran to the end of the corridor and saw an EXIT sign shining above a door that seemed to be a fire exit. He hit the bar latch, and the door popped open to reveal another corridor that continued in the direction he was running. The corridor was made of unfinished cinder block. Exposed pipes ran along the ceiling. Bare light bulbs in yellow plastic cages illuminated the way.

He continued running in what he sensed was the direction opposite to the hospital's 18th Street entrance. He passed a set of service elevators but kept running. He smelled the unmistakable scent of cafeteria food and burst through a set of double-doors that led to a kitchen area.

The kitchen was dark and deserted except for an illuminated EXIT sign over a door set into the back wall of the kitchen. There was some sort of an alarm box on the door, but Devlin didn't hesitate. He punched the door open and found himself outside on a small loading dock. He jumped off the loading dock, turned a corner and saw that he was in a small lot where garbage trucks picked up the hospital's waste. He hid for a moment behind two large garbage bins sitting against a wall.

He could hear distant police sirens approaching from several directions. He didn't want to be trapped back by the garbage bins. He had to reach the street and take his chances.

He ran out to the street and found himself in the middle of 17th Street between Second and Third Avenues. Pony had risked everything for him, but he had only bought Devlin a few minutes. He had to get out of the area before the cops pouring into the neighborhood surrounded him.

Devlin turned right on 17th Street and headed for Third Avenue. He was ten yards from the avenue when a patrol car screeched around the corner, sirens blaring.

He dove down behind a car, figuring the cops would be more intent on making the turn than spotting him. He lay flat on the dirty sidewalk with the parked cars hiding him. The patrol car roared past him. He waited a moment, then stood up, and walked toward Third, exerting every ounce of his will to walk instead of run.

He made it to Third, crossed the street heading downtown and kept walking toward 16th Street. Before he got to the next corner, two more squad cars crossed 14th Street heading up Third Avenue in his direction with sirens blaring. He walked a few more steps and then stood in front of an apartment building watching the police cars as they sped past. Devlin knew a running man would attract attention, and it took a tremendous force of will to stand and wait until they passed.

The longer he stayed on the street the more chance he had of being caught. He thought about ducking into a bar but didn't want to be trapped anywhere. He looked for a taxi, or a bus—anything to get him out of the area, but there was nothing.

He started walking south as fast as he dared. As he crossed 15th, a patrol car was at mid-block, speeding west toward Third. He was sure they had spotted him crossing the intersection, but he just kept walking. There was an apartment building about twenty feet ahead. He thought about ducking into the lobby, but the doorman was standing at the entrance trying to see what had brought so many police and sirens into the area.

Behind him, Devlin could hear the patrol car braking back on 15th Street. He turned and saw the blue and white make a U-turn and accelerate toward him, going against traffic on his side of the street.

He broke into a run, desperately searching for a way out. He could hear more sirens coming east on 14th Street. Suddenly the entire area was being flooded with police. In seconds, he would be blocked in both sides.

He was about ten feet from the 14th Street subway entrance. It was his only chance to get out of sight. He put his head down and ran full speed until he reached the entrance. He grabbed the wooden handrail buried under a thousand coats of paint and jumped down the stairs three at a time.

By the time the squad car screeched to a halt at the subway entrance, and the two cops in the car were out and running, Devlin was vaulting the turnstile onto the subway platform.

Devlin hoped against all odds that at one-thirty in the morning a train would be in the station, but hoping didn't make it happen. There weren't even any people in the station.

The two cops with guns drawn made it over the turnstile and onto the platform just in time to see Devlin jump down on the tracks at the west end of the station and run into the dark tunnel.

Neither cop wanted to run after him in a dark tunnel along the electrified third rail. Instead, they ran to the end of the platform and stayed there, calling in their position and the information that the suspect had fled on foot west toward the Union Square station. Devlin was running along the Canarsie Line tracks, which led west to Eighth Avenue and ended there. The line had only two stops between the Third Avenue station and Eighth Avenue—Union Square and Sixth Avenue. If the cops closed off those stations, he would be trapped.

Devlin looked back at the Third Avenue station. He could see at least five cops on the platform. There was no choice now but to continue west, hoping that he'd get to Union Square before they closed off that station, too. Getting caught now would probably mean getting shot, particularly if more of Kelly's detectives were on the scene.

Devlin ran as fast as he could heading for the lights of Union Square. He tried to land his feet on the wooden ties that crossed the steel tracks. Fatigue and the dim light in the tunnel turned his attempt at running into a stumbling shuffle. But he kept going, moving as fast as he could. Somewhere in the back of his mind he knew that if he fell he could land against the third rail and electrocute himself, but he pushed the thought aside and kept going.

In three minutes Devlin made it to the east end of the station platform at Union Square. He didn't see any uniforms, so he climbed onto the platform and ran toward the first stairway. Just as he got there he heard sirens overhead and the voices of cops coming into the station area above him. He couldn't run upstairs now. He couldn't go back. He had no choice but to keep running west into the tunnel at the other end of the station and try to make it to the Sixth Avenue station before the police sealed that one off.

Devlin ran full speed to the far end of the long subway station. By the time, he got to the west end, cops were coming down the stairs behind him. Devlin jumped down onto the tracks and started to run into the dark, but far ahead in the black hole he could see flashlight beams jerking and moving in the darkness. The police were already in the tunnel, coming east. He was trapped.

Back at the east end of the station, more cops were coming on to the platform. Several were jumping into the tunnel and heading east toward Third Avenue. Devlin hid behind one of the vertical steel girders that ran the length of the station. He looked around desperately trying to figure a way out.

Above ground, more NYPD squad cars were arriving. Fortunately, Union Square served several lines and had subway entrances spread out over an area of almost four-square blocks. The squad cars were racing around in confusion trying to close off every entrance.

Devlin expected policemen to spot him any second. He had to do something. He jumped up and grabbed a thick pipe attached to the column he was hiding behind. The pipe ran from the column to a bank of fluorescent lights. He managed to pull himself up onto the top of the pipe, stand up and grab the bottom edges of an I-beam set into the ceiling of the station. He swung his legs forward and caught the bottom edges of the girder with his feet. Now he was hanging upside down, in clear view of any cops in the station who happened to look up at the ceiling, but he had no choice. Painfully, Devlin inched his way along the bottom of the girder, heading toward the wall that ran along the south side of the station. As his strength was waning, he reached the wall, wedged his foot into a small support girder that angled into the wall, pulled himself forward and lunged, off-balance, far enough to grasp the edge of a large steel trough that ran underneath a grill set into the street above the station. He pulled himself up onto the trough and rolled onto it. He lay on the trough, breathing hard, trying to get his strength back. For the moment, he was hidden.

Devlin was lying in filth. The steel trough ran under the sidewalk grills that provided ventilation for the subway tunnel. The purpose of the troughs, attached under the sidewalk grills with thin steel rods, was to catch the debris that people on the street dropped so the garbage wouldn't reach the subway platform.

After a few moments, Devlin got to his feet. There was only about five feet of clearance from the troughs to the sidewalk, so he couldn't stand up straight.

From his bent-over position he could see that he was shielded from the view of any policemen in the subway, but cops on the street could see him if they looked down past the grills.

He pushed up on the grill, hoping the extra pressure wouldn't collapse the trough beneath him. The grill didn't budge. It was cemented into the sidewalk.

Devlin knew it was only a matter of time before he would be found. But he also knew the litter in the troughs had to be cleaned sometime, and that could only be done from above. One of the sidewalk grills had to lift off.

He shuffled hunched over to get under the next grill. He braced himself underneath it and pushed up. The steel rods holding the trough beneath him creaked. The overhead grill didn't budge. Devlin wondered how long something designed to catch cigarette butts and litter would hold his weight.

He kept going, trying to find the one section in the grillwork that was hinged.

By the time he got to the fifth section, at least a dozen cops were fanning out on the platform below him. If they stood back and looked up they would spot him, but most of them were busy staring into the dark tunnels at either end of the station. Fortunately, there was enough yelling and radios crackling below him that they couldn't easily hear him moving above them. Slowly he kept going, testing each grill as he went. His shoulders, neck, and the middle of his upper back ached unbearably as he continued to bunch his muscles and push up against the grills. He felt as if he were grinding the bones in his upper back, yet the grills refused to budge.

He was almost ready to give up and try to hide where he was when he felt a grill move slightly. Was it just loose? Or was it one of the sections that opened?

He strained harder, convincing himself it had to open. The steel grill cut into the palms of his hands. He used his legs to straighten his body and add more force to the push. He was sure he was straining the metal rods that held the trough in place to their absolute limit. He expected one of them to give way and send him crashing to the subway tracks beneath him, but he kept pushing with all his waning strength. It was his only chance, even though it might be leading him right into the hands of the cops up on the street.

Finally, he felt the grill grind open on one end. The left corner was still stuck so he slammed the open palm of his right hand into the underside of the grill to force it free. Bolts of pain shot through his palm, but he kept hitting the grill until the corner finally broke loose from the packed dirt and grit that held it in place.

The grill was free, but Devlin hardly had the strength to lift it open on its dirty, rusty hinges. It must have weighed two hundred pounds, and his strength was sapped.

The grill seemed stuck. He gasped for breath, able to hold it up but not lift it higher. He couldn't let it down for fear he wouldn't have the strength to lift it again. Sweat ran down his face, stinging his eyes shut. It was his last and only chance to escape the underground trap.

He gathered the last reserve of strength, wishing he could scream, and with one last heave pushed the heavy grill open.

Devlin stood where he was, gasping for breath, trying to let the pain flow out of his shoulders and hands. After taking a few moments to recover, he gripped the sides of the sidewalk and lifted himself up at the corner of the opening. He just managed to thrust himself onto the street, belly down, legs still hanging over the trough. Only then did he look around.

He was just a few yards past the subway entrance on 14th Street where the old May's department store had been. Cops and patrol cars surrounded the entrance, but no one had seen him yet.

He pulled himself out, rolled into the street between two parked cars and crouched there unmoving

The steel grill stood propped open for anyone to see, but Devlin didn't dare try to close it.

He moved out from between the cars, kept in a crouch and duck-walked behind the cars parked along 14th Street. This placed him in view of cops across the street and east of him near Broadway, but they were far enough away that his movement didn't catch their eye.

He made it to the corner of University Place and 14th. He stood up straight, turned left and casually walked downtown on University. He was out of sight of most of the cops.

University Place was well-lit with plenty of stores, restaurants, and bars, and there were several people walking on the street with him, but Devlin kept looking forward and continued walking.

He made it to 13th, then 12th, and then 11th. He began to relax and take stock of himself. His hands were filthy, he was sweating, his clothes were stained and dirty, but no one paid him much attention. His luck held, and when he reached 11th Street, he saw a cab coming west that was free. He stepped into the street, hailed it, and told the cab to take him to Sixth Avenue and 55th Street.

In the cab, he wiped his face and brushed his clothes. It didn't do any good. His new pants and jacket from Bloomingdale's were already wrecked.

The air in the cab was hot and stuffy. He was still sweating. He rolled the window down and let the night air blow on him.

When the cab arrived at 55th, he paid, walked west to Seventh

Avenue and ducked into a bar. His stained clothes were hidden in the dim light of the seedy tavern. He walked straight back to a phone booth near the restrooms.

The phone booth was an old-fashioned wooden one with an accordion door. He shut the door, checked his watch and dialed Pacific Rim. It was eleven o'clock L.A. time. He was going to have to wake William Chow.

Pacific Rim's answering service patched him through to Chow at home.

Chow's houseman answered. Devlin told him who he was and that he needed to speak to Mr. Chow. He waited on hold just long enough to collect his thoughts.

Chow's soft voice came over the line. "Yes, Jack?"

"I need your help."

"Tell me."

"The people responsible for hurting my brother have located him. He's in Gramercy Hospital in New York. They set a trap for me there, but I got away. I should have anticipated this, but I didn't. We have to get George out of there so they can't use him to get to me.

"I need a security team to protect him until we get a doctor to transfer him out. Or maybe you can just send a team up there to roll him out. If you act fast, you might not have any problem. If it takes too long, it's almost certain that detectives from the NYPD will seal him off and it'll be very tough to get him out."

Chow asked, "Do you think the cops are going to try to hold your brother?"

"No. It's just a bunch of rogues working freelance for themselves. They aren't legal."

"I see. What is it, two o'clock New York time?"

"Yes."

There were a few moments of silence. Perhaps Chow was thumbing through a Rolodex instead of his computer database.

He started talking. "The doctor and security people won't be too hard to find. I'll need to get a lawyer, too. Where do you want him taken?"

"To any hospital outside New York City. Connecticut would be preferable."

"We'll need an ambulance service, then."

"Right."

"What's your brother's medical condition?

"I'm not sure. He's recovering from neurosurgery for a fractured skull and a stroke. But he's out of the Intensive Care Unit and on the regular ward."

"We'll have to come up with some permission document from next of kin. What is his wife's name?"

"Marilyn Devlin."

"I'll have our people do this now.

"Thanks. Get him out and hide him."

"Leave it to me. Check back when you can."

The line went dead. Devlin hung up the phone. The booth was stifling. He was sweating again, his knee throbbed and his head ached, but he had one more call to make.

He cringed as he listened to the phone ring at Marilyn's house. It rang five times before she picked it up.

"Yes."

"Marilyn, it's Jack."

"Jack, what's wrong?"

"Nothing. George is fine. Everything is fine, but you may be in danger. You have to take the kids and check into a motel or hotel. Get them out of the house, tonight, now. Don't wait until the morning."

"Jack, what are you talking about?"

"Marilyn, listen to me. I hate having to do this to you. It might not be necessary, but I can't take the chance. The people who hurt George are after me. They might make a move against you in order to bring me out. I've already made arrangements to move George. You guys have to go someplace they can't find you, too."

"God, this is a nightmare."

"I'm sorry, Marilyn. Pick a hotel outside of New York State. Some place in Connecticut."

"Uh, the Hilton near Stamford."

"Good. Check in under the name Williams. I'll call you in the morning."

"Jack, are you sure this is necessary?"

"I'm sure."

"All right. All right."

"Sorry, Marilyn. I'll call you in the morning."

Devlin hung up before she could ask him any questions. He opened the booth with relief and walked out of the bar to Seventh Avenue.

He thought through everything piece by piece as he stood waiting for a free cab. The cops knew where George was, but they couldn't hold him in the hospital or arrest him. Chow shouldn't have any trouble getting him out.

The chances were slim that Kelly's rogue cops would go after Marilyn, but Devlin couldn't take the chance. Even if they didn't try to hold her, they could follow her to George, and they'd get back the leverage to force Devlin to come into the open.

For now, Devlin had escaped their trap and taken away their chances to use his family against him.

He got into a yellow cab and told the driver to take him to Washington Square.

If the cops traced the first cab, chances were slim they would find the second one, but Devlin still didn't take any chances. He had the cab drop him on the south side of Washington Square and walked down LaGuardia to West Broadway to the Pacific Rim loft. Devlin realized he should have been taking such precautions long ago.

It was past three o'clock when he finally finished washing the stink and dirt off his body. The night's episode hadn't done his right knee and the bruises on his hip and elbow any good, but it certainly could have been worse.

He settled down on his bed to try to sleep, but his mind wouldn't stop. It had been stupid of him to think his brother could sit in a hospital under his own name and not eventually be a target for his enemies.

He gave himself five hours before he hit the streets again. He had a lot to do, and it had to be done with a good part of the NYPD looking for him.

He finally drifted off. His last thought was how lucky he had been that James Pony had decided to prove himself without being asked. He'd have to find out how Pony managed to be at the right place at the right time. Devlin couldn't believe Pony had followed him without his knowing it. But how had Pony shown up like that at the hospital? Devlin needed an answer to that question. But any question regarding Pony's courage and capabilities had already been answered. Pony had gone up against two armed detectives with nothing but his hands and feet, and his black T-shirt and jeans.

CHAPTER 33

The next morning Devlin woke at eight. He checked with Chow and found out that moving George had gone relatively smoothly. George was safely hidden in a private hospital near Stamford, Connecticut, under the name Edward Williams.

Devlin hung up the phone and walked to the back of the loft. From a closet, he took out a Halliburton suitcase and began packing it with clothes, money, weapons, and extra ammunition.

His hoard of cash from the Grand Cayman job was shrinking, but he had enough for Susan's $10,000. He was glad Pacific Rim was covering his outside suppliers. Good help was expensive.

He called the car service. This time the driver was an older man whose name tag said, Bill. Bill had a round, pasty face that reminded Devlin of a potato.

The driver didn't initiate any conversation, and neither did Devlin. He gave him Zitter's address and sat back for the ride.

He arrived at Intrepid Investigations, got out of the car, stepped inside the office, and picked up an envelope from Zitter's receptionist. He thanked her, left, and got right back in the car.

Devlin gave the driver the address of William Parker's agency— the one Chow referred him to for skip tracers. He opened Zitter's envelope and scanned the contents while the driver headed east.

Zitter had managed to retrieve a good amount of information on Kelly. The envelope contained an American Express statement, three canceled checks, including a check for a mortgage payment to Lincoln

Savings Bank, and a monthly statement from Chemical Bank showing two checking accounts, a NOW account, and a money market fund. The bank statement had been torn in half but taped together by Zitter. It showed Patrick Kelly's combined accounts in Chemical totaled $67,591. Too much for a cop, even a deputy inspector. The final piece rescued from the garbage was Kelly's telephone bill. There were five pages of itemized long-distance phone calls. Too many again.

The information Zitter had provided on Kelly and Susan's information on Wexler would be plenty for any competent skip tracers. A good skip tracer could start with a phone number and unravel a life story.

The detective agency was on 44th Street near First Avenue. Devlin entered the premises quickly. He waited ten minutes in a reception area before he was called into the office of William Parker.

Parker was in his early fifties. He would have made a good model for an FBI recruiting poster. He sat ramrod straight behind his neat executive desk. He wore a conservative dark suit that went well with his businessman's haircut.

Parker stood when Devlin entered and shook hands with an iron grip.

"Pacific Rim has vouched for you, Mr. Devlin. How can I be of assistance?"

Devlin assumed an air that matched Parker's and laid out the notes and the documents Zitter had gleaned from Kelly's garbage.

He told Parker, "This is information on two individuals who I believe are involved in a criminal enterprise."

"Together?"

"Yes. The first one is a Patrick Kelly. He happens to be an NYPD Deputy Inspector. Among other things, he is in charge of investigating social clubs and after-hours clubs. The detective squad assigned to that job has six two-man teams. I have reason to believe that Kelly is, in fact, running one or more after-hours clubs for his own profit, or at the very least protecting them from any investigation by the police. Several of these clubs are run by a man named Robert Wexler. Here is information I've gathered on Wexler."

"And what exactly do you want us to do, Mr. Devlin?"

"Use this information as a starting point and do a full-blown, in-depth search of any businesses or financial dealings that link these two men. I want computer searches, telephone tracking, document searches, phone interviews, bank searches—anything and every-thing relating to their assets individually or collectively. And I want all your information forwarded to William Chow at Pacific Rim as you develop it."

"Understood."

"Mr. Chow told me your skip tracers are very good."

Parker looked up from scanning Devlin's notes and said, "They're not just very good. They're the best."

"Fine. I want them to use every trick, every snitch, every connec-tion they have. I want to know what these guys own, where it is, and what enterprises link them. I want to know everything that has to do with their assets. I don't care about their family tree, I just want to know where the money is. And I'm afraid I need it very quickly."

"Any particular area you want us to start on?"

'I'd start on New York real estate. And also concentrate on bank accounts."

"I doubt if anything owned by these two will be in their names."

"So do I. You've got to find out whatever dummy corporations or partnerships they use."

"Well, it's certainly nothing we haven't done before."

I'm sure it isn't.

"But even if we get lucky and turn over some rocks fast, this will take time."

"Unfortunately, I don t have more than two or three days."

Parker looked at Devlin to make sure he was serious. "Come on. What you need could take at least a week."

"Put as many on it as you can, and let them work twenty-four hours."

Parker leaned back in his executive chair and stared at Devlin.

"Mr. Devlin, you're in this business. You know how touchy these skip tracers are. They don't share their connections or information with each other. I can't put more than one or two people on it. Otherwise, they'll start getting in each other's way and antagonizing each other."

"Mr. Parker, you know your people. It's your show. Do it whatever way you think is right, but please do it fast."

"All right. I'll do the best I can. I'm afraid this will be at a premium."

"I understand."

"Good."

"Mr. Parker, I have to walk out of here already knowing that in a day or two you'll have what I need."

Parker nodded slowly. "How important is this?"

"This one, sir, is life and death."

"All right. I'll clear the decks and set two of my best men at it. If the information is there, we'll find it."

"Good. Thanks."

Devlin left the agency and quickly ducked into the waiting sedan. He told the driver to take him to the Marriott.

#

While Devlin was meeting with Parker, the men he was trying to link together were enjoying lunch at the same table in a Scandinavian restaurant in midtown.

Wexler had come straight from the Starlight club, while Kelly had come from his office.

The men talked quietly amid the muted bustle of meals being served and dishes being cleared.

Kelly was eating lunch—grilled salmon, salad, and a basket of delicious Swedish dark breads. Wexler was eating breakfast—plain toast and yogurt with black coffee.

Wexler said, "So tell me about this Devlin."

"A bad egg. A rather curious fellow, but not nice. The records we have on him show him to be a professional. He has fairly impressive credentials."

"For instance."

"New York Police, Army, Secret Service. Presently employed by a private security company on the West Coast called Pacific Rim."

"What's he doing in New York?"

"Attending his father's funeral."

"You know that for a fact?"

"Yes, indeed."

"What the hell do we have to do with his father's funeral?"

Kelly wolfed down another mouthful of salmon and bread. Not the father's death. It has to do with his brother's near death at the hands of your lovely bouncers."

"What?"

"Apparently, your boys went a little overboard. They put the man in the hospital with a fractured skull, among other things."

"I wasn't aware of the specific damage done."

"Yes, well, it may be a minor detail to you, Robert, but this time there are repercussions."

"You're telling me all this is out of some pique about his brother?"

"Can't find a blessed other reason for it."

"More macho nonsense. Now he's going to beat up whoever beat up his brother."

"Just so."

"Absurd."

"Absurd, but dangerous. We can't afford to have any attention focused on our after-hours operations."

"I can't afford to have a man on the loose who could track me down, threaten me, and survive Joe and Eddie."

Kelly wiped up the last bit of his meal from his plate and told Wexler, "Yes. Can't argue with you there. We almost had the problem solved last night."

"Where? How?"

"I had two of my detectives stake out the hospital where we found his brother was admitted. Devlin showed up about one o'clock this morning."

"A little late for visiting."

"No restrictions on Intensive Care visitors, don't you know. They like to give the family and friends the chance to be around in the likely event of sudden death."

"And they couldn't grab him when he showed?"

"Apparently not. I haven't heard the whole story yet, but shots were fired, the backups heard the gunshots, called in reinforcements. They almost trapped Devlin in the Third Avenue subway station, but he got away."

"That's ridiculous."

"My sentiments exactly, because now the cat's out of the bag. There's lots of coppers looking for him now."

"So?"

"So it makes it much tougher to do away with him. I'd have preferred to keep it in-house with my squads."

"You just find him, Patrick, and I'll take care of the rest."

"Yes, I figured that would be the plan."

"Catch him. I have some of my people looking for him, too. I'll know if he shows up at our clubs in Manhattan."

Kelly raised his coffee cup in a salute and said, "Well, that's fine, then. Your thugs on one side, my cops on the other." And then Kelly barked out a harsh laugh. "Probably not much difference between them, is there?"

Wexler said, "Mine are generally bigger."

"But mine get to carry guns." Kelly laughed again.

#

When the car service arrived at the Marriott, Devlin told the driver to park on 46th Street and wait for him.

He entered the hotel carrying his gold Halliburton suitcase with his clothes, money, and weapons. He wondered how many other guests checked in with the same items.

He arrived at the hotel suite fifteen minutes past his target time of eleven.

Daryl was sitting in the living room reading *The New York Times.* She had her feet up, shoes off. She was dressed in her jeans and an "I Love New York" T-shirt.

Devlin asked, "How are you?"

Daryl put the paper down and said, "Oh, barely civil I guess."

"You didn't sleep well?"

"Not really, but I'll recover."

"You got yourself a nice T-shirt there.

"I don't like putting on the same clothes I wore the night before. I didn't have anyone to run to my apartment for me. I bought it in the gift shop. You owe me eighteen dollars."

Devlin handed her a twenty-dollar bill. "You got robbed."

"Hotel prices. What's with the suitcase? You moving in with Ms. Absolut Vodka?"

"No."

"So what's in there?"

"Money, guns, bulletproof vests. Stuff like that."

"How nice."

"You going to work?"

"Maybe later today."

"Where's Susan."

"She went to get her hair done. She told me it's the first thing she does when she's hiding out."

"So you two are talking?"

"Yep. Once each of us figured out you didn't spend the night with the other one."

"I see."

Devlin stood up and walked to the window overlooking Broadway and 46th Street. He looked down at the TKTS booth and the huge neon signs that surrounded the area. He saw signs for Sony, Minolta, Canon, GoldStar, Fuji Film. So much for American enterprise.

Daryl asked, "Did you see your brother?"

"No. I went there last night. I couldn't see him because he's out of Intensive Care. I guess that means he's better, but I couldn't get any information."

"I'm sure it means he's better."

"I hope so. What time is Susan supposed to be back?"

"She said she's going blond. That's going to take a while."

"Why?"

"First you got to take the color out, then you got to put the blond in."

"Sounds great for your hair."

Daryl stood up and walked over to Devlin near the window. "Listen, I have to stop with my little bitchy act and come out with what I have to tell you. I don't like the way I feel right now. I don't like any of this. And I want to go home. I said I'd help you, and I did, but I'm finished, Jack. When this is over, and you've done whatever you're going to do to those people, and whatever you're going to do with that woman, you decide if you want to see me, and you let me know."

Devlin didn't argue or explain. He simply said, "Okay."

Daryl looked at him and waited for him to say more. When he didn't, she said, "Do you think I'm running out on you?"

"No. I don't. You're doing exactly the right thing. You don't have any business in this. It makes you feel sleazy, and you aren't comfortable with Susan, and you're absolutely right. I'm grateful for everything you've done. I want to say more, but I can't push everything else out of my mind so I can say it right. Let's just put it aside for now, and when this is over, we'll talk, all right?"

Daryl nodded once and said, "All right."

She picked up her blouse from the back of the desk chair and folded it carefully. Devlin went to the closet in the foyer and took down a plastic bag provided for laundry service. He handed it to Daryl and she placed her folded blouse in the bag.

"Thanks," she said. She put her hand on Devlin's face and started to kiss him goodbye, but instead she kissed his cheek. She touched the back of his head and said, "How's your head?"

"Fine."

"Good."

Devlin held her arm and said, "Listen. I doubt if they can trace me back to you, but it might be better if you went home and filled a suitcase and checked into a hotel for a few days. On me."

Daryl held up her hand. "No, no thanks. You're not stashing me in some hotel. I'm living in my own place, my own way. Maybe in a few days, I'll go out to the Hamptons and sit in the sun for a while. But no hotels."

Devlin knew he couldn't convince her otherwise, so he nodded and said, "Okay, good. Get away for a few days."

As Devlin walked her toward the door, he asked, "Does that bartender at O'Callahan's know your name or where you live?"

"Just my first name."

"Good. But stay away from there for a while."

"I'm never going back in there again."

"That's probably best. Be careful. I'll call you when this is over."

"All right. Enough! Goodbye. And for God's sake, be careful. I'd like to see you again someday."

Daryl turned and walked out of the hotel room. Devlin stood looking at the closed door, aware of how empty the room suddenly felt. And then he did what he was good at doing. He put Daryl out of his mind and did what he had to do. He picked up the suitcase he'd brought to the hotel, opened it, and took out neat bundles of hundred-dollar bills until he had the $10,000 he owed Susan. He took the money over to the desk and divided it into two piles. He took out two envelopes and put $5,000 in each envelope. It wasn't a fortune, but it was certainly enough if Susan Ferlinghetti wanted to disappear on him.

As if summoned by his thoughts, he heard the key card in the door and turned expecting to see Susan walk in. For a split second, he thought Daryl had returned, but then he saw it was, in fact, Susan.

She was a blonde. Her hair almost exactly the color of Daryl's. It was eerie. She almost looked like Daryl's sister. An older, more mature, more glamorous big sister.

She walked to the middle of the room and said, "I like the attention, but you don't have to stare."

"Sorry. It looks good. You look like you should have always been blond."

"I know. It does suit me. It's my alter ego. Did you notice if there was a shower cap in the bathroom?"

"No."

"I've got to take a shower and get some sleep."

"You haven't been to sleep?"

"I never get to sleep before noon. Where's Miss America?"

"She's gone."

Susan smiled and walked toward Devlin. "How convenient." And then she walked into the bathroom.

Devlin called after her, "I brought the money I owe you."

She called out, "Good. Give me a few minutes, and we'll talk." Devlin sat on the couch, and suddenly Susan appeared at the doorway in her bra and panties. They were white lace, and she obviously knew how spectacular she looked in the lingerie. Her full breasts were pushed up into an enticing cleavage, and her dark nipples could be clearly seen behind the lace. The panties were cut high on the hip, accenting the shape and the length of her sleek legs.

She said, "You're not leaving right away, are you?"

"No."

"Can you wait until I finish my shower?"

"Yes."

"Good." She caught Devlin looking at her dark pubic patch and looked down at it herself. "Sorry I didn't have time to dye all over."

She casually walked back to the bedroom, giving him a good view of her shapely rear.

Devlin sat on the couch and laid his head back. He closed his eyes, wanting to take a quick nap while he waited, but the image of Susan made him open his eyes. He kept thinking about Daryl, but he was seeing Susan in that white lingerie.

He was angry and horny and sad, all at once.

He managed to nap for fifteen minutes while Susan showered. The sound of the bathroom door opening woke him. He felt refreshed, but he knew he was running on so little sleep that one of these quick naps might zonk him out for hours. So far, they were working.

Susan walked over and sat on the couch a few feet away from him. She was dressed in a nightgown and a matching robe. There was nothing overly sexy about it, but she couldn't leave him alone.

"Despite the fact that I'm bare-ass naked under this nightgown, let's talk about the money you mentioned."

"Christ, you don't let up, do you?"

"I guess I'm bored."

"Do you really think you should keep coming on to me like this?"

"The sad fact is, Mr. Jack Devlin, that it works with most men. And you're all I've got right now, and I want something to work with you. Doesn't everybody do what they're good at?"

"You don't have to worry about doing what you're good at. I already need you."

"Why? I told you everything I know. What else do you need me for?"

"I don't know yet. This is far from over. There may be more you can do for me."

"Like what, be your bait for Wexler?"

Devlin looked at Susan and realized that he shouldn't have underestimated her intuition. "Maybe something like that."

"You think I'm going to be your sitting duck so you can get Wexler? It's your brother he beat up, not mine."

Devlin stood and walked over to the desk and picked up the envelopes of money. He returned and handed them to Susan. "You're right. I've put you in enough danger. Here's the ten thousand. You want to get out of town and start over now, maybe you'd better do it."

Susan took the money but didn't look in the envelope.

"I don't like this. Not any of it. You said you'd protect me and now you want to pay me off and throw me out."

"You sounded like you want to be done with me."

"I'll tell you when I want out of this."

"Okay, let's start over. If you want to help me, I'll do everything I can for you. If you want to get out of this right now, do it. The money is yours either way."

Susan sat with pursed lips, thinking. Finally, she handed back one of the envelopes to Devlin. "You keep this. I'll keep the other half in case of an emergency. Unless you handle Wexler, I'll never be safe no matter where I go."

"You're right."

"I guess we both need each other for the moment."

Devlin said, "I decided that last night."

"Well, I'm sorry, it just takes me a little longer. I guess we have a deal." She put out her hand, and Devlin shook it. Then Susan put her other hand around his neck and pulled him toward her. She pressed her full lips against his and kissed him with force and passion. "That seals it. I wanted to do that. Tough if you don't like it."

She stood up from the couch and announced, "I'm going to sleep. I'm exhausted. When will I see you again? I'd like to get out of this hotel tonight. How about dinner later?"

"What's later?"

"Say about ten?"

"Fine. I'll see you then."

He watched her walk into the bedroom and close the door. He couldn't see her, but he couldn't help but visualize her taking off the robe and getting into bed.

CHAPTER **34**

Devlin took the car service sedan downtown to Ozawa's dojo and then dismissed the driver.

He stopped at the office to see Ozawa, but he was not in. His wife told him James Pony was upstairs in the dojo waiting for him.

Pony was kneeling back on his heels in front of the shrine at the far end of the room. Devlin removed his shoes, walked quietly across the flawless oak floor, and dropped into the same position next to the young fighter. Pony turned and said, "I see you made it."

"I wouldn't have without you."

"No. Not if that cop had been a good shot."

"Why were you there? Did you tail me?"

"No. Sensei Ozawa told me what you told him about your situation. It seemed to me that if I wasn't with you, I could serve some good by being with your brother. So I went to the hospital."

"When?"

"Shortly after you left yesterday."

"And you stayed there all that time?"

"Yes."

"Did you see my brother?"

"Yes."

"How was he? Was he still in a coma?"

"No. He seemed to be sleeping. Once, when the nurse came to check on him, he tried to reach for her and mumbled something, but she told him to rest and take it easy."

"Christ, maybe he's coming out of it."

"I'd say he was."

"How did you end up in the lobby?"

"They wouldn't let me stay in your brother's room after visiting hours, so I went down to the lobby and kept watch. I sit very still. You didn't see me when you walked in."

Devlin turned toward the shrine. Directly in front of them was an oblong table about three feet high. It was made of a light-colored mahogany. The finish was flawless and the table seemed to merge with the wood floor of the dojo. On the table was a small pedestal on which was placed a cake of sweetened rice called mushimochi, two black lacquer vases filled with green leaves, and a wooden box for burning incense.

Behind the table on a shelf cleverly built into the back wall of the room was a black lacquer stand holding a gleaming Samurai "long sword." Devlin assumed it was Ozawa's family sword, probably made by one of Japan's famous masters and passed down through each generation of the family. Above the enshrined sword was a simple scroll in bold Japanese calligraphy.

The environment of the shrine was at once serene and disturbing. The sword was a sacred object, but to Devlin it was a reminder of sudden, inexorable death.

He realized that the young man next to him was attracted to the intoxicating world of violence and the possibility of sudden death. Nothing made you feel more alive than surviving a brush with death. Pony had somewhere tasted that perilous thrill.

Devlin broke off his thoughts and told Pony, "That was a dangerous thing you did with the cops."

"No, not so dangerous. They didn't see it coming. And neither of them had any training."

"Why did you hold the big guy while you were kicking his partner?"

"I had to. I knew when I started hitting him, he would move. I didn't have time for that."

"Interesting."

"It also anchored me. It gave me more leverage for my kicks to the other one."

"I see. How much do you weigh?"

"One-eighty-five."

"You're strong. And you've got guts. I think. Or you're crazy."

Pony didn't respond to the comment. Devlin asked, "Any second thoughts about working with me?"

"No."

Devlin nodded once and said, "Good. It will probably be two or possibly three days before we move against any of them. Once I start, I don't want to stop until it's over. Right now, I'm waiting for some information to develop. Then I should be able to strike hard. In the meantime, let me tell you everything that has happened so far. Sensei Ozawa doesn't know all of it."

Pony sat almost motionless and listened. He didn't ask questions. He gave Devlin his complete attention. His facial expression didn't change.

Devlin started with the conversation he and his brother had had in the backyard after the funeral. He told Pony about each of the people involved, each event that had occurred and the targets he had in mind.

As he told it all, Devlin realized he was also telling himself. He was trying to explain how he had gotten to where he was. Everything compressed into an hour's narration lent a sense of logic and shape to it. Someone in his family had been hurt. A woman was in danger. The people who hurt them lived outside society's rules and no one was going to do anything about it unless he did it. No cops would. No district attorney. No hero or friend. He was doing it to revenge his brother, yes. To save Susan from a dangerous, degrading man, yes. But as Devlin talked he knew it only *sounded* rational. It wasn't, really. Underneath all the words, Devlin knew as he stared at Ozawa's deadly shrine that the whole truth had to include the fact that he was also doing it because just like with James Pony, and just like Susan, and Daryl and Zitter and everyone else—the danger was attractive. Exciting. And even more exciting, more satisfying was the feeling Devlin got from spitting in the eye of people who thought they could kill him. It just felt goddamn good to stand up.

Neither Devlin nor Pony admitted that to each other. They didn't talk about the real whys behind it all. They talked about the what's. They talked about fighting. Training. Fear. They talked about Devlin's battle with Joe and Eddie. Pony looked at Devlin's hands and knee, his elbow and hip that were still bruised. He looked at the back of Devlin's head. He paid particular attention to Devlin's knee. Devlin let him gently bend and manipulate it. He even let him render a painful adjustment. The young man's hands and arms were incredibly strong. He moved the knee and snapped it quickly. One sharp bolt of pain shot through the tendon on the right side, and when the pain subsided the knee felt better.

They ran around the dojo for twenty minutes. Just enough to work up a light sweat. Then they did stretching exercises. Mrs. Ozawa appeared around four o'clock and served them a light meal of steamed vegetables with slices of grilled chicken and brown rice. Pony seemed to eat just enough to fill his stomach. They drank plain water.

After the meal, Pony spoke. "Good food. No fat. You need sleep. Why not rest for a couple of hours? You have things to do tonight?"

"Yes."

"I'll come with you."

It wasn't a question. It was a statement, said without guile or pretense. The lack of emotion and pretense made Pony easy to work with.

Devlin told him, "Yes, I'd like you to come with me, but for now stay in the background. I can't lose the advantage of people not knowing about you."

"Of course."

Devlin called Marilyn at the hotel in Connecticut. He told her where George had been taken and agreed to meet with her at 7:30 P.M. Then he lay down on a mat Pony set out for him in the corner of the dojo and quickly fell asleep. Pony woke him at 6:00. The car service picked them up and they left for the Hilton in Stamford at 6:30.

Devlin continued his nap in the car. When they arrived at the hotel, Pony stayed in the car while Devlin went in to meet with Marilyn.

Marilyn opened the door of her room, and Devlin was struck by how much she had changed. She had lost at least five pounds since he had last seen her. The weight loss and worry made her look haggard.

She saw Devlin's surprise and told him, "I know I look like hell, but I think the worst is over. I'm finally able to eat again."

Devlin reached for her hand. "I'm sorry, Marilyn. I wish I could have done something. Prevented all this. Are the kids okay."

"Yes. They don't know anything. They think George is on a business trip. I just got back from the hospital. George is much better, that's the important thing now. There's no pressure from the fracture, and the effects of the stroke are fading. He talked to me, and he recognized me, Jack. They say he sleeps most of the time, but he's definitely healing."

Devlin was so relieved he could not speak. All he could do was nod.

"He'll need rehab, but he might survive this nightmare without too much damage."

The hotel room was cool and quiet. They sat and talked. It seemed to Devlin that Marilyn was accepting what happened by looking at it as some sort of horrible accident connected with a dangerous place called New York. He explained that she and the kids should keep their whereabouts private until he took care of the people who had hurt George. He let Marilyn think he was working with the police.

They discussed where they would bring George after his discharge. They worked out a plan for Marilyn to take the kids and move into a summer house on Cape Cod that Marilyn knew about. They had vacationed there before, and she would tell the kids they were going to vacation there again. George would come as soon as the doctors said he was able.

Marilyn said she could make arrangements the next day. If all went as planned, they would be settled in two or three days. Hopefully, George would be with them before too long.

They finished their conversation. When Devlin turned to leave, Marilyn hugged him and said, "Thanks, Jack." Her embrace moved him so deeply he again found himself without words. His fear of being estranged from his brother's family lifted for a moment.

But in the next moment, he thought about how his family would never be the same again. There would never be a time when seeing him didn't remind Marilyn of what had happened to her husband, the father of her children, the pillar of her family. Big, strong, affable George, so terribly hurt and so suddenly diminished, perhaps forever. The frustration and anxiety and anger that Devlin felt returned, simmering and fermenting.

On the way back to Manhattan, Pony and Devlin agreed that Devlin should spend whatever time with Susan that was necessary to keep her quiet, but that she shouldn't leave the hotel.

Devlin thought about getting her settled in a new hotel, but he hadn't made reservations anywhere. And he wasn't sure she would accept packing in the middle of the night and moving. It would have to wait until tomorrow. In the meantime, he would take her to dinner as promised.

They agreed that Pony should wait on the ground floor of the Marriott while Devlin took care of Susan.

Devlin told him, "Just keep an eye out. No one should know she's there but stand guard. Warn me if you see anyone suspicious."

"Right. Room 3417?"

"Yes. By the way, you know you're going to have to wear something besides that black T-shirt and jeans."

"I have other clothes in my apartment."

"Then let's stop there and get them. Shirt, slacks, and regular shoes. You have those?"

"Of course."

Pony's apartment was at 13 West 13th Street. Devlin was amused by the address. Pony was in and out of the building in fifteen minutes. He came out dressed in a black silk shirt buttoned to the neck and black silk slacks. His shoes were black cap-toe, lace on oxfords.

He had put some sort of fixative on his jet-black hair and combed it straight back. With his hair slicked back, Pony looked older. Devlin knew that his exotic good looks and high cheekbones, his clothes and manner would gain him quick entrance into any of the bars or clubs Devlin would need to take him. James Pony continued to impress him.

CHAPTER 35

Susan woke around eight that evening, and the feeling she dreaded happened again. She didn't know where she was or what was happening to her for about thirty or forty seconds. Worse, she seemed paralyzed. Stuck. Unable even to breathe.

At first, she didn't breathe because she was waiting for her memory to click in, and for the background to flow into her consciousness. Then, when her thoughts didn't focus, she became panicky and couldn't breathe. It went on for five seconds, then ten. Then she really panicked and felt as if she might black out. Suddenly, she lurched up in bed, her heart pounding, gasping for air.

Once she got her breath back, she looked around, and the room reminded her where she was. She put her feet on the floor and clutched the edge of the mattress. She took a slow deep breath and shook her head from side to side as if to tell herself she was being silly.

Then she stood up and walked to the bathroom. She turned on the cold water and looked in the mirror. Her brain went completely blank for a second and another wave of panic washed over her because she absolutely did not recognize the image that stared back at her. She had completely forgotten about the change in her hair color.

Christ, she said to herself. Get a goddamn grip. She washed and dried her face, picked up the glass tumbler near the sink and went out into the suite's center room. The ice bucket was there, and the bottle of Absolut had about two ounces left in the bottom. She scooped the remains of melted ice cubes from the bucket and dropped them into the glass. She poured the remaining warm vodka into the glass and swirled it around. The small pieces of ice quickly melted into the vodka.

It was barely chilled, but she sucked half the contents through the remaining ice and swallowed it quickly. The vodka burned her throat and made her empty stomach ache, but it steadied her and helped her settle down.

Knowing the contents of the glass was all the liquor she had didn't comfort her any, but it was a problem that she could focus on and easily solve.

She knew the booze was ruining her memory and stability, but she couldn't face living without its numbing comfort. Especially now.

She set the glass of vodka on the sink and nursed the rest of it as she showered, taking her time and going over her body slowly and carefully. She realized in another six months her body would be showing the neglect and abuse. She'd have to do something when this was over to beat herself back into shape.

She had so much to do when this was over. Get Ceece moved into that school. Make sure her mother was settled. Find an apartment, a job. Stop drinking so much. It was way too much to think about all at once.

As soon as she was out of the shower, she ordered more liquor and ice from room service. Then she put on fresh undergarments and sat in front of the makeup mirror, carefully putting on her makeup base, eye shadow, and mascara. Then she did her lips. First a light outline. Then color. Then gloss.

She began to feel better. This time she wore a black lace bra and matching black panties. She thought about Devlin's reaction to her in the white lingerie and smiled.

Her first plan had been to quickly get him into bed, take control, and make Devlin want her. It hadn't worked. Devlin told her he would help her without that. Even more surprising, she believed him. But that only made her want to sleep with him more.

She looked at her face in the mirror and said, "It's always the fucking same thing after all is said and done, isn't it?"

And so she kept making herself as beautiful as she could. And Susan Ferlinghetti was old enough and wise enough to recognize the signs. She laughed out loud at the idea that she was genuinely attracted to Devlin. Here she was dressing for him and making believe they had a date to go out for dinner.

She looked at the clock. It was nine-thirty. She wondered if he'd be on time.

CHAPTER 36

They came for Daryl like secret police. They did it without regard for time or place or circumstances. It was early enough for plenty of people to be around. A little after ten. Daryl had just gotten into bed about fifteen minutes before. She was tired from the restless sleep in the unfamiliar hotel the night before. She wanted to get a good night's sleep and get up early to catch the jitney for the Hamptons.

They stormed into the lobby of the building, led by Joe, who still considered himself in charge. Smiling Messina backhanded the doorman in the face with his closed fist. No warning, no words. Just a blow fast and hard enough to shatter the cartilage in his nose, crack a cheekbone, and bludgeon the man into unconsciousness.

Eddie followed last. The bruises on his face from the fight with Devlin had turned yellow and purple. His mood and scowl were just as ugly. He was carrying a mean-looking battering ram, the kind used by the police on drug raids. It was an ugly, oblong piece of cast iron with long handles on each side. It weighed about a hundred pounds, and there was nothing sophisticated about the way it was used. Two men would simply slam it into a door until locks, jambs, frames, and doors would bend or splinter or break.

They left the doorman slumped behind his desk, twitching slightly while his basic reflexes struggled to pull air into his lungs.

The three thugs went silently up the elevator and took a position outside Daryl's door. Joe and Eddie each gripped the battering ram with two hands and positioned themselves so they stood sideways to the door with the hundred pounds of cast iron poised between them.

They grimaced at each other as they silently swung the iron ram back and forth, building momentum and force. They wanted to time it perfectly, so that all their strength and weight would be behind one huge, mighty slam that would burst open the door with one blow.

They wanted to do it with one blow as a matter of pride. And as a matter of cunning, since one crash might be heard, but if silenced followed most would simply ignore the first noise.

Messina stood back against the opposite wall so they would have room for their swing.

The two behemoths counted softly to each other as they gathered their strength. Five, swing back, four, swing back, three, two—on one, they smashed the battering ram into Daryl's door with such force the deadbolt snapped out of its socket, all the latches and chains and locks shattered. The door flew open and cracked a two-foot-wide dent in the wall behind it.

Messina wasn't as huge or as strong as Joe or Eddie, but he was quicker. He was past them and through the door before it rebounded. The crash of the forced entry broke Daryl's sleep so suddenly and violently that her heart skipped. She blinked, dazed and disoriented in the cool, sealed-off bedroom.

Then Messina was on her like an attack dog. He grabbed her by the throat and lifted her out of bed. He slammed her hard against the bedroom wall—once and then twice. He released his grip and Daryl collapsed to the floor.

Joe and Eddie entered the bedroom and turned on the lights. When they saw, Daryl sprawled on the floor, wearing nothing but her "I Love New York" T-shirt, their maniacal grins matched Messina's.

They saw her long legs and the dark patch between them. Eddie growled, "Holy shit. Let's fuck her for a while. Look at that nice pussy."

Joe told him, "Not here, dummy. We got to get her out of here."

Daryl was still dazed. It was hard to breathe and she couldn't clear her head. Eddie stooped over her, grabbed her under the arms and lifted her roughly to her feet. He yelled in her face, "Wake up, you stupid bitch! Get dressed. You got one minute, or I break your fucking legs!"

Daryl looked at the three huge men and stood paralyzed with confusion and fear. She had no idea what to do. The thought of trying to oppose them was absurd.

"Move!" screamed Joe.

Daryl staggered over to her closet and found a pair of jeans hanging on the doorknob. She wasn't wearing any panties, but she wouldn't give them the satisfaction of seeing her put them on. She turned her back to them and pulled on the jeans. She zipped and buttoned them and stepped into the closet.

"Hurry up," yelled Joe. "Get some shoes."

In the closet, her bras were folded on a shelf. She took one down, pulled her arms out of the sleeves of the T-shirt, and put the bra on underneath the shirt.

"Come on," yelled Joe.

Daryl kept her back to them, slipped off the T-shirt, pulled a denim shirt from a hanger, and buttoned it up to the collar. She found a pair of white espadrilles on the closet floor. She quickly slipped her feet into them. She was so frightened, she felt as if she were going to evacuate her bowels. She came out of the closet and said, "I've got to go to the bathroom."

Joe grabbed her arm so tightly she was afraid he might break her arm. "No!" he yelled.

He pulled her from the room with Messina leering after them and Eddie following contentedly, carrying the hundred-pound battering ram as if it were a suitcase.

They hustled her out of her apartment, leaving the broken door gaping on its twisted hinges.

As Wexler ordered, they took Daryl to Susan's apartment, which was close by on 65th and Second. The entire operation, from the moment they walked into the lobby of the building until they roughly pushed her onto Susan's living room couch, had taken only eighteen minutes. Two tenants who had found the doorman at Daryl's building dazed and bleeding, had just dialed 911.

#

It was almost 10:30 when Devlin arrived outside Susan's hotel suite door. He checked himself. He was wearing black slacks, a white Polo shirt, and an unconstructed Armani jacket of gray silk. The jacket fit his wide shoulders and was loose enough to cover the bulge of the Caspian Arms 1911 holstered under his left armpit.

He decided he was presentable and slipped the card key into the door.

Susan was sitting in her bedroom when she heard the key card in the door. For a second, she imagined she was back in her apartment waiting for Wexler, and he had come for her before she was ready. She felt the panic and loathing so strongly she had to close her eyes and make herself realize she wasn't in her apartment.

In the doorway, Devlin stopped and called her name. He felt presumptuous walking in on her.

"Susan, are you decent?"

She stood up and answered from the bedroom, "Yes," and walked out, smoothing her dress and trying to take the nervousness out of her voice. "Yes," she said, "I'm decent. By some standards, I guess."

Devlin closed the door and stood looking at her. She wore a simple black dress. It was so basic and unadorned that it transcended its simplicity and became simply elegant. The dress had thin shoulder straps that swooped into a low neckline and bare back. The dress artfully emphasized Susan's full breasts and shaped itself nicely around her small waist and rounded hips.

Her bare shoulders and back seemed to have a sheen that made her skin translucent. She wore a simple pearl necklace and on her wrist a thin silver bracelet. Her blond hair set off the dark color of the dress and the white of her skin. Her hair seemed softer and looser than when Devlin had seen her after she had it dyed. She had done something with it, but he couldn't tell what.

The dress ended just above the knees, long enough to be respectable, short enough to show the shape and length of her legs.

Devlin shook his head almost imperceptibly.

"I'm sorry. It seems I always find myself staring at you."

"Well, at least this time I'm not in my underwear." She moved toward him and took his hand. "Don't stand still. Come in. Do you want a drink?"

"Make it something soft."

"Are you trying to set an example for me?"

"No. I just can't afford the luxury of it right now."

Devlin sat at the couch and Susan made them drinks. Two tall glasses. Devlin's club soda over ice with lime. Hers half club soda, half vodka. Susan came and sat next to him. "So, how was your day, dear?"

Devlin smiled, "Fine. How was yours?"

"When you sleep during the day, things are rather uneventful. Not much to report."

"How did you sleep?"

"Sleeping wasn't bad. Waking up was a little hard."

"Really?"

Susan took a long sip from her drink. "Yes. It's disorienting for me being in a strange place."

"I see. Well, I guess that doesn't make it any easier to tell you I think we'd better move. Tomorrow I'd like to set you up at the Carlyle."

"How nice. Another suite?"

"If you like."

"One bedroom or two?"

"I think one should do it. No one else will be spending the night with you."

"What about you?"

"I don't, uh . . ."

Susan said, "Look, we said no more come-ons, so I'll skip being coy. You and I are going to sleep with each other eventually. It might be for different reasons than I first expected, but it's going to happen."

Devlin looked at her calm, beautiful face, her womanly body in that simple black dress and knew she was right. "Then I guess there's nothing for me to say."

Susan smiled. "I guess not."

"Yes. Well, how about if our next move is dinner?"

"Good idea. I'm starving."

Devlin stood up. "If you don't mind, I reserved a table in one of the hotel's restaurants. I think the food is good. And I don't feel comfortable spending too much time out on the streets."

"I was hoping to get out of the hotel."

"Tomorrow."

Susan picked up a small handbag on the bar and said, "All right. What the hell. I'll pretend we just took a long walk to some place way on the other side of town."

"Good."

Instead, they took a long elevator ride down to the lobby, then another long ride up to the revolving restaurant on the top of the hotel. It was a tourist trap of sorts, but Susan seemed to like the out-of-town atmosphere. She had more vodka before dinner, drank half a bottle of Australian chardonnay with her meal, and took her time with her Grand Marnier after the coffee.

At first, Devlin had an overwhelming urge to drink with her, but the very strength of his urge was enough to create a backlash in him that rejected the desire to slide into a woozy alcohol haze with Susan.

The dinner conversation centered on Wexler and Devlin let Susan go on about the man. It suited Devlin to sit and hear about Wexler. He asked an occasional question, but he mostly listened. He wanted to know everything he could. Susan was too ashamed to give

Devlin details, but she told him enough to let him know how degrading her months with Wexler had been.

Finally, Devlin couldn't stop himself from asking, "Why the hell didn't you leave him?"

"Oh, it's not so hard to figure out. At first, I didn't leave because I thought I could have what I was getting out of him and keep him at arm's length. The money, the apartment. Working the club was somewhat interesting. But Wexler isn't one to give without getting what he wants, no matter how disgusting. I may have a lot of faults, but denial isn't one of them. I knew exactly what I had become. I was determined to get out, but I didn't want to burn the bridge before I had a way out. I started putting money aside. Planning. But before I was quite ready I saw him do something that terrified me."

"What was that?" Devlin asked.

Susan grimaced and said, "I don't want to even talk about it. But after that, it didn't seem so easy to just walk out on him. When I found out he knew where my money was, where my family lived, even what I was planning in my own head, it seemed impossible. And then you came along."

"I'm glad I did."

"Why?"

"Because you deserve better."

"Where have I heard that before?"

"It happens to be true."

"That doesn't mean I'm going to get it."

"It doesn't mean you're not, either. Let's go for that walk you wanted."

CHAPTER 37

Joe locked Daryl in Susan's bedroom and left her there while he, Eddie and Messina waited in the living room for Wexler to arrive.

Eddie kept talking about raping Daryl. "You think fuckhead Wexler will let us have her for a while after he's done?"

Joe said, "Why? You like sloppy seconds?"

"Hey, fuck you. I'm going first."

"Hey, grow the fuck up, will you?"

Eddie said, "The only thing I want growing around here is my dick."

Joe stood up and paced the living room. "Yeah, well, just keep your dick in your pants until Wexler tells us he's done. I don't want him walking in here with some ruined bitch hiding under the bed."

"Relax."

During their exchanges, Messina just watched them and listened, his slightly demented half-smile never wavering. Neither Joe nor Eddie knew what he was thinking, but both assumed from his look that he was enjoying the conversation about raping Daryl.

The sound of Wexler's key in the door stopped their conversation. He entered the apartment and simply said, "Where is she?"

Joe answered, "In the bedroom."

"The three of you, come with me."

Eddie winked at Joe and smiled as they followed Wexler.

Daryl was sitting in a chair near the window of the bedroom. She had her feet folded under her. While they were out she had looked through Susan's drawers for a weapon. She found nothing useful, but she did find some of Susan's cotton panties and had put on a pair.

Wexler stood at the doorway and told Joe and Eddie, "You two, bring her over and put her on the bed. Hold her down."

They were on top of her before she could even think about resisting. They grabbed her under the arms and lifted her like a sack of flour and threw her across the width of the bed so they could hold her from either side. Eddie simply sat on her thighs. If she hadn't been on the soft mattress, his 260 pounds would have broken her knees. Joe kneeled on her arms and held her hips to the bed. The only thing she could move was her head and her hands.

Wexler pulled his chair near the foot of the bed and said to her, "Now, my dear, this is beyond any heroics or resistance. I'm going to ask you one question, and if I don't get the answer I want, I am going to hurt you beyond imagination. Where is Devlin?"

Daryl answered immediately, "I don't know. I have no idea." Wexler motioned to Messina to come to the foot of the bed. He pointed to Daryl's hand that was near that end of the bed. He held up his little finger and pointed to the middle knuckle and told him very quietly, "Break her little finger right there."

Messina immediately grabbed Daryl's little finger and cracked it as if it were a chicken neck. The pop and crack of the splintering joint was sickeningly audible. Daryl screamed. The pain shot through her finger all the way to her shoulder. She turned white and broke into a cold sweat. Wexler gave additional instructions in the same flat, emotionless voice. "Get off her. You cover her mouth. You lift her legs. I don't want her going into shock."

Joe and Eddie did as instructed. Eddie grabbed both her ankles with one hand and lifted her legs.

Messina's half-smile had grown into a leering grin. He thoroughly enjoyed her screams and enjoyed seeing Joe muffle them under his big hand.

Wexler told Messina, "Grab her wrist."

In seconds, Messina was holding Daryl's right hand in the air by her wrist. The joint of the little finger was completely broken apart. The finger jutted out at a crazy angle.

Wexler slapped Daryl to attract her attention. Aggravated, he hissed at her, "Now you shut up and listen to me." He slapped her face again, harder. "Shut up!"

Daryl struggled to control herself. She clenched her teeth to stop from screaming. Her eyes filled with tears, not just from the pain but from the terror welling up inside her.

Her fear mixed with the pain to the point where she felt she was losing control. She stared at Wexler as if to show him she was trying to cooperate.

"Now listen to me. I am going to ask you again. This is your last chance. If I don't like your answer, I will have him break every finger on your right hand before I ask you again. Do you understand?"

Daryl nodded. She couldn't imagine bearing the agony of another broken finger. She kept staring at Wexler. She couldn't bring herself to look at her hand.

"Are you ready?"

She nodded yes.

"Where is Devlin keeping Susan Furlong?"

For a second, Daryl didn't know who he was talking about. She had never heard Susan's assumed last name. Panic swept over her. Then she realized he was talking about Susan, and she immediately gave Wexler the answer. "The Marriott Hotel on Broadway."

"Good," said Wexler. "Now concentrate. What is the room number?"

Daryl was breathing rapidly now. She desperately tried to remember the room number. She remembered the floor. She remembered that you had to turn right at the elevator. Wexler started to say something, but she wouldn't let him speak. She said, "The room is on the thirty-fourth floor." She pictured the door and tried to visualize the numbers on the door. "It's . . . it's number 3417." She repeated the number.

"Very good," said Wexler. "You see how easy it is when you try?"

He nodded to Messina to release her hand. Messina very slowly lowered it to just above the bed, then grinned at her and slammed the hand down right on the broken finger. Daryl screamed again, Joe clapped his hand over her mouth, and she passed out from the pain.

Wexler stood up and walked to the living room. He motioned for the others to follow him.

"I'll stay here and take care of this. You three go to the Marriott and get into that room. If Susan is there, Messina, you bring her back here. Joe and Eddie, wait for Devlin to show up. See if this time you can finally take care of that idiot. If you don't do anything stupid you can surprise him. Beat him, but don't kill him. You can cripple him, blind him, maim him, but don't kill him. When you're done, call me."

Joe asked, "How do we get in the room?"

"One of you pose as room service, then let the other two in."

CHAPTER 38

When Devlin mentioned taking a walk, Susan quickly stood up and headed out of the restaurant.

Devlin paid the check and walked quickly to catch up to her at the elevator. They stood waiting and suddenly Susan turned to him and said, "Thank you for dinner."

Devlin answered, "You're welcome." He was amazed at how much Susan could drink and still speak without slurring her words.

When they reached the ground floor, Devlin looked for James Pony, but before he could spot him, Pony appeared at his side as if he were waiting to follow them out the door.

Susan started through the revolving door and Devlin quietly told Pony, "Just going for some air. Stay here."

He stepped into the revolving door and caught up to Susan. She grabbed Devlin's arm as if it were something she did every day and hugged it to her body. Devlin felt the soft fullness of her breast against his arm. She leaned into him and breathed deeply. She said, "I never thought I'd want a lungful of this air. Let's walk up one of the theater streets."

"Fine."

They walked to 44th Street and turned west. They kept walking to Eighth Avenue, and Susan stopped at a deli on the corner. She bought a carton of Parliaments. Then as they passed a liquor store, Susan insisted they go in and buy vodka. "Do you know room service charges you forty-seven dollars for a bottle of Absolut?"

"That's a lot."

"It's ridiculous."

Susan asked for two liters of Absolut and a liter of Grand Marnier. Devlin paid. They walked back to the hotel with their purchases and took the elevator to the thirty-fourth floor.

Devlin hadn't seen Pony in the lobby, but he knew he was around.

They entered the room, and Devlin placed the liquor on the bar. When he turned, Susan stood in the middle of the living room staring at him. One thin strap had fallen off her shoulder. She said, "You know, you must really be something."

"Why?"

"I'm standing here realizing I don't know which I want more, you or another drink."

Devlin said, "Tough choice, huh?"

Susan walked toward the bar but stopped in front of Devlin. She rested her arms on his shoulders and pulled him toward her for a kiss. Devlin had been wanting to have her in his arms, and he held her tightly, trying to feel all of her against him at once. He let his hands roam over her bare back, down to her buttocks and up again.

She squirmed when he caressed her backside, so Devlin reached down and massaged each round full cheek. She ground her pelvis against him, and he became erect. She worked her tongue into his mouth and reached behind his head to pull him more to her.

As she grabbed a handful of hair, she pulled at the wound healing on the back of his head. Devlin winced, pulled away from their kiss and gently took her hand away.

"What's the matter?"

"Sorry. I've got a cut healing back there."

Susan bent around to see the back of Devlin's head. She carefully pushed aside the hair that covered the wound. "Oh, poor baby," she said. "I'm sorry. Come with me."

She took Devlin by the hand and started walking backward toward the master bedroom. She was bent over, showing more of her lovely cleavage. She was drunk and playful and sexy. She smiled coquettishly and tried to tease Devlin as she led him toward the bedroom. "Let me take care of you tonight, Mr. Devlin. I'll make all that hurt go away. I promise."

Devlin imagined getting lost in her, but the damn cut in the back of his head was a nagging reminder of Daryl. He thought about resisting Susan, and as if she had read his mind Susan said, "Come on. Please don't make me beg, honey. Please."

She had him. He was gone. There was no more need for Susan to pull him toward the bedroom. They were both breathing hard, and then the phone rang and shattered the moment.

It so startled both of them that for a couple of beats they stood motionless in the doorway to the bedroom. The phone rang again and again. Devlin finally pulled his hand out of Susan's grasp and grabbed the phone.

He picked up the receiver and said, "Yes?"

The voice at the other end was Pony's. "Three men. Big. Two of them like you described. They just went into the elevator."

"Shit."

Devlin stood for a moment thinking, reacting, pulling himself out of Susan's intoxicating presence. Pony couldn't wait for an answer. He asked, "Did you hear me?"

"Yes. Yes! Okay, listen to me. I'm not running. You want to fight? We're going to fight. Get up here quick. They won't get in easily. Get up here and get behind them. Take out whoever you can. Move! Now!"

Devlin hung up the phone and told Susan. "Trouble. Wexler's men are in the hotel."

"What!"

"They're on their way up here."

"Oh God, what are you going to do?"

"Stop them. Go into the bedroom. Lock your door. I'll lock the door on this side. Don't open any doors for anyone except me. If they get past me and try to take down the door, lock yourself in the bathroom. There's a phone in there. Call hotel security first, then the police. Go. Now!"

Just then, Joe, Eddie, and Messina stepped out onto the thirty-fourth floor. All forty floors of the hotel were constructed around a huge atrium. From where they stood near the elevators they could look down and see the empty hotel corridors running around the atrium for five floors below.

Two floors below, Joe spotted a room service cart with dirty dishes and a half-empty bottle of red wine, parked outside a room. He told Eddie, "Go down and bring that cart up here."

Downstairs Pony was waiting for the elevator on the ground floor. No matter how hard he willed it to arrive, there was nothing he could do but wait.

Up on the thirty-fourth floor, Joe and Messina waited for Eddie and the cart.

The elevator door opened and Eddie stepped out pushing the room service cart. He had a ridiculous grin on his bruised ugly face.

Joe took off his suit jacket and folded it over the handle of the cart. He straightened his tie and wheeled the cart toward the room. He told the other two, "Stay out of sight. When I get to the room, I'll try to get her to open the door. As soon as she does, we bust in and take her."

Eddie followed behind him with Messina taking up the rear.

Pony was finally in the elevator going up. It was packed with people. When it reached the eighth-floor lobby, most of the people got off, but five or six more got on. There were eight people besides Pony, and they punched in five stops—all below the thirty-fourth floor. The delays were excruciating, but he stood quietly, breathing slowly, exerting all his training to stay in control.

Joe arrived at 3417 and knocked on the door. Devlin stood to one side of the door with his .45 in his right hand and the small wooden fighting stick in his left. At the sound of the knock he answered, "Yes?"

When Joe heard Devlin's voice, he turned to the others whispering, "Shit, he's in there. Get ready." Then he said to Devlin, "Room service."

Devlin stood with his back pressed to the wall beside the door. He said, "Just a second." He put the fighting stick in his mouth and set the chain latch on the door. In the hallway, Joe smiled as he heard the chain being attached. The thought of a small chain stopping him was very amusing. He pulled back the food cart to get momentum. Devlin turned the doorknob and opened the door to the end of the chain, then grabbed the fighting stick and flattened himself against the wall.

He got out of the way just in time as Joe rammed the food cart into the door with all his weight behind it. The chain snapped like a string, and Joe came charging through the door with Eddie fast behind him.

Devlin timed his first blow perfectly. He stepped out from his protected spot next to the door and smashed Joe squarely in the teeth with the barrel of his Caspian Arms. Joe's four front teeth shattered. He sucked blood and pieces of tooth back into his throat and stopped dead in his tracks gagging, trying to cough out the broken teeth.

Eddie, rushing in fast behind him, couldn't stop and slammed into Joe, sending him crashing into the room service cart. Joe went down hard, but Eddie stayed on his feet and turned to face whoever hit Joe. Devlin stepped forward and calmly shot Eddie in the right knee, blowing out the entire knee joint and sending him crashing to the floor.

Devlin turned and saw Messina standing in the hallway. Messina took one look at Devlin and his gun and bolted to his left. As he turned the corner, he ran head-on into Pony and shoved him out of his way with a sweep of his huge arm.

Pony stayed on his feet, but he hit the wall hard. Since Messina was rushing away, he let him go and hurried to help Devlin.

Back in the room, Joe was sprawled on top of the overturned room service cart. Eddie was struggling to get up on one leg. Joe suddenly got to his feet, turned, and charged at Devlin. He was so fast,

Devlin couldn't shoot him anywhere without being sure he wouldn't kill him. He lashed out with a fast front kick to meet Joe's charge. He hit him square in the chest, but the big man took the blow and fell forward, grabbing Devlin's leg and charged right into him. He shoved Delvin backward. Devlin went down. Joe landed on top of him and managed to pound a heavy chopping blow to Devlin's chest. Joe's mouth was filled with blood, which he spit into Devlin's face as he grabbed for Devlin's hand holding the .45.

The blood and spit blinded him, but Devlin swung at Joe and rammed the end of the fighting stick into his temple. The crack of the blow could be heard in the bedroom, but it didn't knock Joe off him.

Eddie was now crawling forward, dragging the leg with the ruined knee. Joe had been knocked to the side by the blow to his head, and Devlin used all his strength to shove him off. He managed to do it just in time to roll away from Eddie's fist, headed toward his face, but he didn't avoid all of the punch. Eddie managed to deliver a stinging blow to Devlin's left ear.

Joe tried to grab Devlin's leg, but Devlin kicked him off and managed to get back on his feet.

Just then, James Pony appeared in the doorway. Devlin saw him and yelled, "Get the third one." Pony turned and disappeared.

Joe was struggling to stand up, but he was too disoriented from the blow to his temple. He lost his balance and fell back down.

Devlin stepped forward and kicked Eddie full in the face, breaking his jaw and knocking him on his back.

Joe finally managed to get up on his knees. He was a heavyweight desperately trying to beat the count. He shook his head and spat out more blood past the stumps that used to be his front teeth. The exposed nerves in the broken teeth screamed with pain.

Eddie was down, and Devlin wanted to finish him off. He kicked Eddie hard between the legs and heard a painful grunt. Eddie reached up, weakly trying to grab Devlin, but Devlin jumped up and came crashing down on one knee landing all his weight landing on

Eddie's solar plexus. The big man buckled, his sternum cracked, and he lost consciousness.

Devlin spun around to face Joe. He still had the .45 in his hand. He pointed it at Joe. "Move and you're dead."

Joe yelled, "Fuck you! Shoot me." He stood up on his feet. "Come on, you fucking pussy. I got no weapons, no guns. Come on. Take me if you're so tough. I'll fucking break you in two."

Devlin holstered his gun and tossed the fighting stick on the couch. He calmly said to Joe, "It's time you had a beating."

#

As Devlin and Joe squared off, Pony pushed the elevator button for the third time. He didn't think he had much chance to catch up with the ugly one who had swatted him aside as though he were a child.

Messina, however, had made a mistake. When he got in the elevator, he had pushed the button that said LOBBY and had gotten off at the eighth floor, expecting to be on the street level. When he realized his mistake, instead of waiting for another elevator with the crowds in the lobby, he found the escalators and started running down them to get to the street-level exit.

An elevator finally appeared, and Pony rode it nonstop to the eighth floor. A crowd filled the elevator, but then it continued straight down to the street level.

Pony stepped out of the elevator just in time to glimpse Messina going through the revolving doors out to the large throughway that ran past the hotel at ground level between 45th and 46th Streets.

Pony ran toward the exit doors, keeping Messina in sight.

Messina emerged out of the hotel not knowing which direction to turn. He wanted to catch an eastbound cab but couldn't tell if the eastbound street was to his right or left. He hesitated, then turned left, which gave Pony enough time to close the distance between them before he made it out the street.

Messina heard the footsteps behind him and whirled around.

When he saw Pony, he immediately lashed out with a quick right hook. The punch came at Pony without a second's hesitation, thrown with such speed it would have connected with anyone slower than Pony. The young fighter ducked under it, but Messina's big knuckles raked across his back. Pony stayed down, moved in toward Messina, bobbed up, and landed a solid uppercut that hit the bigger man square on the underside of his jaw.

The punch snapped Messina's massive head back but didn't slow him much. He snarled, stepped back from Pony, and swung a lightning fast backhand punch. This time the blow caught Pony coming in to land another punch. He saw the blow coming and tried to block it with his left forearm, but Messina was so strong the punch came through and hit the side of Pony's head.

For a split second everything went black, and then Messina's next punch landed on Pony's left shoulder. He felt his arm go numb as the blow knocked him off his feet. He landed hard on the concrete but rolled with the punch and got back on his feet just in time to deliver a straight kick at the charging Messina. The big man blocked the kick with his forearms, but Pony followed it instantly with a dangerous leaping roundhouse kick that caught Messina on the side of his head.

For a moment, the action stopped. Fighting a man like Messina, who was so fast and so strong, was both exhilarating and terrifying. A crowd had already gathered around them, but Pony concentrated totally on the man in front of him.

Messina circled with his leering grimace. His left ear was ringing from Pony's kick. He shuffled forward with his hands in front of him. Pony shifted his stance to get the best angle, and then suddenly Messina was on him.

They locked arms, grappling for leverage. Messina was surprised by the young man's strength. He tried to throw Pony against one of the huge pillars running along the passageway, but the young fighter was too well trained and countered the move and delivered a sweeping leg kick that knocked Messina's front leg out from under him. Messina lost his balance and went down hard. Pony had enough strength to rip free from his grip, but Messina grabbed at him and tore open the front of his black silk shirt.

As Messina hit the ground, he lashed out with a kick that caught Pony full in the thigh, knocking him backward.

Messina was on his feet quickly. He dropped all finesse and charged ahead, ready to take the blows until he could land his own. Pony punched and moved back, punched and blocked and kicked and backpedaled. Messina blocked the blows or absorbed them and swung back with devastating roundhouse punches, most of which Pony was fast enough to deflect with his upper arm and shoulders, but every blocked punch hurt.

Pony kept fighting off the larger man. He felt his knuckles cracking into the man's flesh and bone, but Messina seemed oblivious to the pain. Pony was quicker and more accurate, but no one punch could stop Messina.

Two strikes to the jaw rattled Messina, a kick to the ribs, an elbow to the side of the head, and Messina started to slow his charge. Pony gathered his strength to finish off Messina with carefully aimed blows.

Just then Pony heard a strange noise and sensed a huge shape looming up on his right, but he couldn't take his eyes off Messina, and in the next instant he felt himself shoved to the ground by a force so strong he was stunned more by the impact and size than by the blow. As he went down, he felt as if he had been pushed aside by a giant.

He hit the sidewalk hard, but rolled into the direction he had been thrown and managed to get back on his feet. As he stood and turned, he saw that a mounted policeman had ridden his horse right between him and Messina.

The cop had wheeled the horse around, knocking Pony down and driving Messina backward.

Messina didn't hesitate for a second. He ran north, toward 46th Street. Pony stood his ground looking at the cop.

The cop yelled at him, "Don't move!" Pony obeyed. The cop asked, "Did he have a knife or a gun?"

Pony said, "I don't know. He jumped me from behind."

The mounted policeman said, "Stay here."

Without another word, the cop turned his horse and tried to make his way through the crowd to chase down Messina.

Pony moved off quickly in the opposite direction, ran through the passageway across 45th Street and into Shubert Alley. A souvenir shop was just closing, and he ducked inside and asked if he could buy a T-shirt.

The man behind the counter told him, "We're closed.

Pony said, "Sir, I need a shirt. Here's twenty dollars, just hand me one. No receipt, no bag."

The clerk admired Pony's chest for a moment and then said, "Oh, all right. Here's a large. It should fit."

Pony took the T-shirt, stripped off the remains of his silk shirt and slipped it on. It bore the *Phantom of the Opera* logo.

He looked down at his pants and saw that there was a tear in the left leg. He tried to brush off the dirt around it. The clerk asked, "What happened to you, honey?

"Somebody tried to mug me.

"Oh, you poor thing. Are you hurt?"

"I'm all right. Thanks."

Pony left before he drew any more attention.

From where he was, he could see that the crowd around the hotel entrance had dispersed now that the fight was over. He walked quickly back, checking himself for damage. Nothing was broken, but he knew he would have plenty of pain from a fight that had taken less than two minutes.

#

Up in the hotel room, Joe grimaced and spat out more blood. He stood with his hands up, slowly moving toward Devlin. All he wanted to do was grab and smash. Eddie was unconscious on the floor to his left. His breaths came out in quivering rasps. Joe kicked Eddie's shoulder and yelled, "Get up, you fuck. Get up, you useless fuck." But Eddie wasn't moving. Devlin was. He did the one thing Joe didn't expect. He came straight at him and flicked a lightning jab right at his mouth. It landed squarely, snapping back the bouncer's head and releasing a torrent of pain in his broken teeth. The big man growled and charged at Devlin, who deftly stepped aside, grabbed Joe under the armpit and shoved him in the direction of his charge, smashing him into the wall. The entire room shook with the impact. Joe slid down along the wall to his knees leaving a trail of blood and spit.

Devlin moved quickly toward him and kicked hard into his right kidney. Joe grunted at the excruciating pain, but he was far from done.

He twisted away from the wall and swung a backward blow at Devlin with all his strength. It caught Devlin squarely on the right side of his ribcage, knocking Devlin sideways. He went down on one knee, struggling to drag air into his lungs. Joe threw himself at Devlin, slamming him to the ground with a horrible thud. He scrambled forward and shot a vicious right hand to Devlin's face, Devlin managed to turn away from the punch, but Joe's fist caught him solidly on the side of his head. It was a tremendous blow. Two of Joe's knuckles cracked hitting Devlin's skull. Joe was half on top of Devlin, pinning him under his weight. He tried to get up on one hand to hit Devlin again, but Devlin slammed the V of his open right hand into Joe's throat. Joe's mouth flew open. He grabbed his throat, unable to breathe.

Devlin pushed off the bigger man, rolled away from him , and stood up.

Devlin didn't want the fight to last a second longer. Just hitting the huge man caused pain, but he wasn't going to kill him with the gun, or risk the sound of another shot to disable him.

He didn't want to break his hands on the man either, so he went to work with kicks. Joe was up on his knees but still bent over, struggling to breathe, a stationary target for the moment. Devlin stepped forward and delivered a roundhouse kick to the side of the man's head, knocking him down on the carpet. Joe teetered on the edge of consciousness, but unbelievably he once again struggled to his knees. Devlin watched him, thinking of how he had beaten his brother. He heard the words of the neurosurgeon, Dr. Wu, describing how George's brain had slammed back and forth in his skull causing enough damage to send him into coma and stroke and paralysis.

Devlin looked around for something to use. He saw the hotel's ice bucket sitting on the bar. He picked it up. It was filled with ice and water.

Without hesitating, he took the heavy bucket in his right hand and approached Joe from behind. He reared back and with all his strength smashed the ice bucket into the back of the man's head. Devlin's ribs screamed with pain, the handle of the bucket broke off. Cubes of ice and water sprayed all over the room.

Joe went down and stayed down.

Now the second man, Eddie, was coming back to consciousness. The shock of the bullet wound to his knee was setting in. He felt weak and dizzy. Even though the room was spinning into focus, he lay unmoving in a cold, clammy sweat.

Eddie struggled to get up on one elbow. The pain in his knee was enough to make him want to cut off his leg. When the room finally came into focus, Devlin was squatting next to him holding the barrel of the .45 an inch from his head.

Eddie turned to look at him, and Devlin pressed the barrel hard against the middle of his forehead.

Devlin looked him in the eyes and said, "You have one chance to live. Tell me where Wexler has her."

Eddie shook his head and said, "What?"

Devlin took the barrel away from his head and smacked the shattered knee. It felt as if someone had tightened the vise that was already crushing it. Eddie screamed.

Devlin slapped him across the face and told him, "Shut up! Listen to me. One more time. Where is Wexler keeping the girl? She's the only one who could have told you this location."

Devlin saw Eddie's eyes look at something behind him, and he heard Pony's soft voice tell him, "It's me, Mr. Devlin.

Without looking, Devlin said, "Good. Close the door, James."

The door closed and Devlin said to Eddie, "Answer me, or I do the other knee. Then the elbows. Then your feet. Then your hands."

"All right, all right," Eddie yelled. "I'm no fucking hero. He's got her in his bitch's apartment."

"Susan's apartment?"

"Yes."

Devlin stood up, grabbed one of the liter bottles of Absolut off the bar and with all his might smashed Eddie in the back of the head with it. The heavy bottle shattered. Eddie's skull fractured and the skin on the back of his head split wide open. Glass, blood, and vodka sprayed one wall of the suite.

Devlin turned to look at Pony.

"Did you get the third one?"

"We fought. The police broke it up and went after him. I don't know if they caught him. I doubt it."

"Shit."

"You took out two of them," Pony said with quiet admiration.

"The gun helped."

Pony asked, "How did they find you?"

"Daryl. She's the only other person who knew we were here. They must have run her down and gotten the information out of her. They have her at Susan's apartment, but I doubt if there's time to get there before that third guy warns them."

Devlin ran quickly to the adjoining bedroom door. "Susan, we have to get out of here. Open up."

Susan opened the door holding her suitcase. She was ready.

"Let's go," she said.

She came out into the center room of the suite and looked down at Wexler's two huge bouncers broken and bleeding on the floor. The room looked as though it had been bombed while Joe and Eddie were in it. Furniture was smashed. Even the walls were dented. There were smears and splatters of blood everywhere.

Devlin got her attention and said, "Susan, this is James Pony. He's helping me. He's going to take you to another hotel. The Carlyle. I want you to check in as Mrs. Johnson from the Pacific Rim Corporation. They'll know what to do. Don't give them any credit cards or other names. Just Mrs. Johnson. Make up an address, check in, and stay in your room until I come for you."

"Okay."

"Give me your apartment keys. I might need them."

Susan handed Devlin the keys without a word. She had all she could do to keep from looking back at Joe and Eddie, beaten and broken on the floor.

Devlin said to Pony, "Take my suitcase with you. It's over in the closet."

Pony picked up the gold Halliburton case, gently took Susan by the elbow and led her out of the hotel suite.

When the door closed, Devlin went to the couch and pulled off one of the thick seat cushions. He went over to Joe and placed the cushion over his right knee. He pressed the muzzle of the .45 deep into the cushion and pulled the trigger. The noise was muffled enough to stay inside the soundproofed room.

Devlin lifted the cushion to survey the damage. His shot had gone right where he imagined the center of Joe's knee was under the cushion. The knee joint was obliterated.

Devlin stood up and holstered the pistol. He looked down at Joe and said, "You decide to come after me, I want to hear you limping."

CHAPTER 39

When the doorman announced that Messina was downstairs, Wexler was sitting in Susan's living room drinking a mediocre glass of Beaujolais and rereading a favorite section of William Shirer's *The Rise and Fall of the Third Reich.*

Daryl was in the bedroom, crying at the effort it took not to scream from the pain caused by the broken finger. Even through the locked bedroom door, Wexler could hear her intermittent weeping, and he was beginning to get tired of it.

When he told the doorman to send up Messina, he found himself intensely anxious to see Susan. Messina walked in alone and bruised, and Wexler knew he wouldn't be seeing Susan. He immediately felt enraged, but he calmly asked, "What happened?"

"Walked into a fuckin' setup, that's what happened. That guy you're looking for was there, and he knew we were coming."

"Impossible."

"Go tell that to your two boyfriends."

"Joe and Eddie?"

"More like dead meat and goner. At least one of 'em got shot."

Wexler stood up so fast his wine sloshed over the rim of the glass. "What are you talking about? How could he know you were coming?"

Messina answered, "Don't fuckin' ask me. That guy Devlin let them into the hotel suite and shot at least one of them."

"What did you do?"

"Tried to get the fuck out of there, that's what I did. Almost got caught by the cops outside the place trying to fight off some little asshole working with Devlin."

"Who was that?"

"Have no idea, but the son of a bitch knew how to fight, I'll tell you that. Listen, no one told me anything about guns and shit. I ain't walkin' into no more fucking gun fights unless I got a gun."

"I agree."

"This guy you're after knows what the hell he's doing, and he ain't afraid to do it. You better get some muscle besides those pretty bodybuilder boys you're using."

Wexler sat down. He had to think this through, but first he had to decide what to do in the next few moments. It clearly wouldn't take Devlin long to figure out that Wexler had Daryl. It was likely Eddie or Joe had told him where.

Daryl was still moaning in the bedroom, interrupting Wexler's train of thought.

Wexler told Messina, "Go find something to shut her up. Look around for some painkiller or something. Or a bottle of booze. Anything. Her whining annoys me."

Messina went into Susan's bathroom and rummaged around the medicine chest for something to ease Daryl's pain. He found a bottle of 10-milligram Valium and a bottle of Nuprin. He took the medicine and a fifth of Chivas Regal he found in the kitchen and brought everything to Daryl in the bedroom.

Daryl was huddled on the bed, cradling her hand in her lap. When Messina walked in, she twitched and put her good hand up.

Messina tried to disarm her with a smile, but it only made him look more creepy and frightening. He said, "Stop squirming around like a little shit and take some of this stuff and shut up." He held up the Scotch and the pills. "Swig it down with some booze here, and you'll feel fine."

Daryl said nothing. Messina dumped everything on the bed and told her, "Hurry up and stop making that pitiful noise. If you don't shut up, Wexler is gonna make me come in here and do a lot worse to you than fuck up your little finger."

Daryl said nothing. Messina stepped forward and slammed his hand into her crotch and squeezed hard. Daryl grunted in pain and disgust. He lifted her off the bed and said, "You hear me, goddamn it!"

Daryl screamed, "Yes."

"Then answer me when I talk. Take that shit and shut up."

Messina released his grip, turned, and left.

Daryl picked up the bottle of Chivas with her good hand and took a long swig. The liquid burned down her throat and into her stomach.

It almost made her gag, but she forced herself to swallow another mouthful. Then she swallowed three Nuprins with the saliva in her mouth and took another swig of Scotch.

She was worried about taking the Valium but decided feeling woozy and out of it was better than feeling the pain. She forced one pill down. She hoped it would help keep her from looking at her broken finger. Every time she saw the finger jutting out at such a strange angle, it made her sick and nauseated.

When Messina entered the living room, Wexler was just hanging up the phone.

"What did you do about the girl?"

"I gave her some booze and some Valium and shit. She should be out of it soon."

"I suppose I'll have to get that finger set if I'm going to keep her." Wexler paused to think that over and then said, "Well, we shall sit tight for a little while in case Mr. Devlin comes to the rescue."

"He shows up, you'd better have more than me to throw at him. I'm not armed."

"Reinforcements should be here very soon."

Messina asked, "Who?"

"The police."

Messina stood up with an amazed look on his face. "The police? What are you, fucking crazy?"

"Relax. These are my police."

#

Devlin got out of the cab on 65th and Second and started walking toward the apartment building on the opposite side of the street.

Susan's building was a tall black obelisk with sheer glass sides that rose fifty stories high. The entrance to the building was set back and fronted by a U-shaped driveway on 65th Street. As he approached the building, he saw the two cars pull into the driveway. One car was a blue and white squad car. The second car he recognized as an unmarked police sedan. Two uniformed cops got out of the squad car and two detectives wearing suits got out of the unmarked sedan.

The uniformed patrolmen and detectives huddled for a moment outside the building. The two uniforms went inside. One of the detectives got back into the unmarked sedan, and the other into the squad car. After he parked the blue and white squad car, he joined the other detective who had parked across the street in front of the building.

Devlin went inside a video rental store across from the building.

He pretended to shop for a tape while he tried to figure out a way to get past the two cops outside and get Daryl away from the two cops he figured would soon be with her in the apartment.

His mind was made up for him when another unmarked sedan pulled up with two more detectives. One of them got out and joined the two already watching the building. He was the short, heavyset cop who had tried to arrest Devlin at the hospital. Devlin figured his taller partner was still recovering from his thirty seconds with James Pony.

The fourth detective walked into the building and took a seat in the lobby. That made at least six cops on the scene. Too many.

Devlin left the video store with his head down and walked east on

65th Street. At First Avenue, he hailed a cab and took it to the Carlyle.

It was almost one o'clock in the morning when Devlin walked into the suite. Susan and Pony had checked in forty minutes before. James Pony sat silently near a window. Susan sat alone on the couch.

Nobody moved, which seemed appropriate in the more elegant surroundings. The rooms were smaller than at the Marriott, but the furnishings were more expensive, the colors more vibrant. Yellow drapes, blue carpet, sofa and chairs upholstered in an ivory brocade. At the Marriott, everything was shades of tan and brown and all straight lines instead of rounded edges.

As soon as he walked in, Susan asked, "They got her, didn't they?"

"That's the way it looks."

"It had to be her. No one else knew we were there, did they?"

"No. I shouldn't have let her go back to her apartment alone."

"It's tough taking care of two women at once."

Devlin sat at the room's writing table. He didn't respond to Susan's comment.

She asked, "What are you going to do now?"

"Get her away from them."

"How?"

Devlin rubbed his face and eyes as if he were trying to generate an idea. He felt tired and slow. The fight with Joe and Eddie had taken too much out of him. He hurt in too many places—ribs, knee, head, fists.

He asked Pony, "How are you doing?"

Pony turned to Devlin and said, "Fine."

"Any damage?"

"Knuckles, mostly. Some bruises."

"Thinking about it?"

"Yes."

"You may get another shot at him."

"I hope so."

"They have Daryl in Susan's apartment. It's at 265 East 65th Street.

There are two detectives in an unmarked car across the street, one or two in the lobby, and at least two uniformed cops in the apartment. We can't go up against them, but we still have to watch the building to see if they move her. I have to know where she is. Do you think you can do it?"

Pony stood up slowly. "Yes."

"You might be standing out there most of the night."

"I know."

"Okay. Got the address?"

"Yes."

Pony glided out of the room.

"Now what?" Susan asked.

"Like I said, I have to get her free."

"Like I said, how?"

Devlin walked away from where Susan was sitting and tried to piece together a plan.

Susan tried to let him alone, but she couldn't stay silent under the pressure. She asked, "How the hell did they know about her? How did they find her?"

Devlin turned back to her and said, "Through that goddamn bar where this all started. That bartender must have led them to someone who knew her address. Daryl was their only lead. I got my brother away from them and his family. Daryl was the only person they could connect to me."

Susan said, "She gave us up awfully fast. I don't even want to think about what Wexler did to her."

Devlin turned and moved toward the phone. "What's the phone number in your apartment?"

Susan was startled by his sudden burst of movement and gave him her number without thinking.

Devlin dialed it. Wexler answered on the second ring. Devlin concentrated on getting the anger out of his voice. "Wexler, this is Jack Devlin."

Wexler's voice came over the line sounding relaxed and eerie. "Jack Devlin."

"Wexler, your business is with me. I want Daryl Austen out of it."

"What did you say?"

"I want the girl out of it."

"Are you actually stupid enough to think I care about what *you* want?"

"Not really. It'll just be a lot easier for us to get together if the girl is out of the way. You want me, not the girl. Let her go, and I'll meet with you anywhere you say."

"Oh, what a brilliant negotiator you are. I let her go home, and you'll be over shortly."

"Name the time and place."

"Listen, you fool, I'm going to find you anyhow."

"I wouldn't be so sure."

"Well then, let's see. How about instead of sending you the whole girl—I start sending parts of her until you show up. I could start with a finger. I've already had one of them nicely broken. It's hanging on by the skin. I can easily tear it off and put it in an envelope. Where should I send it?"

Devlin closed his eyes and tried to breathe steadily. "That won't do anybody any good at all, Mr. Wexler."

"Don't bore me with veiled threats."

"Wexler, you and I are going to meet face to face before this is over. Why not get the others out of the way and get down to it? You bring Daryl, I'll bring Susan. The women walk, you and I settle our differences."

Wexler didn't answer.

Devlin pushed a little harder, "Come on, Wexler. It'll be interesting. You can try to kill me when we make the exchange. The women are just bait anyhow, right? A simple exchange will speed up the game."

Wexler's voice turned a notch serious. "I'm not going to try to kill you, Mr. Devlin, I *will* kill you."

"Sure. It'll be fun."

"Don't patronize me, you idiot, or I won't even send you a finger. And you can do whatever you want with that drunken slut you've got."

"Make up your mind, Wexler. It's the best offer I'll give you. It's the only one I've got."

"All right, macho man, call me tomorrow at this number at six o'clock. I'll tell you where and when."

"Fine. Just one more thing."

"What?"

"Now that we've reached an agreement, I don't see any more need to hurt the girl."

"Only if I feel like it."

Devlin heard the click and then a dial tone. He put the phone on its cradle and looked up to see Susan storming into the bedroom. He followed her and saw her furiously throw her suitcase on the bed. She started fumbling with the catches to open the case. But her hands were shaking so much she couldn't open the locks. Devlin grabbed her arm and tried to turn her toward him.

"Susan, stop."

She spun toward him and slapped him hard across the face. She burst into tears and yelled, "Don't touch me, you son of a bitch. Trading me like a piece of meat. You bastard! You liar!"

"Stop it. Listen to me."

"Why? So you can lie to me more? Tell me how you're going to protect me!"

She swung at him again, but this time Devlin didn't want any more pain inflicted on the bruises that Joe and Eddie had created. He blocked her swing with his left hand and grabbed Susan's other arm with his right hand. He gently forced her down until she was sitting on the edge of the bed.

He put his face in front of Susan's and said, "Please stop this and listen to me. Unless we bring Wexler out into the open, he will kill you and me and Daryl."

Susan stared at him, and Devlin slowly released her arms. He talked in a softer, calmer voice. "I don't want you screaming at me or hitting me or running out of here until you listen to what I have to say. I'm not trading you. I'm not turning you over to Wexler. I'm asking for your help. *Asking.* If you don't want to do it, you can go. But I had to contact him. I had to take away his reason to hurt Daryl. He's ready to start cutting that girl up and sending me parts."

Susan tried to steady herself. She rubbed her arm where Devlin had gripped her.

"I'm not lying to you, Susan. Do you hear me?"

"Yes."

"Do you believe me?"

"Maybe I do," she said, "maybe I don't. It doesn't matter. I can't help you anymore. I can't be sure you can protect me. I can't risk letting him get me. I have a mother who depends on me. I have a sister who is very ill. She needs my support. In a few months, she will be in a place where she can be taken care of, and unless I help my mother it will never be done. Even if Wexler finds me in a few months, I've got to risk it."

Devlin said, "I understand."

"You know where that girl is. You have the Indian watching to see where they take her. You call the fucking police, and you get her back without me. I'm sorry."

Devlin tried one more time. "The police aren't going to help me. I have no evidence. No way to get a warrant. And even if I did convince them to move on Wexler, they could kill her before I get her out. It's too risky."

"It's not my problem. I can't risk my life for hers."

Devlin stood up and backed away from Susan. He held up his hands. "All right. All right. I won't ask you again."

"And I'm not staying here. I'm getting as far away as I can from this right now."

"Susan, it's two o'clock in the morning. You don't know where you're going. Even if you did have a place to go, you can't catch a plane at this time of night. Stay here. You're safe. No one knows you're even here."

Devlin watched her think about what he said. She pushed her suitcase aside and lay down on the bed. She covered her eyes with her arm and said, "I don't know how the hell I got into this, but in the morning, I'm getting out of it."

Devlin left the bedroom and quietly closed the door. He walked out to the living room and slumped down on the couch. He hurt all over. He felt exhausted. The fight with Joe and Eddie, the nights without sleep, the loss of Daryl and now Susan—it had all taken too much out of him.

He lay back and tried to think of what to do. He pictured putting on his Kevlar vest, loading up with guns and ammunition, and shooting anybody who got in his way until he made it into Susan's apartment and got Daryl out.

The stupidity of that made him feel even worse. He felt a dark force invade him, enervating him. He knew if he didn't fight it, didn't move, do something – he would lose everything.

He forced himself to stand up, put one foot in front of the other. He walked to the closet and picked up his Halliburton case. He opened it and found a small box with an assortment of pills. He picked out two 50 milligram pills of powerful non-narcotic pain-killer. He went to the bathroom and swallowed them with a handful of water. By the time he walked back to the main room, he was ready to continue. He sat at the desk. He started writing notes on a pad of hotel stationery. Thinking. Planning. He refused to fall asleep. He refused to give up. He wasn't going down without a fight. If necessary, a fight to the death.

CHAPTER 40

Out on Second Avenue, Pony stood in the darkness of the video store's alcove. Over an hour ago he had spotted the detectives sitting in their unmarked cars. They watched for anyone entering the building; he watched for anyone leaving. He was sure that none of them would see anything, but he stood in the darkness, waiting for the second hour to pass, surprised at how difficult it was.

He spent much of the time reliving his fight with Messina. Devlin had talked about bouncers who got their jobs mostly because of their size. He had envisioned fighting such big men. His assumption had been that they would be very strong and powerful, but not very fast. Messina was both. Very fast. Very powerful. It was exhilarating fighting a man who could knock you out with one punch.

The fight told him that most of Messina's training had been as a conventional boxer. He had very good hand speed, and he was so strong that stopping his punches meant hitting them away rather than blocking them. Pony wanted the standing and watching to be over. And he wanted to fight Messina again.

Upstairs in Susan's apartment, Messina lay sleeping on the couch in the living room. The Irish cop Donovan, who had run into Devlin at O'Callahan's, sat playing gin rummy with another cop who was part of Kelly's crew.

Messina was a night owl, but he didn't like being around cops, so he had put himself to sleep on the couch. Before long, he woke up with a fierce erection. He wanted to go into the bedroom and fuck

Daryl, but he knew the cops wouldn't let him. He also knew the cops wouldn't be there forever. He'd bide his time and play with the idea in his mind.

If Messina had come into the bedroom, Daryl wouldn't have known it. She had passed out from the Scotch and Valium. The pain in her broken finger had subsided to a dull ache, buried under the numbing alcohol, tranquilizer, and pain reliever.

Outside, Pony waited patiently in the dark.

#

By four in the morning, Devlin had covered every angle. No matter how he tried to figure it, the key was Susan. He couldn't figure out a way to do what he needed to do without her, but he believed he'd finally had a way to convince her to help him.

He went to Susan's bedroom door and knocked softly. He heard her respond, "Yes?" and quietly opened the door.

Susan was sitting up in the bed, wearing the same black dress she had worn to dinner. She was smoking a Parliament with the ashtray on her lap. She looked as if she had been doing some thinking, too.

Devlin asked, "May I come in?"

Susan answered quietly, "Yes."

Devlin approached and sat on the edge of the bed. Susan didn't move to make room for him. Her legs were almost touching his bruised hip.

"Susan, I'm sorry about before. I just couldn't—"

She interrupted, "It's all right. I'm sorry I carried on like that. It was stupid."

"I've got to ask you a few questions, and then, whatever you decide, that will be it."

"What?"

"When we first talked, you told me that Wexler knew about your savings, your money, your family. Even what you were thinking. Does he know about your sister?"

"Yes."

"You said your sister was ill. Can she travel?"

"Yes, she can travel."

"Will you be able to take her with you? Can you take care of her?"

For a moment, Susan didn't say anything. She took a deep breath and let it out slowly. Her face didn't change. In fact, there was virtually no expression at all, but Devlin saw a tear well up in her right eye and slide silently down her cheek.

Susan quickly wiped away the tear and began to talk quietly and carefully.

"My sister is not ill. My sister has Down syndrome. She is twenty-two years old. She will probably live into her middle-age years, but not much longer. She's already got some physical problems that are common in Down syndrome people. They'll get worse as she gets older. My mother is seventy-eight, and she isn't in very good shape. She'll never live long enough to take care of Ceece. We've been waiting a long, long time to get my sister into a residence where she can live and be taken care of for the rest of her life. We finally got the final notice. A place will open for her in about six months. Probably sooner. It's as good a place as we'll ever get for her. It won't hurt to see her there.

"I can't take care of Ceece. And even if I wanted to take her with me, I couldn't. The school could call her any day, and I can't risk letting Ceece lose her place on the waiting list."

Devlin listened without moving. He had the feeling he was the first man Susan had ever told this to.

Susan kept talking. "Now you're going to tell me that if I run, Wexler will go after my sister and my mother. You're going to tell me Wexler will hurt my sister to get back at me. My sister is the most innocent angel, the dearest, sweetest person I've ever known. She's probably the only human being I know who wouldn't ever hurt anybody. She doesn't even know how to hurt somebody. And you're going to tell me Wexler will hurt her to get back at me."

"I believe he will."

For the first time since Devlin entered the room Susan looked at him. "Then I want you to promise me something."

"What?"

"If I can't kill Wexler, if he kills me first, do you promise me that you will kill him before he hurts my sister?"

Devlin sat silently for a few moments. Then he took Susan's hand and looked her in the eye and told her, "I know enough about killing to know that I hate it. Taking a life is not something you ever recover from. Ever. But I promise you, I give you my word, as long as I am alive, Wexler will die before he hurts you or your family."

Susan blinked slowly once. She set her ashtray and cigarette on the night table next to the bed. Then she told Devlin, "I guess there isn't much more you can give me." She leaned toward Devlin, put her hand carefully on the back of his head, and kissed him lightly on the cheek. She touched the side of his bruised face and told him, "You're a good man, Jack Devlin. You're a good man in a very bad world," and then she rested her head against his chest.

Devlin held her gently while she lay against him. After a few moments, she pushed herself up and looked closely at his face and the side of his head. "What did Joe and Eddie manage to do to you?"

"Nothing's broken."

She looked at his hands and his face again and slowly, carefully slid his jacket off his shoulders. She lifted off his shirt and gently touched the bruises forming on his ribs where Joe had hit him.

She told him, "Stand up, honey." She slid off the bed and stood in front of him. She saw the scraped and discolored skin on his left hip, and she carefully unhooked his belt, unzipped his trousers and let them fall to the floor. She looked at the black-and-blue hip and then knelt down and helped Devlin step out of his pants.

She gently let her soft hands rise up his legs and buttocks and back while she softly told him, "They've already hurt you too much. I want to give you pleasure instead of pain. I want to sleep with you. I've wanted to since I saw you at the club. I've been fighting with you and yelling at you and you're the only one who's helping me. It's crazy. I'm so stupid. But you have to understand it's because I was afraid. I was alone and afraid."

"I know."

Hardly moving, she slid the straps of the black dress off her shoulders, unzipped the back and let the dress fall to the floor. She let Devlin look at her body for a moment, then said, "I'm going to do whatever you tell me to do so we can stop Wexler. But I want you to explain it to me. To tell me your plan. I don't want to do anything blindly, just because you say so."

Devlin answered, "I understand."

Susan reached behind and unhooked her bra, slid her arms out of the straps and held it in front of her. "I hope your plan works." She removed her bra, revealing her full lush breasts. "But if it doesn't work . . . " She stepped into Devlin and embraced him. Her skin felt silky and hot. An erotic jolt sparked through Devlin's body as he held her next to him. ". . . If it doesn't work, I'm not going to die without the two of us sleeping together once and for all."

CHAPTER 41

Dawn was just beginning to break when James Pony heard the footsteps coming from around the corner.

A young man turned onto Second Avenue from 65th Street and peered into his alcove.

Pony was instantly ready to disable the man, but he looked confused and a little embarrassed. He spoke in a stilted Slavic accent. "You please come to the car. Mr. Devlin ask for you."

Pony relaxed and followed the Russian around the corner and saw a black Ford LTD parked at the curb. Devlin was in the backseat. From where the car was parked Devlin had a clear view of the apartment building entrance.

Pony got into the backseat. Devlin asked, "Tired?"

Pony answered with a nod, "Yes. Very."

"Anything happen?"

"No. Two cars are outside." Pony pointed them out to Devlin. "I didn't see any woman who matched your description go in or come out."

"Okay. Good. Go home and sleep. Catch a cab over on First Avenue. I don't want anyone to spot you."

Pony nodded. "When will you need me again?"

"Tonight. Not before six at the earliest. I'll call you at your apartment or the dojo. Will you be anyplace else?"

"No."

"Go."

Pony slid out of the car and drifted down 65th Street.

Traffic was beginning to build on Second Avenue. It was almost six o'clock. Devlin picked up the car's cellular phone, dialed the Parker agency and got Parker's home phone number from the agency's answering service.

When Parker answered, Devlin said, "It's Jack Devlin, Mr. Parker."

"You're calling me at home. Is this an emergency?"

"Yes. I've got one innocent person kidnapped, another in danger, and my ass on the line. I've got one possibility to end this situation, and it depends on you and your skip tracers coming through for me."

"They're working on it."

"I need to see what they've got today."

"You said we'd have three days."

"I know, but I need to see what you've got now."

"I'm not sure we have that much."

"Whatever you have."

"All right, when?"

"Noon."

"Give us until after lunch. It might make a difference. How's two o'clock?"

"I'll see you then."

Devlin hung up the phone and continued watching the apartment building. He had spoken to one of Chow's assistants at Pacific Rim an hour ago, telling him he needed a surveillance team in front of Susan's apartment building. Even though he was fairly sure Wexler would set up the exchange, he still wanted to keep track of Daryl.

At eight o'clock, all the cars on his side of the street had been moved because of parking regulations, and Devlin began to feel he was becoming too conspicuous. He stayed watching and fighting sleep until almost nine when the surveillance team finally showed up.

It was two operatives driving a van that looked like a plumber's truck. Devlin approved of the idea. It was just the kind of truck that would park outside an apartment building for hours while the plumbers worked inside.

He got out of the car service sedan and knocked on the truck door. A man opened it who looked like an old hippie cowboy. He was tall and lean. He wore jeans and a denim work shirt. He had long gray hair tied in a ponytail. His partner was a short, skinny black man who wore a blue jumpsuit.

The tall one extended his hand and introduced himself, "Hank Dixon." The black man in the jumpsuit leaned forward and shook Devlin's hand. "I'm Vincent."

"Jack Devlin. Glad you guys made it."

Devlin pointed out the cops in their unmarked cars. Dixon looked at them through a set of high-powered binoculars.

"We've got 'em. They stay on their side of the fence, we'll stay on ours. What do you figure the chance of them expecting us to be here?"

"Very slim. Cops don't think about people watching them. And they probably won't be around much longer. I think they were mainly worried about something happening last night. I'd say around eleven o'clock, look for them to move her."

"And you want to know where they take her?"

"Just as soon as it happens."

Devlin hoped that once they moved Daryl, Wexler would use fewer men to guard her, assuming Devlin wouldn't know about the second location.

"Okay, boss. We'll be on her."

Devlin thanked them, got back into his car and headed downtown.

The car service dropped Devlin off at the Pacific Rim loft. Devlin told the driver to wait.

He showered, changed clothes, and got on the phone. He spoke to William Chow, updated him on the latest developments and discussed his plan. Chow responded in his quiet voice, telling Devlin, "If your plan has any chance to work, Parker's people must come up with ironclad evidence for you. I'll notify Parker we'll give his skip tracers a five-thousand-dollar bonus if they succeed. Bon courage, Jack."

Chow hung up before Devlin had a chance to thank him.

Next, Devlin called Marilyn and learned that she had made all the arrangements for the house in Truro on the Cape. She told him the doctors hoped to discharge George in two or three days.

Devlin got back into the car service sedan and rode to the Carlyle. It was just before noon when he walked into Susan's suite.

She was having a room service lunch of chicken salad, fruit salad, and iced tea. Susan looked alert and bright and tense. She told him he looked tired and strung-out. He told her that's what happens when you only sleep two hours a night.

She wore a simple print dress, one gold bracelet on her wrist, and very little makeup.

Devlin wore light-green linen slacks, a beige rayon shirt, and a light-blue blazer to cover his holstered .45.

He asked her, "How are you doing?"

"All right, I guess."

"You're up early. Did you sleep at all last night?"

"No. I haven't switched to regular hours yet. I spent my time looking at all your scars and thinking."

"About what?"

"About a lot of things. About your plan. About how I have to stop drinking if I'm going to help you at all."

"You have to tackle the drinking one day at a time."

"What's that, AA stuff?"

"Yeah."

"You know about them?"

"A little. I know it works for some people."

"One more thing to do when this is all over."

"Things will be a lot easier for you when this is over. Just hang in. It won't be long now."

Devlin looked at the food Susan was eating and realized he hadn't eaten in a long time. He picked up the phone and told Room

Service, "This is room 418. You know the last order that came up here? Send it all again, but double it. Right. And hurry, please."

"You're having lunch with me?"

"If you don't mind."

"Of course not. Then what?"

"I disappear for a while. I'll be back to call Wexler at six."

"That should be interesting."

Devlin said, "Will you be all right until I get back?"

"I'll try to sleep in a little. I can't go out, right?"

"No sense taking chances now. But I'll tell you what. When I leave, I'll tell the concierge to send up a masseuse. It'll be easier to fall asleep after a massage."

Susan smiled and said, "Now why didn't I think of that?"

"Because you're too busy thinking about Wexler."

Devlin's meal arrived, and he wolfed it down. He spoke to the concierge on the phone, making arrangements for Susan's massage. Then he sat with her on the couch and told her, "You hang in. I'll see you later." Susan kissed him quickly and told him to leave. The car service sedan was waiting outside and Devlin ducked into the backseat. He gave the driver the address of Parker's office.

When he arrived, shortly after two o'clock, Parker handed him a folder with seven single-spaced pages of information.

Parker said, "I haven't read it yet myself. I suggest we sit and see what we've got."

Both men sat and read. By the second page, Devlin realized that Parker's skip tracers had uncovered so much information they were almost buried in it.

They had started with the properties Susan told him Wexler owned.

They quickly discovered that the buildings were held by the Colville Corporation. From there they had searched databases that listed every incorporation in every state of the U.S. They found Colville Enterprises, Colville Construction, Colville Incorporated, and Colville Partners, all incorporated in Delaware. Each of the Colville entities was a subsidiary of the other. They hadn't yet uncovered the major stockholder.

Once they found the corporate entities, they started searching for bank accounts. They found accounts for the various Colville corporations in New York State, Nevada, California, Grand Cayman, and Liechtenstein.

A search of property records in Manhattan, the Bronx, and Brooklyn listed thirty-seven properties owned by four of the Colville corporations they had uncovered.

They went back to the banks that held Colville accounts and crosschecked them with Patrick Kelly's three accounts at Chemical Bank in New York. The skip tracers found several wire transfers of money from the Nevada and California banks to Kelly's account. It was obvious to Devlin that one of Parker's skip tracers had a connection at Chemical Bank. Otherwise, it would have been nearly impossible to find the wire transfers. The problem was, they didn't have a similar source at the Nevada and California banks. They had no proof who was behind the transfers. They couldn't prove that Kelly was obtaining money from Wexler.

They had started to search through other records emanating from the Colville corporations and the properties they owned. They poured through Dun & Bradstreet reports, insurance company title records, credit surveys, loan applications, mortgages, and other financial records. There was even a page listing all the companies or individuals whose phone numbers were on Kelly's long-distance bill. But there still was no definite link between Kelly and Wexler.

The last page of the report listed eighteen of the thirty-seven properties owned by Colville: six in Manhattan, six in the Bronx, and six in Brooklyn. Some of the properties listed housed legitimate clubs, restaurants, or bars.

Of the six in Manhattan, two properties housed after-hours clubs that Devlin had visited: Eternity and the Starlight Club. Devlin was sure that at the very least Wexler and Kelly were partners in both clubs, with Wexler acting as the front man to hide Kelly's involvement. But so far Wexler's name was buried too deeply in the paper trail.

The properties in the Bronx and Brooklyn also had tenants that were clubs or restaurants or bars. Devlin assumed some of the buildings also housed after-hours clubs.

The final interesting piece of information came from an analysis of the Colville accounts at various banks. Not one of the accounts held more than $15,000. It was almost certain that a great deal of the money had to be hidden offshore in places like Grand Cayman or Liechtenstein. Millions could be wire-transferred in seconds. Given enough time, the skip tracers would probably find it, but Devlin didn't have any time.

He looked up from his reading and said, "Your people have done a remarkable job. An incredible job. But I've got nothing here that links these two for sure."

"I know. It's just a matter of time until they tie that part up. Some piece of paper or bank account or corporate document will pop up that links them."

"Mr. Parker, I wish I could give you more time, but I've got to have something by tonight, tomorrow at the latest."

Parker looked at his watch. "We've only got a couple of work hours left on the East Coast. We won't break this today. We'll be damn lucky to have something by tomorrow."

Devlin started pacing the room. "All right. Your people are doing great, but right now they've got too much. They'll get buried before they get what I need. Tell them to forget about digging into the bank accounts. We know Kelly is getting funds from Colville. We know Wexler is behind Colville, but they can't waste any more time tracing backgrounds on the corporations. Unless one of your people has an in with a bank officer at one of the Nevada or California banks, we won't get the proof at that end.

"Tell them to concentrate on the New York properties. If something happens to Wexler, Kelly has to have access to the properties and the money. There's got to be a link."

"If that's the way you think we should go at it, fine."

"Don't straightjacket them. Just try to keep them from wasting time on anything that won't link Kelly and Wexler."

"Call me tomorrow."

"I'll *see* you tomorrow. Five o'clock and then it's all over."

Parker nodded. "All right. We'll work until the bell sounds."

"One last thing," said Devlin.

"What?"

"I've said it before, but I'll say it again. Lives depend on this."

"I understand."

Devlin left the agency. He knew a lot more about Wexler than he had before. He also knew that if he had to bet his life that Parker's skip tracers would succeed, he'd be riding a long shot.

#

Uptown, the men Devlin was trying to link together were having tea at the Ritz Carlton on Central Park South. They weren't happy either.

Kelly handed Wexler copies of the Bellevue Hospital admission forms on Joe and Eddie. "The Manhattan North boys were called into one hell of a holy mess at the Marriott. Your boy Devlin made shit out of them."

"Apparently he had some help."

"Yes. A godawful big gun was his help. Why the hell didn't you call in my boys? At least they'd have been armed."

"I didn't know that Devlin would be there. Not to mention you've had your chance to find him and not come up with a damn thing."

"And not likely that we will, thanks to you. He's buried deep now, my friend."

"Only figuratively. I want him actually buried. Broken and buried somewhere nobody will ever find him. I want him buried alive."

Kelly pointed his finger at Wexler. "If you want Devlin, you damn well better go ahead with this exchange he wants."

"Fine."

"My men will be there. We'll take him. You just show up."

"Fine."

"Where are you keeping the girl?"

"I've moved her to an empty apartment in my Sixtieth Street building."

"Is she in any kind of decent shape?"

"She's got a broken finger, that's all."

"I'll send a man to fix it. Are you feeding her? Keeping your thugs away from her? I want her walking and presentable. If Devlin sees her damaged, he might try to shoot you then and there."

Wexler said, "What are you, afraid of that fool?"

"Listen to me, Robert. This fellow Devlin is no fool. He's a professional. He's already done a hell of a lot of damage. And if he has the balls to meet you, he's a dangerous man."

"Well, isn't that your specialty? Taking care of dangerous people?"

"Yes. So don't try and do anything with those amateurs of yours." Kelly looked at his watch. "Give me tonight and tomorrow to get the men I need for this. Set it up for tomorrow night. Ten o'clock."

"Where?"

"Pick someplace nice."

"How about the Plaza? The Oak Room Bar."

"Fine. I'll have the place covered."

Kelly finished his tea and left.

CHAPTER **42**

After leaving Parker's office, Devlin checked his answering machine and got the message that Daryl had been moved to an apartment on 60th Street. The car service took him to the address, and he quickly spotted the plumber's van parked across the street.

He walked up to the van and knocked twice. Hank Dixon popped open the door, and Devlin got into the passenger seat. The old hippie sipped from a cardboard cup of coffee. His partner was asleep in the back.

Devlin asked, "How are you doing?"

"Fine. They moved her about noon like you figured. They have her in that four-story building across the street. Front apartment. Third floor."

"How do you know?"

"Saw 'em pull the shades down when they got in there."

"Who's with her?"

"Two guys. I'd say one of 'em was a cop, plainclothes. The other one's a straight up thug. Dark hair, big head, mean lookin' son of a bitch."

"How'd she look?"

"Couldn't tell, really. She was walking all right. I think they did something to her hand. She had it wrapped in a towel."

"Any way we can find out what's going on in there?"

"Well, I been thinkin' about that. There's no sight lines into the place. I called in about an hour ago and ordered some equipment—a small mic and a transmitter. Shouldn't be too hard to get it on the front door of the apartment. No problem broadcasting from there to here, so we can keep it small enough so they won't see it. We won't hear much, but if she starts screaming or something, we'll know."

"You think you'll have any problem getting it placed?"

"Nope."

"Okay. Do it as soon as you can."

"Will do. But that's it. Our specialty is surveillance, Mr. Devlin. If something goes down in there, we ain't chargin' in to stop it. What do you suggest we do?"

"Call 911. Tell them a cop needs assistance. Say it's a 10-13. Tell 'em you heard shots. Send them to that address, that apartment. That should raise enough hell to stop whatever's happening. Then call me." Devlin handed him a matchbook from the Carlyle. "Room 418. That's the best we can do. I'm planning to have her out of there sometime tomorrow."

"Okay, boss. We'll keep an eye on her."

"And an ear."

"You got it."

Devlin headed downtown. Twenty minutes later, he was sitting with Sam Zitter in his office at Intrepid. He told him the latest developments.

"How many people they got guarding her?" Zitter asked.

"It looks like one detective and one of Wexler's bouncers. I think it's the third guy who jumped us at the Marriott."

"So how's the girl?"

"The surveillance team said she looked okay. I know that they broke one of the fingers on her hand."

"Why the fuck don't you get some real cops and go in and get her out?"

"Like who? I can't be sure I'll end up with dirty cops working for Kelly who will arrest me instead."

"How about your pal Freedman?"

"I don't want to get him involved in this. More important, if I take Daryl out of there now, I lose my chance to get to Wexler."

Zitter leaned back and considered everything Devlin said. He had on a white shirt, brown tie, and brown pants. His jacket was a weird purplish color. Devlin thought the man should stick to suits. At least the jacket and coat wouldn't clash.

"I guess you're right. Pretty fucking dangerous game. Especially if they're being rough on the girl."

"My people are going to try to get a mic on the apartment. If they hear any screams, they'll break it up."

"So what do you want me to do?"

"Two things. Find Kelly and set up a meeting with him for tomorrow at seven o'clock."

"Seven o'clock?"

"Yes. Just you and Kelly."

"And what happens at that meeting?"

"I'll tell you tomorrow at six."

"Tell me now."

"It depends on what I find out tomorrow by five."

"You're playing it awful fucking tight, Jack."

"I wish I didn't have to. You think you can find Kelly?"

Zitter waved his hand at Devlin and said, "Find him? Sure. But I don't know if he'll want to talk to me."

"That won't be a problem. By tomorrow he'll want to talk to you."

"What are you going to do?" asked Zitter.

"You don't want to know."

After Devlin left Zitter's office, he picked up James Pony and went back to the Carlyle. The living room was empty. Pony sat down on the couch. Devlin walked into the bedroom and found Susan sitting in a chair reading the newspaper.

Devlin asked, "You get any sleep?"

"Some. It's been a long afternoon. You're a little late. You should have made that call by now."

"He can wait five minutes." Devlin picked up the phone and asked Susan the number. She recited it, and Devlin dialed.

Wexler answered, "Talk."

"Devlin here."

"Tomorrow night, Devlin. Bring the slut. Oak Room Bar at the Plaza Hotel. A comfortable public place where we'll all be safe. Ten o'clock."

"Fine. Just us, Wexler, and the women."

"Of course. We'll have a nice double-date."

Devlin hung up, turned to Susan and said, "Done. Ten o'clock tomorrow night."

"One more day."

"And part of a night," said Devlin.

Susan walked to the window in the bedroom. A quiet summer evening was settling over the city. She stood in the red sunset, her golden hair gleaming, her white skin turning rosy. Without looking at him, she asked Devlin, "When are you going out?"

"Late. About one-thirty or two."

"Have you slept yet?"

"No."

"You'd better get some rest."

"I will.

"When this is over and you get Daryl back, I'm never going to see you again, am I?"

Devlin walked over and stood next to her by the window. "That depends on quite a few things."

"Like what? How Daryl feels about you?"

"No. I'm not getting her away from Wexler for myself."

"But you can't stop thinking about her, can you?"

"Not really. Not until she's safe."

"Oh God."

"What?"

"How the hell am I going to make it through another night and another day? I want a drink so bad my fucking bones ache. I want you. I want a job. I want my sister safe. I want a place to live. Something. Anything. And I can't have any of it."

Devlin turned her so she was facing him. "There's no reason you can't have all of that."

"What if I want you in my life?"

"Decide when this is over."

"Christ, I can't stand hearing that anymore— 'when this is over'." Susan leaned into Devlin's arms and said, "Let me lie next to you while you sleep. We don't have to make love again. I just want to feel you against me. I just want you with me for now."

Devlin stretched out on the bed with Susan next to him. He held her with his right arm, wishing he was a giant magnet that could draw all the fear, pain, addiction and anger out of her. At one point she seemed to shiver, but she didn't say a word. And Devlin didn't stop holding her, even after he fell into an exhausted sleep.

CHAPTER 43

When Hank Dixon saw the man with the black doctor's bag get out of the cab in front of the 60th Street building, he knew it was his best opportunity.

He picked up the small microphone and transmitter and quickly walked across the street. He timed his approach to the front door so that as the man with the doctor's bag was buzzed inside, he was able to move forward, stop the door before it closed, and step into the lobby. Dixon had a ring of keys in his hand as if he were about to unlock the lobby door for himself. The doctor turned around and saw him come in after him, but the keys in the man's hand deflected any protest he felt like making.

Dixon walked up the stairs slowly, letting the doctor get a flight ahead of him. He stopped when he heard the doctor turn into the hallway. He waited in the stairwell and listened. He had been right. The doctor was going to the apartment where they were keeping the girl.

As the door on the top floor closed, Dixon ascended quietly up the last flight of stairs and walked down the hallway to the door. He counted on the voices of the men inside to mask his footsteps.

He waited quietly the door, straining to hear if the voices moved to the other room.

Inside, Messina and Donovan were taking the doctor in to see Daryl, who was lying motionless on the bed. She had taken so much aspirin and Valium that her ears were ringing. The finger still throbbed. She hadn't been able to keep any food or liquids down. She hadn't been able to shower or bathe for almost two days. Her skin looked chalky and sweaty.

She rested the hand with the broken finger on her hip, the thumb hooked inside her belt to hold the hand in place. The broken finger jutted off at such a strange angle that it pointed toward her foot. Most of the little finger was purple. It had swollen to three times its normal size.

The doctor was a retired police surgeon named McDermott. Kelly called on him for injuries that couldn't be seen in hospitals. The money Kelly paid him supplemented McDermott's pension checks.

McDermott's brow furrowed when he looked at the finger. He set his doctor's bag on the bed and went to work quickly. He used Novocain to numb her entire hand. He carefully examined the finger. It was so swollen and misshapen he could hardly move the finger back into place. He pulled and adjusted the bones the best he could. A skilled hand surgeon might have been able to set the break hours ago, but not now.

When he got the finger into what he guessed was the best position, he wrapped it in a flexible bandage. He couldn't risk taping it. The pain from the swelling would be unbearable. He knew the finger would never heal properly without surgery, and maybe not even then.

He finished his wrapping, then went to the bathroom to soak two rolls of plaster of paris. He brought the rolls back and molded a cast to protect the finger and hand.

When he was finished, he roused Daryl gently and told her, "Listen to me, dear. I've done what I can for your hand. When the Novocain wears off, it will hurt. I'm leaving some painkillers for you. They told me they gave you Scotch and Valium. Don't drink any more alcohol or take any more Valium." He held up a small vial of pills. "If you can't stand the pain, take one of these every four hours. It's Tylenol with codeine. Don't take it if you don't need it. And keep the hand elevated. You've got to keep the swelling down."

"Okay," said Daryl. "When do I get out of here? What's going on?"

"Soon, I'm sure. Then get to a hand surgeon so you can have this taken care of properly. I haven't fixed it. I've only done enough to stabilize it for the moment. Do you understand?"

"Yes."

By the time Kelly's doctor appeared again on 60th Street, Dixon was already back in the van listening to the audio transmission with his partner, Vincent. He had placed the microphone above the small opening between the jamb and the top of the door. He couldn't quite make out the words. But if anyone screamed or there was any other loud noise it would come through loud and clear.

CHAPTER 44

At ten o'clock Devlin ordered a room service dinner at the Carlyle for himself, Susan, and James. If Susan couldn't drink, at least she could eat.

Pony and Devlin ate sparingly. Susan ate more than both of them.

She sat back on the couch and announced, "Even if I had some booze there's no room for it."

"That's the idea."

Devlin got up and went into the bedroom. He was there for almost an hour. When he returned, Susan asked, "When are you leaving?"

"About an hour."

No one said much after that. Pony dozed. Susan read the *Times* again. Devlin sat quietly, deep in thought. At 12:57 A.M., Devlin asked Pony to come into the bedroom with him.

Devlin motioned to Pony to sit in the chair near the window. He reached under the bed and pulled out the Halliburton suitcase. He placed it on the bed, turned to Pony, and said, "Tonight, we fight."

Pony smiled and said, "Good."

Devlin sat on the bed facing him. "I'll explain what's going to happen as we go. I can't be sure of everything, but just follow my lead, and it should be fine. You'll see exactly what I'm going to do when it happens. We're going to have to move fast. Hit hard. The focus will be on me. But I need you to cover my back."

"What exactly are we going to do?"

"We're going to make it very expensive for anyone to be in business with Robert Wexler."

Devlin stood up and turned to the case. He snapped open the lid and revealed a cache of weapons. He picked out two, three-ounce cans of Cap Stun spray, which was more powerful than any tear gas or Mace, one pair of brass knuckles, a fighting stick about two feet long, and a small chain with weighted ends called a Manriki Gusari. He laid everything neatly on the bed and lifted out a lightweight bulletproof vest made of Kevlar.

He told Pony, "I can't offer you any of these weapons, or a vest. You have to stand up to a frisk."

"I don't want them."

"If you ever get the chance, wear the vest. It'll stop a bullet and make it very hard to get a knife into you."

"I've never worn one."

Devlin was already stripping off his shirt and putting on the vest. It fit very tightly around his torso and closed on the sides with Velcro straps.

Pony watched asked Devlin, "How many times have you been wounded?"

"I've been shot twice. Stabbed a couple of times and cut up pretty bad once."

"Don't want any more of it, huh?"

"No. Most of it you hardly feel when it happens. Especially the stab wounds. More like a hard punch. Slashes burn, you feel the blood making your clothes wet, but you don't feel the cut very much until later. Not much later. And while they heal. They take a hell of a lot of time to heal." Devlin asked Pony, "How are you against knives?"

"Very good, I think. I don't like knives."

"Good. Seems like in every crowd somebody has a knife."

Devlin looked at Pony. He was dressed much like the night before. Black silk shirt buttoned to the neck, black pants, black shoes.

Devlin worried for a moment about bringing Pony into tonight's battle with no weapons or armor. Devlin knew Pony's skin under his shirt had yet to be scarred. He hoped it would stay that way tonight.

"When do we go?" asked Pony.

"Right now."

They walked to the door together, but Pony waited in the hallway when Devlin turned to tell Susan, "If I don't get back, you've got the money. Take it and go someplace until things cool off."

"I'll expect you at dawn," she said. "Don't talk about not coming back."

"Just in case. If I don't get back by the morning, get out, leave a message for me here under the name Mr. Johnson telling me where you are."

"I told you—don't even talk about not getting back here."

Devlin nodded once and left.

Outside a car was waiting, but this time it wasn't from the car service. Chow's people had arranged something different. The car was a gray, four-door Chevy Caprice, rented under a fictitious name through Pacific Rim. If they had to abandon it, there would be no link back to anyone.

The driver was Mike Trey from the car service. Devlin gave him the first address. It was for a club called the Tomb on the five hundred block of West 21st Street. It was one of the six listed as being owned by Wexler's Colville Corporation on Parker's report.

It was 1:15 A.M. when Mike drove up to the club entrance. Devlin told Mike, "Pull up and double-park about twenty feet ahead there. Leave the engine running and the back doors closed but not shut. Don't double-park too close. We want to be able to get in on both sides."

"You got it, boss."

Devlin put his hand on Mike's shoulder. "You wait for us. When we get in, pull out fast, but don't hit anything."

"Yes, sir."

They got out of the car, and Devlin told Pony, "You go ahead and get in before me. You've got the right look, they should let you in.

Once you get in, stay near the entrance and wait for me to get inside. There'll be trouble when I come in, so if they gang up on me near the doorway, help keep them off me so I can get all the way inside."

"And what happens inside?"

"Keep as many of the bouncers off me as you can. When I leave, help me fight my way out. I'll have my gun and weapons, so let me clear the way."

Without another word, Pony floated down the street.

At the door to the club, three bouncers stood guarding the velvet ropes. A small ferret-faced man in a baggy suit sat on a stool next to the door. He worked the door, telling the bouncers who was allowed to pass the ropes and enter the club. He sat hunched on his stool, his dark hair oiled and pulled back into a ponytail. He wore eyeliner under eyes that constantly darted around the crowd.

When Pony walked up to the entrance, the doorman nodded to the bouncers, and they unhooked the rope for Pony to pass. There were at least a dozen hopefuls who waited to be nodded in with Pony, but they didn't even get a glance from the doorman.

Pony walked into the darkened doorway and found himself standing in a small foyer. Another bouncer, dressed in black pants and a tuxedo shirt, ran a hand-held metal detector around Pony's body. When the bouncer finished with the metal detector, he patted Pony down with his other hand, just to be sure there were no non-metallic weapons. Pony stood and felt the big hand forcefully pushing around on his body. He tried to gauge the man's strength without offering any resistance. These were the big men Devlin had told him about. It seemed the strategy was to position enough human tonnage around these places so that the mass of muscle and bone automatically kept everyone in line. Pony figured the man patting him down weighed at least 250 pounds.

Devlin waited up the street for Pony to get all the way inside. He took one deep breath and let it out slowly. He squared his shoulders and walked straight for the club entrance.

When the skinny, intense doorman saw Devlin coming, he muttered to the bouncers, "No way. Not this guy."

The three big bouncers perked up like huge dogs smelling meat. The biggest of the trio stood right behind one of the stanchions that held the ropes. He purposefully clipped the rope in place as Devlin approached. He wore a leather jacket over a black T-shirt and black jeans. Devlin figured him for about six five, 240 or 250 pounds. The bouncer crossed his arms to make them look bigger and swelled out his chest as Devlin approached.

The second bouncer was parallel to the one near the stanchion. He was much shorter but very stocky and broad. He looked like a skinhead: shaved head, sleeveless T-shirt, black jeans with suspenders, and combat boots. His huge arms were covered with dense blue tattoos.

The last bouncer was next to the door, just to the right of the doorman. He was the last line of defense outside the club. Devlin didn't bother to look at anyone other than the biggest bouncer. He was locked into an eyeball to eyeball stare with him.

Devlin kept looking right at him, waiting for him to waver. Devlin let the fury swell up in him—bringing the fire that would fuel his movements and give him strength.

He kept walking toward the entrance, not breaking stride.

The fighting stick was in his back pants pocket. Both of Devlin's hands were full. He kept staring at the big bouncer's eyes so the man wouldn't see his hands.

The bouncer motioned for Devlin to stop. Devlin didn't even hesitate. He stuck the Cap Stun canister an inch from the bouncer's nose and sprayed him in the face. The big man bellowed and staggered back, rubbing at his face and gasping for air.

Devlin kicked over the stanchion to knock the velvet rope down. The shorter, skinhead bouncer was already charging, head lowered, arms spread wide to grab Devlin and knock him down. Devlin stepped slightly back and to his left and twisted a tremendous left hook into the bouncer's bald head. The force of it stopped the bouncer in his tracks. Devlin's hand would have been shattered under the impact with the man's skull if he hadn't been wearing the brass knuckles. As it was, Devlin felt the jolt of the impact all the way up into his shoulder and neck. The bouncer's scalp split open, he spun in mid-air and landed on his knees. Blood sprayed across the sidewalk. He wasn't knocked out, but he stayed on his knees trying to get his bearings.

Devlin kicked him in the sternum, doubling the man over. He fell forward on all fours gasping for air. Devlin used the same foot to kick him hard behind the ear, knocking him into oblivion.

The ferret-faced doorman was already yelling into a walkie-talkie for help. The first bouncer was still incapacitated by the spray, but he was also enraged. He charged at Devlin, swinging a wild roundhouse right. Devlin ducked, twisted, grabbed the man's extended arm with his left hand, and punched his right fist into the big man's ribs just under the armpit. Then he added his force to the bouncer's forward momentum and rammed him into a parked car. The bouncer's head took most of the impact, and he was out.

The third bouncer suddenly found himself alone against someone who had just wiped out two of his partners in less than a minute.

Devlin walked toward the entrance, and the doorman ran past the bouncer to get inside. Devlin snarled at the third bouncer, "Move."

The bouncer had enough bravado to stand with his hands up ready to fight, so Devlin sprayed him with the Cap Stun, kicked him in the balls, then shoved him away.

The bouncer with the metal detector had been alerted by the doorman. As Devlin stepped into the foyer, he rushed Devlin, hitting him hard mid-chest with his shoulder, driving Devlin against the wall. Devlin absorbed the impact and the bouncer made the mistake of straightening up to hit Devlin, who he figured would be paralyzed from being slammed into the wall. Devlin banged his forehead into the man's nose, knocking him back. He punched his brass-knuckled fist into bouncer's throat and jaw with a vicious uppercut. The bouncer went down hard, and Devlin charged into the club.

Inside the club the doorman was screaming for help. The club was basically one huge room with a bar on the side and a bandstand at the far end. A heavy metal band was playing deafening music, but somehow the doorman's calls for help had gotten through and Pony could make out several large men heading for the entrance. They were pushing and knocking people out of the way. The crowd was opening for them, but closing behind and following the bouncers. The excitement of seeing a fight was drawing everyone toward the back of the club.

Pony stepped out of the crowd and met the first bouncer rushing toward the door. He had the advantage of surprise and timed a powerful spinning backhand punch that hit the man right on the jaw, sending him down hard enough so that his head bounced on the concrete floor.

A second bouncer following the man sidestepped his falling partner and lunged at Pony, trying to grab him around the neck. Pony ducked and swept the man's feet out from under him with his right foot. The bouncer went down hard. A third bouncer grabbed Pony in a crushing bear hug from behind.

Pony grabbed the man's arm and shoulder and rolled forward, pulling the big man over him. They both hit the floor hard. The bouncer's grip was broken. Pony rolled free and onto his feet.

Pony tried to move deeper into the club to draw the men away from Devlin, but the bouncer who had Pony in a bear hug was up on his feet. He grabbed at Pony's arm before he could move away. Pony turned and exploded into a flurry of punches to the man's face, chin, sternum, followed by fast Muay-Thai kicks to ribs.

Devlin was inside now, just as two more bouncers made it to the entrance. Devlin pulled out the fighting stick and cracked one of the onrushing men squarely on the bridge of his nose, breaking the cartilage and causing immediate pain. Devlin shoved the two-foot fighting stick into the bouncer's gut, taking away his breath. In the same movement, he pulled the stick back, spun down into a crouch, and caught the other onrushing bouncer squarely in the shins with a baseball swing of the stick that cracked his feet out from under him.

It was now total chaos in the dark club. The band was still wailing away on stage, unable to see what was happening beyond the lights shining on them. People were screaming and yelling. Dozens were running toward the front exit. Others were massed around the fallen bouncers. Two or three fights were breaking out among the patrons.

Devlin could just make out Pony ahead of him amid the shoving, pushing crowd. He didn't know how many more bouncers were in the club, but he saw two of the bartenders leap over the bar with small bats in their hands. Both were coming right for him.

Devlin took out his Caspian Arms .45, pointed it toward the ceiling, and squeezed the trigger twice. The booming blasts from the gun exploded against the brick walls and concrete floor.

The sound was deafening, and the effect instant. Hundreds of people screamed, ran, or dropped to the floor. One bartender stopped, but the other one was crazy enough to come at Devlin with his upraised club. Devlin ducked the blow, punched him in the stomach with a brass-knuckled fist, and slapped him across the head with the heavy barrel of the .45. The bartender collapsed.

Devlin jumped over the bar, took his fighting stick, shoved it into the shelves behind the bar, and raced down the length of the bar knocking down and breaking practically every bottle of liquor on display.

He came back the other way smashing mirrors and breaking glassware. The gunshots had silenced the band. Almost all the club-goers had fled out every exit. Devlin saw two doors pop open near the front. Two of the bouncers had recovered and were heading toward the bar to trap Devlin. Devlin pointed his .45 at them and yelled, "Get down."

Both put up their hands and stopped.

"Get on the ground. Face down. Now!'

The bouncers did as they were told. Devlin looked around. Nobody else was coming after him. The place was a wreck, and less than five minutes had elapsed since Devlin fought his way in.

Pony had finished off the first bouncer he'd stopped from charging Devlin with an elbow to the throat and moved toward the front entrance so he could find Devlin.

Devlin tried to see where Pony was, but Pony's black clothes made him hard to spot in the darkened club. He finally saw Pony making his way toward him. Devlin waved at him and pointed to the front exit. He still had the brass knuckles on his left hand and the .45 in the right. The two bouncers near the bar watched him but stayed down on the floor.

Devlin ran toward the exit. A few patrons still in the club gave him a wide berth. Pony followed behind, covering his back. Devlin holstered the .45 and surged out the door into the crowd outside the wrecked club.

Before he could move past the crowd, Devlin felt someone slam into him from behind—knocking him forward into a group of people. They all went down, with the first bouncer Devlin had sprayed on top of him.

The bouncer, screaming and cursing, grabbed Devlin's hair and tried to slam his face into the sidewalk. Luckily, there were two people trapped under Devlin, and instead of the sidewalk, Devlin's face hit someone's back. It still hurt.

Pony came out of the crowd and saw Devlin go down. He had let happen exactly what Devlin had asked him to prevent, an attack from behind.

For the first time in Pony's life, he felt rage surge through him. He flew at the bouncer straddling Devlin and slammed his knee into the man's kidney. The bouncer grunted in pain, but still held Devlin's hair. Pony grabbed the man's throat and began crushing it. The man let go of Devlin and desperately clutched at Pony's hands.

Pony, with a strength born of fury, lifted the man off Devlin, let go of his grip and delivered two open-handed blows to the bouncer's ears, exploding both eardrums. He slammed two punches into the man's ribs, then grabbed the man's pants at the ankles and wrenched his feet out from under him. The big man fell back and hit full-length onto the pavement, cracking open the back of his head. Devlin got to his feet, grabbed Pony, and headed for the car.

Devlin didn't hear any sirens, but he expected them any second. He shoved his way out into the street and spotted the Chevy parked where he had told Mike Trey to wait. He and Pony ran to the car and got in without a word.

Devlin yelled, "Go!"

Mike pulled out and drove to the corner. Traffic was stalled, so he bounced up on the sidewalk, passed all the stopped cars, bounced down the curb, and headed north on the West Side Highway.

Mike turned and asked, "Shit, are you guys all right?"

Devlin calmly told him, "Watch where you're driving."

Mike looked at them in the rearview mirror to see if they were damaged or bleeding. "Christ, what happened in there?"

Devlin said, "Drive to Eighth Avenue and 35th Street." Mike stopped asking questions and drove.

By the time Devlin's car was on the West Side Highway, a call was being made to Wexler at the Starlight reporting what had happened. In two seconds, Wexler knew the man being described was Devlin. He cut off the caller, cleared the line, and dialed Kelly's private number while making a mental list of his clubs that he would call and warn.

Devlin sat in the backseat taking deep breaths. It had been close. Very close. He felt the back of his head to see if his cut had opened. It hadn't. He pulled the brass knuckles off his fist and flexed his hand. His knuckles were scuffed, but no serious damage had been done to his hand. His shoulder twinged a little, but nothing else felt damaged. More pain would come tomorrow.

He turned to Pony and asked, "You all right?"

He nodded. "Yes."

"Your hands okay?"

Pony smiled and said, "Yes. It takes so many hard blows to knock one of them down."

"You can't hit them in the face or head. It doesn't do it."

"Hard to get enough room to use my feet. I'm sorry I let that one get you from behind."

"You got him off me, that's what counts. You did goddamn great, James. Unarmed in there? Goddamn great."

Pony nodded and drifted back into himself.

Devlin closed his eyes, willing his heart to stop pounding, wondering if they could survive another battle like the one they had just gone through.

When they pulled up to 35th and Eighth, Devlin checked his watch. It was 2:15 A.M. He told Mike to park about ten yards past a bar called the Dead Bait Club.

Devlin walked quickly toward the entrance with Pony following close behind. The door to the bar looked as if it belonged on a farmhouse in Mississippi. There was a hubcap nailed to the door and under it the initials DBC, painted in red.

There were no bouncers outside. No ropes or stanchions. No crowd waiting to get in. Devlin and Pony walked into the bar. At the entrance, a bouncer looked them over but didn't speak to them or frisk them. He was about six three and looked like a college athlete except for his Elvis haircut and sideburns.

Devlin took a quick look around. A long bar was on the left. Opposite the bar was a wall covered with signage from small town diners, country gas stations, and hardware stores that were in business during the forties and fifties. After about thirty feet the room opened up into a wider area with tables and chairs. A small bandstand filled the back of that room, and a five-man band was on the stage playing Zydeco music. The place was packed with yuppies. The joint was making a lot of money for the Wexler/Kelly empire.

Devlin told Pony, "Just make sure that bouncer doesn't try to be a hero."

Pony nodded. Devlin made his way through the crowd until he arrived at the bathrooms situated on the left, down a short hallway off the dance floor.

He went into the men's room. A young man in suspenders and tie was using the single urinal. The toilet stall was empty. Devlin told him to get out. He looked at Devlin and decided not to argue.

Devlin used his fighting stick and the weighted metal chain, the manriki gusari, to pull apart the water supply pipes for the toilet, one urinal, and the sink. Hundreds of gallons of water poured out of the broken plumbing.

He burst into the ladies' room, yelling for everyone to get out and did the same to the plumbing in there. The women in the bathroom were screaming. Water started flooding into the club. People standing near the restrooms bumped and shoved each other to get away from the flood. The manager of the club ran over trying to figure out what the hell had happened. The bouncer headed toward the commotion, but Pony stepped in front of him and told him, "Don't go back there."

The bouncer put his hand on Pony's chest and tried to shove him out of the way. Pony grabbed the back of the man's hand, twisted it counterclockwise and pulled it down, stopping just before the bouncer's wrist snapped. The pain immobilized him, Pony spun the bigger man around and brought the arm up in a hammerlock. He calmly told the bouncer, "You don't want to go back there. Just walk out the door, and I won't have to hurt you."

The bouncer knew he was overmatched and did as he was told.

The water reached the dining room. People jumped up from their seats trying to get away from it. The band stopped playing. Three drunks trying to get away from the water fell into a table sending food and drinks flying. Two guys started shoving each other. More tables turned over. The Zydeco band unplugged their instruments and hurried into the kitchen.

Devlin picked up beer bottles off the bar and threw them at the mirrors and liquor along the back bar, yelling for everyone to get out. Some people stood back and watched Devlin, but most cleared out. The bartender jumped over the bar and ran.

The manager yelled at Devlin, "What the fuck are you doing? I'm calling the cops, you asshole! I'm calling the cops!"

Devlin tipped over the jukebox, smashed the club's soundboard with his fighting stick, and threw a chair into the lights overhanging the small stage.

The manager was hysterical. He wouldn't stop screaming. Devlin picked up the phone on the reservations desk, rammed it into the manager's stomach, and yelled, "Then shut up and call them!"

The blow doubled over the manager, and he dropped to his knees in the dirty water still running out all over the floor.

Devlin walked along the bar, raking off glasses and drinks with his fighting stick. Near the exit, he picked up a bar stool and walked out the front door.

The place was destroyed. The manager got to his feet. His shoes and pants were soaked. He felt like throwing up. Water, food, broken glass, and liquor covered the floor.

Just as the manager started to dial 911, Devlin threw the bar stool through the front window, breaking the bar's neon sign and sending the manager sprawling into the water, soaking the rest of his clothes.

The whole thing hadn't taken less than ten minutes.

By the time Devlin left the Dead Bait Club, Kelly had reached three of his detective squads. He dispatched each team to a different club. Wexler was at the Starlight methodically calling each of their properties and warning them to be on the lookout for Devlin.

Pony and Devlin were back in the car heading uptown on Eighth Avenue. Devlin checked his watch. It was 2:47. The next place on his list was Eternity, the after-hours club on 56th Street. He told Mike, "Drive as fast as you can."

He turned to Pony and said, "One more. We'll do one more, and then we disappear. If we're lucky, we'll still be ahead of them. This next place is much more dangerous than the others. The guys running it will definitely have guns, so stay out of the action except to keep any spectators out of it who want to get in the way. Really watch out in there, okay?"

Pony nodded and asked, "Do you want me to go in first again?"

"Yes. And I'm going to leave you in there a few minutes so no one connects you with me. Nurse a beer at one of the tables. The place has two levels. Don't sit upstairs. Stay in the bar area."

Pony nodded and for the first time felt a ripple of fear hit him.

When he walked in, Pony was frisked by the same man in the tweed cap Devlin had met the first time he was there. Pony guessed the man was Irish. By the liquor on his breath and his fumbling touch as he frisked him, Pony was sure the man was drunk. He would be no problem if it came to a fight. Pony looked up at the top of the stairs and saw the real problem—the big, long-haired kid in the army fatigue jacket. Pony felt uneasy at having him loom so large from the height of a double flight of stairs. He pictured the bouncer charging down the stairs and knew there would be no way to stop him, and no way to avoid him in the narrow stairwell.

As soon as the Irishman finished frisking him, Pony paid his ten dollars and hurried up the stairs into the club. He wanted to get off the stairway and past the bouncer as quickly as possible.

For the first time that night, Pony realized he was worried. Devlin had told him to stay out of the way, as if this one would be too dangerous for Pony. But why send him in here if he didn't want him to do anything? Watch his back, he'd said. Keep the spectators out of it. It didn't explain much, but one thing was clear—there was no way Devlin could make it up those stairs once the doorman at the bottom frisked him and found his weapons.

Was he coming in without them? Pony shook his head hard once to banish the questions in his mind, went up to the bar, and asked for a beer. The bartender put a wet can of Budweiser on the bar and took his ten-dollar bill.

Pony picked up his change and walked away to find a place to sit. He found a table with an empty chair near the far end of the bar and sat down.

Pony's table was at the corner of the L-shaped room. He could see everything from the entrance to the stairs that led to the upper level.

This was nothing like the other two places they had been in that night. It was dark and furtive and populated by a weird mix of people. There were working men in T-shirts and businessmen in suits. One person sitting at the bar seemed to be a transvestite. It was noisy, but only in bursts. Most of the noise came from the gambling area to his right where a few people played the big wheel and the slot machines.

Sitting in a chair next to the slot machines was the man in charge of the gambling. He was tall and thin with a hawk face. He wore a brown fedora, a white silk scarf, and a light sweater over designer jeans. He had on tinted glasses and watched more than he spoke.

The man moved in quick spurts, getting up and going to the big wheel to make a payment or collect money for chips. Coming back to his seat and sitting quickly as he checked on the slot machines.

He handled the money very swiftly and easily, keeping the chips and markers in a cigar box. Pony had a feeling that if the man decided not to pay someone, he would make it stick and that would be that.

Pony was beginning to understand what Devlin meant. The whole place felt dangerous. Perhaps that's why so many people came.

Pony sat waiting for Devlin. He kept his eye on the door watching for him. Each passing minute made him feel more uneasy.

And then suddenly, the sound of gunfire exploded in the stairwell. Pony saw the bouncer in the army jacket jump up. He heard the big bouncer's footsteps thundering down the stairs.

The bartender and the gambler also moved as soon as they heard the shots. The bartender grabbed a handgun from under the bar, and the gambler stood up and pulled a gun out of a holster at the small of his back.

Downstairs, Devlin had done his work very quickly. When the drunken doorman let him in, Devlin waited for him to close the door, and when he turned to frisk him, hit him as hard as he could with a fast right hook. The punch lifted the man off his feet, bounced him off the wall and sent him crashing into an unconscious heap.

The big kid was already charging down the stairs with a baseball bat when Devlin drew his gun, spun around, aimed carefully, and shot him in the right thigh. The kid's leg collapsed under him, and he tumbled and fell down the stairs. He came rolling down at Devlin like a human boulder, and there was no place for Devlin to get out of the way. Despite the crashing tumble, the bouncer still held on to the baseball bat, ready to hit Devlin with it.

The sliding mass smashed into Devlin's legs, and Devlin landed hard on the bouncer's chest. Even though his femur was shattered, the big kid had enough strength and rage to swing the bat at Devlin's face. Kneeling on the bouncer's chest, Devlin was able to block the blow with his left forearm, but he couldn't grab the bat to stop the kid from rearing back and aiming another shot at him.

Devlin didn't want to have to absorb another hit from the bat, so as the bouncer reared back, Devlin smashed the butt of the Caspian straight down and hit the bouncer between the eyes.

It didn't slow the kid much at all, and the second swing of the bat came right at Devlin. This time Devlin managed to block the bouncer's right arm, but the bat was long enough to catch him on the side of the head and shoulder. It was enough. Devlin couldn't waste any more time. His skull would be split any second. He shoved the muzzle of his gun at the point where the bouncer's right shoulder met his chest and pulled the trigger.

The shoulder separated from the body, the arm and the bat fell away, and the spitting, snarling fight went out of the bouncer. In an instant, Devlin was on his feet. He picked up the baseball bat and ran up the stairs as fast as he could.

In the bar, almost everyone was down on the floor or trying to take cover behind a corner or a table. The bartender crouched behind the bar with his pistol aimed at the entrance. The lean, mean-looking guy running the big wheel stepped over people and in front of Pony. He took cover behind the curve of the bar. He yelled at the bartender to turn up the lights.

Pony knew that if Devlin came charging through the entrance, he would be shot by both of them. The guns scared him, but he had to do something. He was sitting directly behind Hawk Face. He silently stood up, moved behind him, grabbed the man's head from and pulled him back, kicking his feet out from under him, and shoving him to the floor. Hawk Face fired his gun, and the bullet went straight up, catching Pony along the outside edge of his right arm, digging out a trail of flesh and blood before it lodged in the ceiling.

Hawk Face hit the ground hard. Before he could recover, Pony grabbed the hot barrel of the gun and twisted it out of the gambler's hand. He stomped hard once to the man's solar plexus and once to the temple to knock him out. Just to make sure he wouldn't get up, Pony stomp-kicked his knee.

The gun shot had made the bartender turn his head in Pony's direction. He started to take aim at Pony, but just then Devlin burst through the doorway and threw the baseball bat with all his strength at the bartender. The bat sailed through the air, spinning handle over end. The fat part of the bat caught the bartender in the head just as he was about to shoot Pony. The bat hitting the bartender's head made a sound like two bats cracking together.

The bartender crashed into the back-bar, but he still pulled the trigger of his revolver, sending a bullet right through the window near Pony. Black-painted glass sprayed out on the street below.

Devlin was over the bar like a big cat. He kicked the gun out of the bartender's hand and pounded brass-knuckled, left-handed punches into the man's face until he was inert.

Pony's arm was stinging and burning with pain, but he made his way through the customers, most of them on the floor, to the doorway. Devlin saw him and motioned for Pony to keep moving. From his position behind the bar, Devlin aimed his .45 at one of the slot machines and pulled the trigger once, then again, destroying the machine and sending anyone thinking of being a hero back down on the floor.

Devlin jumped back over the bar and headed for the doorway in front of Pony.

He turned into the stairwell just as the drunken Irish doorman staggered to his feet and drew his gun, a small snub-nose revolver.

Devlin ducked back before the first shot crashed wildly into the wall at the top of the stairs.

The doorman was snarling, "You motherfucker. I'll kill you, you fuck." Two more shots exploded in the narrow stairwell spraying plaster and wood fragments on Devlin near the door at the top of the stairs.

Devlin thought he might wait for six shots then take his chances, but the Irishman must have gotten his wits about him and stopped shooting. He didn't stop yelling, "Come on, you fuck. You're dead. You're dead."

Devlin and Pony were trapped at the doorway. Pony held the gambler's gun and faced the crowd to prevent any rush from behind. Devlin couldn't let any more time pass before they got out. The shot that blew out the club's second-floor window would surely bring the police. And Kelly's cops were probably already on the way.

Devlin switched the .45 into his left hand and grabbed the stool the bouncer had been sitting on with his right hand.

He pointed the .45 into the stairwell and aimed down the stairs, high enough so he wouldn't kill the Irishman by accident and let off two booming shots. The Irishman ducked, and Devlin leaned into the stairwell and threw the stool at the Irishman as hard as he could. The stairwell was so narrow the barstool bounced off the wall on the left side, but it crashed into the Irishman with enough force to knock him down.

As he went down the Irishman pulled the trigger on the cocked revolver and almost shot the bouncer lying on the stairs. Devlin charged down the stairs taking them three or four at a time.

But the Irishman wasn't quitting. He was tangled up with the bar stool and the downed and bleeding bouncer, and his jaw was broken from Devlin's punch, but he still had enough fight in him to get to his feet, cock the revolver and get off a shot before Devlin slammed into him full force. The bullet just clipped Devlin on the left hip and buried itself in the stairs.

Devlin didn't feel the bullet but felt himself spin as he smashed into the Irishman with his right shoulder. The impact was incredible. It had all of Devlin's weight, magnified by the rush down the stairs.

The Irishman was flattened and crushed against the door. He collapsed, and Devlin almost did, too, but Pony was right behind him and helped Devlin up as he frantically pushed open the latch that released the exit door.

They both staggered out on the sidewalk as an unmarked police sedan screeched to a halt. Two of Kelly's detectives burst out of the car with guns drawn. More police sirens were wailing in the distance.

Devlin told Pony, "Run!"

Pony ran east, and Devlin fired his remaining three shots over the detectives' heads. They both dropped down behind the cars parked in front of the club, and Devlin ducked back into the club's doorway. He was amazed to see that Mike, his driver, had stayed double-parked right where he had left him. The guy had guts. If he could make it to the car, Devlin figured he had a chance.

He slammed a fresh clip into the Caspian and turned back to face Kelly's detectives. They were both peering over the cars they hid behind with their guns drawn. Between them was the open door of their police sedan.

Devlin stood up straight and walked toward them, alternating slow, precise shots at each detective. The bullets slammed into the sheet metal of the cars right where they were crouching for cover. Devlin counted on the cops not having the guts to stand up and shoot back at a man walking at them and firing. He was right. But would he make it to his car before his clip ran out? And then, Mike Trey surprised Devlin again.

He was about ten feet in front of the police sedan. He threw the big Chevy Caprice into reverse and backed up full speed. The heavy car slammed into the police sedan, shoving it back five feet. The open driver's door smacked into one detective. The other one stood up to get out of the way, and with his last bullet, Devlin calmly shot the man's hand that held his service revolver.

The hand and revolver disappeared, the man collapsed. Devlin ran to the car. The back door on his side was smashed shut, so he ran around and jumped in the front. Mike floored the accelerator just as two blue and white police cars turned onto 56th Street at Third Avenue.

The light at Second Avenue was still red, and Devlin yelled at Mike, "Stop!"

He slammed on the brakes. Devlin prayed the cops would stop in front of the club before they chased after a car waiting at a red light.

His gamble paid off. The cops screeched to a halt in front of the club just as a group of patrons spilled out in a mass on the sidewalk.

Just then the back door of the Caprice opened, and Pony quietly entered the car. Devlin smiled for the first time the entire night.

The light turned green, he leaned forward and told Mike, "Nice work. Now go straight, then left, then back to the Carlyle. Slow and easy."

When they were halfway through the intersection, Devlin noticed the Mike Trey's hands were shaking.

CHAPTER 45

Mike dropped them off at the Carlyle with Devlin's thanks and an extra five hundred dollars. Devlin knew he was lucky. Not many would have stood up the way Mike had.

Susan was dozing when they entered the suite, but she woke up immediately when she heard the door open. She waited in the bedroom for about five minutes, then got up, put her robe on, and found Devlin and Pony in the bathroom.

Devlin's Halliburton case was open on top of the sink. Inside the case was a first aid kit with everything he needed. Pony's bloody shirt was on the floor, and Devlin sat on the closed toilet seat swabbing out a nasty wound that ran from near the young fighter's elbow almost to his shoulder. Pony's face remained impassive against the pain.

Devlin heard Susan but didn't turn to look at her. He said, "We'll be out of here soon. Nothing too serious."

"You've got blood all down your left leg."

"I know. I'm all right. Just want to take care of James here."

Susan left and sat out in the living room. The blood and the ugly tear in Pony's arm made her feel queasy.

After he finished with Pony, Devlin peeled off his pants and rolled down his bloody underwear to see how bad his wound was. It burned like hell but didn't hurt enough to cause pain when he walked.

He looked at a spot on the top of his left hip and saw that the skin had been torn away deep enough to reveal the bone underneath. He stared at the small piece of his hip bone visible beneath the bloody furrow gouged out by the bullet. He was transfixed for a moment, amazed at how bright white the bone appeared. It was so white and pristine it didn't look real.

He knew that the bullet hadn't touched the bone. Otherwise, the force of it would have shattered or at least cracked his hip. And since there wasn't much pain when he walked, he assumed there were no fractures.

He covered over the white bone with a thick disinfectant cream, carefully laid a sterile gauze pad over the wound and taped everything in place.

He washed the blood off his leg and kicked his bloody pants into a pile. He was too tired to wipe the blood off the floor.

He walked out of the bathroom and saw Pony already asleep on the living room couch. Devlin made it to the bedroom, lay down on the crisp white sheets and let Susan pull a light cover over his bruised naked body. He was totally, utterly, drained. Before he closed his eyes, he told Susan, "Wake me up this afternoon. Two o'clock. No, make it three."

Before she could answer, Devlin was asleep.

CHAPTER 46

Two o'clock found Daryl miserable and angry.

The pain in her hand was finally bearable. The cast made the broken finger seem more distant, and she didn't have to be sickened by the sight of it sticking out. But the Tylenol with codeine the doctor gave her made her stomach hurt, and the room was stifling hot. She felt grungy and dirty and wanted a shower more than anything, even though she had no clean clothes to put on afterward.

She sat up and swung her legs off the bed, then stood up slowly. She felt shaky, but she had to get more air into the room. She went to the window, which was blocked by sliding gates secured with a padlock. She reached between the slats and tried to shove the window open farther but only managed to push it up a couple of inches. She was breathing hard from the effort and became even more angry at how weak and helpless she felt.

She went into the bathroom, determined to clean herself up.

The bathroom seemed as if it hadn't been used in a long time. There was a toilet, sink, and tub. Two white hand towels hung from a small rack opposite the sink.

She closed and locked the door behind her and stripped off her clothes using her one good hand. She ran the water, adjusted the temperature, and stepped under the cleansing shower, holding her cast outside the shower curtain.

She was tired and hungry, but worst of all a stench seemed to have seeped into her, and she had to get clean.

She did the best she could using a half-bar of soap that was in the tub and her one good hand. She didn't dare take too much time in the shower. She turned off the water, stepped out and dried herself with one of the towels. She longed to wash her hair, but she didn't have any shampoo.

She picked up her clothes and started to leave the steamy bathroom so she could dress in the bedroom. When she stepped into the bedroom, cold fear and disgust paralyzed her. Messina stood in the middle of the bedroom. His fly was open, and he was fondling his fully erect cock. He cackled a vicious laugh and flicked his tongue out at her. "Hey, Blondie. Time for fun and games."

Disgust and anger finally overtook Daryl's fear, and she yelled, "Get away from me, you disgusting pig!" and spit at Messina's face. He was stunned just long enough for her to turn and dash back into the bathroom, slam the door, and lock it.

Messina yelled, "Fuck! Fucking disgusting bitch!"

He stuffed his disappearing erection back into his pants, ran over to the door and slammed a fist into it, cracking one of the panels. "Open this fucking door, or I'll break it down, you cunt!"

Wexler entered the bedroom and barked, "Stop it."

Messina turned with his upraised fist, and Wexler told him in his icy, quiet voice, "Put your hand down and get away from the door." Messina was shaking with rage. Wexler told him, "When I tell you, you can do anything you want to her, but for now I need her in one piece. So please step away and go into the living room. Now."

Messina put his raised fist down and backed away from the door with great difficulty. He went over to Wexler and told him, "She is going to die in pieces, man."

Wexler smiled and answered, "Fine. Soon I'll give you two women to kill any way you want, but not now."

Messina nodded once and left. Wexler walked to the bathroom door and tried the handle. It was locked. He knocked once and told Daryl, "Come out of the bathroom, now."

Daryl yelled back through the door, "That pig tried to rape me. I'm not dressed. I'm not coming out."

Wexler spoke through the door. "You will dress and come into the living room in three minutes, or I will send him back in here to finish what he started. Three minutes."

Daryl went to the sink, rinsed her face, and dried it. She dressed quickly in her dirty clothes, unlocked and opened the door. She half expected to see Devlin or Messina standing there, but the bedroom was empty. She walked out into the apartment's living room.

Wexler was sitting on the couch. Messina and Donovan sat in chairs by the door. Wexler looked her over and said, "You look like hell."

"What do you expect?"

"Didn't the doctor take care of your finger?"

"He said I have to see a surgeon today or tomorrow or I'll lose the finger."

"If anybody has lost anything significant around here it's me. And I have you and your friend Devlin to thank for it."

Daryl stared at him, trying to focus with eyes that didn't seem to want to work. Through her dry mouth she said, "I don't know what you're talking about. I don't have anything to do with you or what Devlin did to you. I need clothes and something to eat, and I have to see a real doctor."

Wexler stood up and told her, "I'll tell you what you need and when you're going to get it. Shut up and do exactly as I say or I'll have more than your finger broken."

He waited for Daryl to answer back. She didn't move or speak. He nodded once and said, "I take it you understand me?"

Daryl answered, "Yes."

"Good." Wexler pointed to the cop Donovan and said, "This man will take you back to your apartment. You clean yourself up, do whatever you need to do to make yourself presentable. Be ready to leave at nine-thirty tonight. You will then be taken to meet Mr. Devlin. Do you understand?"

"Then what?"

"Why then, your terrible ordeal will be over, and you'll be reunited with your friend, Mr. Devlin."

Wexler stood up, walked toward the door, and told Messina, "Come with me." To Donovan, he said, "Take care of it."

Wexler left the apartment with Messina following.

CHAPTER 47

It wasn't easy for Susan to wake Devlin. He was so deeply asleep, it was as if he had passed out. Even though she shook his shoulder gently, it hurt. He held up his hand and with his eyes closed croaked, "Okay, okay, I'm awake. I'm awake."

"Are you all right?" Susan asked.

"Yeah."

"Do you need help getting up?" she asked.

"No," he said, "Just give me a few minutes. Wait outside, okay?"

Devlin did not want Susan to see him try to sit up or stand. It took him a full minute to get his feet on the floor and sit up straight. He hurt all over. His left arm was deeply bruised and tender where he had blocked the bouncer's baseball bat at Eternity. The knuckles on his left hand were jammed and cut from so many hard hits with the brass knuckles. His right shoulder hurt all the way into his back and ribs from slamming into the Irishman at the bottom of the stairs. He was afraid to stand up and see how his hip felt.

Still sitting, he called Zitter. The receptionist put him through, and Zitter bellowed over the phone, "Devlin! What the fuck happened last night?"

"Why?"

"Fucking Kelly called me this morning foaming at the mouth. He threatened me ten different ways if I didn't bring you in or tell him where you were."

"You don't know where I am."

"No shit. Where are you?"

"You don't want to know."

"Yeah, all right. What did you do? Wreck his clubs?"

"Not all of them. Did you tell Kelly you want to see him at seven?"

"Yeah. He wanted to meet right now."

"Not until seven."

"Yeah, yeah, don't worry. I told him seven."

"Where are you two meeting?"

"An Irish fucking bar, where else? McMahon's on 59th near Lex."

"Okay, Sam, before you meet him, meet me at a place called Mulholland Drive at six-thirty."

"Where's that?"

"63rd and Third."

"Okay."

"Make sure none of Kelly's people follow you."

"No shit. How many of his places did you wreck last night?"

"Three."

"What's the point?"

"Pressure. Listen, let me ask you one more favor."

"What?"

"Do you know anybody in Internal Affairs? Any brass you can trust?"

"To do what?" asked Zitter.

"Arrest a bunch of rogue cops."

"Not on my say-so. You got evidence?"

"Okay, forget it. We don't have enough time anyhow. Just meet me at six-thirty."

Zitter said, "I'll be there," and hung up.

That done, Devlin decided to try to stand. And then to walk. The left knee was stiff and sore again. His hip creaked with pain. His knees, ankles, hands, shoulders, every joint seemed to fight him. He was getting too old for this damage. A few inches more on center and his hip would have been shattered like a piece of glass.

But he kept moving and kept fighting off the pain. He showered, letting the hot water seep into him and ease away some of the hurt. By the time he finished his shower, he was moving almost normally. He changed into his last pair of fresh clothes, took two more painkillers, and walked into the living room of the suite. Pony was sitting in his usual place by the window, and Susan on the couch reading *The New York Times*.

Pony cradled his arm in his lap. Devlin noticed his right cheekbone was swollen and scabs were forming over the cuts on his knuckles. Otherwise, he looked relaxed and alert.

Sunlight streamed into the room, illuminating infinitesimal pieces of dust floating in the air. Somewhere Devlin had read that most dust is actually tiny planetary debris from somewhere in space. For a moment, he felt out of place, stuck in a spot that wasn't anywhere near the natural orbit of things. He couldn't imagine an odder couple sitting in a sun-filled living room at the Carlyle. Susan, the austere beauty. Tense, vulnerable, blond. James, darkly handsome, young, strong, seemingly removed from all emotion. And all three of them trapped in a situation that could only be resolved with more danger and bloodshed.

When he walked in, Susan said, "You made it."

"Barely," answered Devlin. "How are you, James?"

"Face hurts. Hands hurt. Arm. But nothing serious."

"How are you, Susan?"

"I feel like shit, and I can't stop grinding my teeth."

"It won't last forever."

"Says who?"

"Well, the rest of it is going to be over tonight. You've come this far. Don't stop now. You've got to be clean, sober, and alert at ten o'clock."

She held up one hand and said, "I know."

Devlin returned to the bedroom and called Parker's office. When Parker got on the phone, Devlin said, "Tell me your guys did it."

"I'm just reading it now. I think they nailed it. Amazing."

"How? What's the connection?"

"One lazy insurance agent. You'll read it when you get here."

"I can't risk coming to your office. Can you send it to me by messenger?"

"Where?"

"Leave it at the front desk at the Carlyle Hotel."

"Fine."

"Rush."

"What a surprise."

"Parker."

"What?"

"Thank you. Thank you very much."

CHAPTER 48

At exactly 6:30 P.M., Devlin walked into Mulholland Drive and saw Sam Zitter sitting at the bar nursing a Budweiser.

When Zitter saw Devlin, he stared at him for a moment and said, "Man, you look like shit."

Devlin said, "You should have seen me a couple of hours ago."

"What happened to you? You can't even walk straight."

"I'm all right."

"What the hell were you trying to do last night?"

"Piss off Kelly."

"Mission accomplished. He's out for blood."

"Good."

Zitter said, "Guy like Kelly has enough brass to come down hard, Jack."

"Kelly is nothing but a goddamn crook and a coward is what he is." Devlin dropped a copy of Parker's report on the bar. "I just finished reading all of this. It's fifteen pages of information about bank accounts, corporations, title searches, mortgages, property deeds, et cetera, et cetera."

"Yeah?"

"It shows that Deputy Inspector Kelly uses Robert Wexler as a front man. Wexler is the one who had my brother beat up."

"Right. Wexler. How does he front for Kelly?"

"Wexler runs at least a dozen clubs, bars, and after-hours joints using a bunch of dummy corporations and companies. Wexler is the name on all public papers, but Kelly is the real power behind the scene. Kelly provides protection for the illegal clubs. Probably helps cut corners on the legal ones, too. They share the income."

Zitter asked, "You got proof of all that?"

"Enough to hook Kelly into it. There's a lot of information in there that shows stuff like transfers of money from a Colville Corporation to accounts held by Patrick Kelly. I know Colville is controlled by Wexler. But I couldn't connect Kelly to Colville or Wexler until now. Here's the break—the people I had working on this found out that about half the properties owned by the dummy corporations are insured for fire and liability by the same company, Kingsborough Insurance of America. They kept tracking through on the insurance and found that the beneficiaries on all of the insurance policies after the corporations are none other than Patrick Kelly and Robert Wexler."

Zitter raised his eyebrows and said, "Bingo. I'd say the Manhattan D.A.'s office would sink their teeth into that, not to mention Internal Affairs. How much you think is involved."

"Millions. And once you connect Kelly to Wexler, you connect them to all sorts of crimes, criminals associated with the after-hours clubs. Throw in tax evasion and money being transferred across state lines and foreign banks, the feds can jump in, too."

"So now that you got a fuckin' stick, how do you want to hit Kelly with it?"

"Here's the way I see it. We busted up those clubs good enough to bring the cops down hard on them. Especially that after-hours joint. There'll be plenty of investigations trying to find the owner. Normally, Kelly would have a pretty good chance of hiding behind Wexler's corporations. But with this" . . . Devlin held up the typewritten pages . . . "we can lead the cops to Wexler and from him right to Kelly."

Zitter said, "So now Wexler's a liability instead of an asset for Kelly."

"Right."

"What's next?"

"I want you to show Kelly what we've got here."

"Because you want Kelly to know that when they find Wexler, he's fucked."

"Exactly."

Zitter raised his eyebrows and told Devlin, "You got Wexler's death warrant in your hand."

"I'd say so. If Kelly gets rid of Wexler, the authorities are going to have a much harder time finding his part in all this."

"But what's going to prevent Kelly from just going after you, so the information doesn't get to the cops?"

"When you meet with him, you let him know that if anything happens to me, or Susan Ferlinghetti, or Daryl Austen, Pacific Rim makes sure this information gets followed up and presented in a neat package to the NYPD, the feds, IRS, Manhattan D.A., the works."

"How's he gonna know you aren't going to turn the information over anyhow?"

"I'd say he's smart enough to threaten going after the women if I do that."

"A stalemate?"

"Should be."

"Or maybe he'll just say to hell with it and take everybody out."

"I don't see it that way."

"Jeezus, I don't know if you've got more balls than brains, or what. And you still have to get the women free of Wexler."

"Ten o'clock tonight, I'm meeting Wexler at the Oak Room bar in the Plaza. We've agreed to exchange the women. He gets Susan Ferlinghetti, and I get Daryl Austen."

"And both of you get to double-cross each other."

"Right."

The grizzled detective took a swallow of his beer.

"Pretty goddamn dicey, my friend. Wexler ain't gonna let you walk away with both women. And you won't know where Kelly is going to come out on this until your neck is in the noose."

"Sam, just drop this report in front of Kelly, tell him what I've told you, and let me take care of the rest."

"You got a plan for that?"

"We'll see."

Zitter sat for a moment twisting his watchband around his wrist, his jaw jutting out, and his lips pursed. Finally, he said, "I don't know if I'm helping you, or hurting you."

Devlin turned to Zitter and said, "It's all I've got. It's the only way. In the last week I've lost my father, almost lost my brother, and I'm not going to lose anybody else. If Wexler wants to take me on, let him. If Kelly wants to back him and come after me with his rotten cops and his fucking rank and whatever else he's got—let him. He's a thief, and he lies with scum, and if he comes after me, I guarantee you I won't die alone. But I've got to get those women free of Wexler."

Zitter said, "All right. Enough talk." He reached for the report. "You want me at the Plaza at ten?"

"You've already done enough. More than enough. Just deliver this to Kelly and get out in one piece. You don't need any more trouble with this. Call me at the Carlyle when it's done. Room 418."

Zitter looked at his watch and jumped up from his bar stool. "I'm late. Kelly leaves, and it's over right now."

Zitter rushed out of the bar and Devlin watched him go. He paid the tab and went back to the Carlyle to wait.

Five minutes later Zitter walked into McMahon's and sat next to Patrick Kelly, who was sipping a glass of Scotch and soda at the bar.

Two of Kelly's detectives sat a few feet away in a booth.

Kelly told Zitter, "You're late."

"Five minutes late is on time."

"What have you got to tell me?"

"I don't know where Devlin is, but I know what he plans to do."

"What?"

Zitter laid the neatly typewritten pages on the bar. "This is a copy of information he's gathered on you and somebody named Wexler. I haven't read it. I don't want to read it. Apparently, it connects you to Wexler, and I gather that's not good for you."

Kelly didn't touch the papers, but he slowly turned to look at Zitter.

Zitter continued talking. "I'm also supposed to tell you that the trouble at your clubs last night were caused so the authorities will investigate those clubs. I assume enough ruckus was made so that plenty of cops, building inspectors, and fire marshals will be trying to find the owners of those places. And, I am told, that means they'll eventually be knocking on the door of somebody called Robert Wexler. If they don't find Wexler fast enough, my client will tip them off."

Zitter pointed to the typewritten pages on the bar. "With this information in the wrong hands, Wexler apparently becomes a problem for you. My client wants you to take care of that problem yourself. And he also wants a guarantee that nothing happens to Daryl Austen or Susan Ferlinghetti. If anything happens to them, or my client, this information goes to the feds, the D.A.'s office, NYPD, and others. There are enough copies for lots of people."

Kelly nodded and quietly muttered, "Sweet mother of mercy, isn't this a wonderful thing to see. Instead of coming in here to help me find that bastard Devlin, you've come in delivering his blackmail threats and dirty lies."

"The only thing I'm delivering is information my client wants you to know about. You do what you have to do, now that you know about it. Make sure nothing happens to my client, or his interests, and the information stays private."

Kelly turned to Zitter. His face twisted into a venomous sneer. "You two-bit Hebe bastard. You think you can threaten me with this? You think I'm gonna swallow this shit? You fucking, washed-up Judas. You turn against your own? You go against a brother cop?

I'll destroy you in this town, you kike fuck."

Zitter stood up off the bar stool and turned to Kelly. He spoke softly. "You're not my brother cop. Not on the job or off—not now, not ever, because what I hear is you're a fucking thief, Kelly. You're a crook, and I'm not.

"Now, you want to hear a threat? Listen to this—you fuck up and go after the wrong people, the word goes out on you. And I don't care how much brass you got, you know the minute you get connected to those clubs you're the one who's dead in this town.

"*That's* your problem. If you want to make *me* your problem, I'd think twice about it. I know where you live, you bastard. You send any of your rotten cops against me, including those two pieces of shit sitting in that booth over there, I'll fucking kill them. And then I'll fucking kill you. Don't make me your problem, Kelly, because you've got enough of them right now. Start cleaning your own house and maybe you'll make it out of this."

Zitter unbuttoned his jacket, put a hand on his gun, and walked backward away from Kelly, keeping an eye on his two detectives. Kelly didn't say a word, and nobody moved except Zitter. When he got near the door, Zitter turned and left the bar. He jumped into the first cab he saw, got out three blocks later, found a payphone, and dialed the Carlyle. Susan answered the phone and Zitter told her, "Tell Devlin it's done."

CHAPTER 49

The Oak Room bar was crowded. The host standing at the entrance to the room was a distinguished man in a tuxedo who looked Devlin over carefully as he walked in. Devlin wore a black Polo shirt and black slacks with his gray linen jacket. The lack of a tie raised an eyebrow, but the tall, elegant blonde with him added more than enough glamor to gain entry. Susan looked stunning. The tension and sobriety made her eyes sparkle. Her beautifully cut linen suit fit her striking figure perfectly.

The host seated them at a table in the middle of the room. Devlin carefully looked around. Nearly all the stools at the bar were filled: two businessmen talked deals; a glamorous couple in European clothes sipped snifters of brandy; a young couple who looked like out-of-towners enjoyed a nightcap.

There were ten tables in the room—big wooden tables with big wooden chairs finished in red leather. Two couples occupied a table for four. A black woman sat alone at a table for two, her back against the wall. She wore a green silk suit with a string of pearls and a fixed smile. Devlin took her for a hooker. A little over the hill, but friendly, willing, and patient, waiting quietly for a prospect to approach her.

Those were the civilians amid the dark woods, big oil paintings, and tall glass windows looking out on Central Park South. Mixed in with them were six of Kelly's detectives. A pair of them covering each of the three entrances to the room.

Devlin spotted the stocky detective and his tall partner, whose face still showed the results of his brief encounter with James Pony. They sat near the exit to the lobby.

At a table near the Central Park South exit sat the team that had staked out Susan's apartment where they had taken Daryl.

Finally, there was an exit that led to the larger Oak Room next door. The redheaded cop, Donovan, sat near that doorway with a man Devlin assumed was his partner—a short, quick-eyed cop who looked Italian. They all wore cheap suits and sport jackets. None of them looked happy to see Devlin.

Devlin had taken Susan into a room where he was one man against six. For a second, he felt like taking out the Caspian and holding it in plain view. His nerves were strung so tight every ache in his battered body throbbed. In the next few minutes, somebody was going to get hurt. Waiting to find out who was excruciatingly nerve wracking.

If the room had been a crowded, noisy place, Devlin might have walked right up to one of Kelly's men, stuck the gun in his face, and demanded they turn over Daryl right then and there. But the Oak Room bar helped ease the tension. Devlin turned inward, forcing himself to relax, and let the next move unfold by itself.

The bar had the quiet, comforting air of a once grand place gently sliding downhill ever so slowly. The high ceilings, the wood paneling, the tall windows framed by heavily scrolled woodwork—all surrounded Devlin and Susan and let them pretend they were simply out for a late drink.

Devlin thought about sitting in this barroom with a character like Zitter and drinking through a long lunch on a winter afternoon. A crisp winter afternoon with snow outside in Central Park and cold sun streaming in through the tall windows and lots of intense New Yorkers outside rushing to meetings that had started five minutes ago.

But instead, he took a seat in the middle of a nasty trap, on a dark, humid night with no sign of any friend or any help from anyone inside or out.

Susan sat across from him and smiled. She said, "What are you drinking?"

Devlin looked at her tense, beautiful face, and admired her courage. She felt the danger that surrounded them, but she kept a smile fixed in place and remained determined to hang on no matter what happened. He smiled back and said, "Club soda with orange juice."

She answered quickly, "Me, too." As if to say, whatever you do I will, too. Devlin felt a surge of affection for Susan. He wanted her out and away and safe—now.

There was no waiter in sight, so Devlin got up and went to the bar to place his order. Six heads swiveled as he walked the short distance to the bar. The bartender was a trim black man old enough to have gray hair but youthful enough to pass for fifty. The man listened to the order and told Devlin, "Have a seat, sir, I'll bring it right over."

Devlin went back to his table and waited. In a few minutes, the bartender appeared with two glasses filled with ice, a small pitcher of freshly-squeezed orange juice, and two small bottles of Seagram's club soda—all neatly arranged on a cork-bottomed serving tray. One by one he put down the items and finally laid a computer-printed check upside down on the table.

Before the bartender poured the orange juice, Robert Wexler entered from the hotel lobby. He was alone.

The bartender filled the glasses with a bubbling mixture of club soda and orange juice as Wexler approached, all smiles and conviviality.

Wexler wore a pressed seersucker suit, blue shirt, and red bow tie with a matching breast pocket handkerchief. He looked as if he didn't have a care in the world.

Devlin watched him and felt the trap tightening.

Wexler took a chair at Devlin's table with a superior smile on his face and told the bartender, "I'll have one of those, too, my good man. It looks quite refreshing."

The bartender finished serving and said, "Yes, sir." He seemed to like Wexler's look. Perfect gentleman for the Oak Room bar.

Wexler smiled at Susan and said, "Good evening, dear. How are you?"

Without returning the smile, Susan answered, "Fine."

Wexler waited a beat, then said, "How nice. You sound sober, Susan. Could that be?"

"That would be none of your business, Robert."

"Oh my, some assertiveness training in addition to the course on sobriety. Plus, a new blondes-have-more-fun hair color. How inspiring! How Pygmalion."

Devlin interrupted Wexler's scorn. "Susan is here, where's Daryl Austen?"

Wexler looked at Devlin as if he were seeing him for the first time and just noticing he was sitting there. "Oh, Mr. Devlin. How are you? What was the question?"

"Where's Daryl Austen?"

"She hasn't arrived yet?" Wexler asked innocently.

"Wexler, I'm not in the mood for your bullshit. I thought we understood each other."

"*I* understand. You're the one who's too stupid to understand what's going on. You know, Mr. Devlin, frankly you disappoint me."

"Wexler, if she doesn't appear now, Susan and I will walk out of here, and you'll be the first one I kill if anyone tries to stop us."

"Oh, so macho. So big and tough. Is that what you see in him, Susan?"

"Robert, don't talk to me. Keep fucking around, and I walk out of here, and I don't give a damn who doesn't like it."

Wexler looked at Susan for a moment and decided that she wasn't bluffing. She *had* changed. He turned away from her and said, "Threats. Ultimatums. You two are terrific negotiators, aren't you?"

Susan stood up, but Wexler held her arm. "All right. All right. Enough. If you can't cope with a little civilized bantering, the hell with you. Sit down, and we'll get on with it."

Susan firmly pulled her arm from Wexler's grip and slowly

sat down. Wexler turned and motioned to the stocky detective sitting near the lobby entrance. The detective got up and left. In a few moments, he appeared with Daryl and Messina.

Daryl looked gaunt and haggard. Messina walked behind her. His leering grin and hulking presence seemed to threaten everyone in the room.

Daryl's arm was in a sling, her hand covered with a cast that looked thick and slightly grotesque. It made her look wounded and vulnerable. Devlin thought about the pain Wexler had inflicted. The pain he had done nothing to stop or prevent. Daryl's entrance seemed to give Wexler even more confidence.

The stocky detective returned to his seat. Daryl and Messina approached the table. While most eyes were on Daryl, James Pony unobtrusively entered the room from the Central Park South entrance and took a seat at the bar. The pieces of a very dangerous game were falling into place.

Daryl reached the table, and Devlin stood. Wexler motioned to the fourth chair and said, "Sit, my dear. Sit. You've had a trying time, but we're almost done."

To Messina, Wexler said, "Be kind enough to sit by the door over there. Be alert. I may need you."

Devlin smelled Messina's cheap hair oil as he moved away from them. He glanced at the thick back and the muscles that ran up into Messina's neck and thought about shooting him in the head.

They all sat down, and Devlin asked Daryl, "Are you all right?"

"No. I am not all right. I have to get out of here, and I have to get to a hospital."

Devlin said, "Daryl, I'm sorry—"

Daryl interrupted. "I know. I know. You warned me, I got involved. I don't want to talk about it now or say anything now. I just want this over, and I want to get out of here."

Susan, suddenly flushed with anger, demanded from Wexler, "What the hell did you do to her?"

"I thought we weren't talking."

"What did you do to her?"

"Me? I didn't do anything. That man sitting over by the door did it. He just broke her little finger." Wexler shrugged. "Just one little finger, broken in two. On the cosmic scale of life, certainly no big deal. I could have had him break much more, but Ms. Austen was very cooperative. She told me what I needed to know right away, so we didn't need to waste the energy. Right, Miss Austen?

"When do I get out of here?" asked Daryl.

Susan reached across the table and took Daryl's hand. "Now," Susan said.

Wexler's voice took on an edge as he said, "Don t be so hasty, Susan. We men have some business to conduct, and you're not to leave."

Susan and Daryl were about to stand, when Devlin reached out and said, "Easy now. Let's do this right."

Wexler spoke up. "Ah, there—you see. Mr. Devlin is so much more experienced in these exciting hostage exchanges. Let's listen to what he has to say, girls."

Daryl clenched her teeth and stared straight ahead. Devlin could see she wasn't going to hang on much longer. Susan looked ready to claw Wexler's eyes out.

Devlin looked directly at Wexler and told him, "Nobody moves but the women. They stand up and walk out of here together. You and I sit and finish our business."

Wexler pursed his lips, steepled his fingers under his chin, and stared at Devlin. He relished the opportunity to be difficult. "I don't know, Mr. Devlin. That seems rather sudden. I have unfinished business with Miss Ferlinghetti. I'd rather not trouble myself looking for her."

Susan spoke. "Robert, you know where I live. You won't have to look for me. I'm leaving, and I'm taking Daryl with me."

Wexler dropped his facade. "Oh for God's sake, stop trying to act so tough. It's unbecoming to a helpless drunken whore. Go on and get out. I know where to find you now, and I'll know where to find you later. And believe me, you and I have unfinished business, and you're going to pay for all the trouble you've caused me."

Susan pushed her face toward Wexler and said very slowly, "Robert, fuck you."

Devlin interrupted, "Okay, let's not lose sight of why we're here. Daryl, Susan, just get up slow and easy, and leave."

The two women stood up. Daryl spat at Wexler and turned to leave. Susan moved quickly to catch up to her.

Wexler smirked at the departing women, calmly took out his handkerchief and wiped the spit off his shoulder.

Susan linked arms with Daryl, and both of them walked through the room toward the Central Park South exit.

At the doorway, Messina stood and waited for them to approach. Daryl shrank back from him, but Susan kept moving toward the exit.

All eyes were on the women. Without moving his head, Devlin looked for Pony. He was just exiting into the hotel lobby.

Susan and Daryl were already half-way to the door, but Devlin knew he had to give Pony time to get around to the Central Park South side of the bar. Devlin called out, "Susan." Both women stopped and turned.

Wexler told Devlin in a quiet voice, "Don't make another move, Devlin, or you're dead where you stand."

Susan turned to Devlin. He motioned her toward him. Susan came back to the table; Daryl stood where she was. Devlin told Susan, "I just wanted to say, thank you."

Susan looked at him, not quite understanding what he was doing. Devlin said, "Okay, go ahead."

Susan turned back, went to Daryl, took her arm again, and walked. As they went down the stairs to the door, Messina fell in behind them. As soon as they stepped outside onto Central Park South, Messina moved quickly and grabbed each woman by the arm. Randy, Wexler's driver, had the Mercedes parked right in front of the entrance. He stood next to the car's open back door. Two of Kelly's detectives were also waiting outside. They closed in on Messina and the women.

Susan and Daryl were surrounded. Messina had their arms in a crushing grip. He started to muscle both women into the car, but Daryl dug her nails into his hand, and Susan struggled and fought to get her arm free. Messina yelled, "Cut it out, or I'll break your fucking arms!"

Kelly's two detectives came closer to help Messina. Daryl was too weak to fight, but Susan's fierce resistance gave Pony the extra seconds he needed to reach them before Messina got them into the car.

Pony ran full speed and threw his body into the knot of men surrounding Susan and Daryl. He managed to knock down one cop and land an elbow smash on the back of Messina's head that stunned him just enough for Susan to break free.

She grabbed Daryl and tried to pull her away from Messina, but his grip held. The second cop couldn't get to Pony because Messina and the fallen cop were in the way. Pony kicked the downed cop in the face and landed a vicious knee kick on Messina's kidney. His grip on Daryl loosened, and Susan pulled her free.

The first cop was back on his feet, taking out a blackjack. The second cop had his gun out, and Messina was up now, too.

Pony stood between the three men and the women. Randy tried to grab Susan from behind. She turned and punched him in the face and kicked and snarled at him, "You fucking touch me, and I'll kill you." She was so fierce he backed away.

For a second, no one moved against Pony. Then the first cop tried to step around him, and Messina lunged at him. The young fighter was lightning quick. He jumped out of Messina's way and threw a punch at the cop trying to get past him. The punch missed but made the cop duck. Susan and Daryl ran around the Mercedes out into the street.

Suddenly, a van that looked like a plumber's truck screeched to a halt in front of Susan and Daryl. The van's sliding door flew open, and Vincent yelled out to Daryl and Susan, "Get in! I'm with Devlin!"

Susan and Daryl bolted for the van. The first cop went after them. Messina moved toward Pony again, and the second cop aimed his gun in the direction of the van.

Susan helped Daryl into the van and scrambled in after her. The cop got to them in time to grab Susan's arm to pull her out. Vincent kicked him in the face. He let go of Susan. She fell into the van; Vincent slammed the door, and his partner Hank Dixon floored the accelerator. The van roared east on Central Park South.

The cop with the gun took aim at the van. Pony lowered his shoulder and ran into Messina, shoving him into the cop. All three hit the sidewalk hard, but Pony was on the top of the pile and got to his feet first.

Kelly's men were out of it, but Messina was up and moving toward Pony, who backed away from him, turned and jogged across Central Park South, drawing Messina away from the Plaza. At the park entrance Pony hesitated, letting Messina get closer, then he continued running, keeping just enough distance from Messina to lure him deeper into the park.

Messina had lost the women, lost a chance to smash Pony, and now was being tormented. Rage pounded in his head. He ran faster, determined to close the distance. Finally, Pony stopped in a small clearing near the Wollman skating rink. Messina saw that Pony was going to stand and fight, so he stopped running, tried to catch his breath, and slowly closed in on Pony. Pony watched the big man advance under the ugly yellow glare from the park's high-intensity lights. Deep shadows cut into Messina's face, but Pony could still make out his demented grin. Pony stood his ground, waiting for the final battle.

But Messina wasn't interested in fighting Pony again. When he was within ten feet of Pony, he pulled out a snub-nosed revolver and fired one shot that hit Pony in the middle of his chest. The impact knocked Pony back five feet. He went down hard.

Pony lay on his back, gasping for breath.

Messina, still grinning, walked over to Pony, aiming the gun at his head. He wanted to put one more right in the middle of Pony's face. He bent over to see if Pony's eyes were open.

Pony's eyes were wide open. He saw the muzzle of the revolver coming at him. When the gun was within reach, he swept his left hand across, grabbed Messina's right wrist, and pulled Messina to his left while he rolled in the same direction. He ended up on his feet behind Messina. He punched Messina's elbow with his right hand. The big man bellowed in rage and pain as the gun fired a bullet into the ground. Pony struck another blow at Messina's elbow, and the gun dropped. Pony shoved Messina to the ground, picked up the gun, and threw it deep into the bushes surrounding the clearing.

Messina scrambled to his feet, furiously rubbing his arm, trying to get back some feeling.

Pony stood bent over. He couldn't straighten up. Devlin's Kevlar vest had stopped the bullet, but the impact felt like the hardest punch Pony had ever weathered.

The two fighters circled each other in the eerie glow of the Central Park streetlights. Messina's leer had turned into an ugly snarl. Suddenly, Messina lunged, and Pony saw the knife just in time.

Pony jumped away from the blade and spun a roundhouse kick that hit Messina on the hip and knocked him back. But Messina was too quick. He slashed at Pony's leg. The blade cut across Pony's thigh, but he still snapped off another roundhouse kick that caught the side of Messina's head.

Messina spun like a bull and slashed again at Pony, who danced back out of his reach, then leaped forward to chop a hammer punch on Messina's forearm. Messina's right arm was becoming useless, but still, he held onto the knife.

Messina charged Pony with the knife held in front of him. Pony grabbed Messina's right wrist to deflect the knife. He was strong enough to stop the knife from stabbing him, but now Messina had contact and simply bulled forward, grabbing Pony around the waist with his left arm and driving him to the ground.

Pony kept his grip on Messina's wrist. Despite landing hard on his back with Messina's weight on him, Pony kept Messina's knife hand pinned to the ground. Messina lifted himself up with his left arm and reared back to smash Pony in the face with a head butt. Pony did the only thing possible—he jackknifed up and smashed Messina with his forehead first.

The blow shattered Messina's nose. He reared back, and Pony used all his strength to push him off and roll on top of him. Pony still held Messina's wrist to keep the knife away, but with his free hand, he pounded three hard punches into Messina's face and broken nose.

Messina growled in agony, reared up, and grabbed at Pony's throat. Pony tore himself free and sprang to his feet, moving away from Messina.

Messina staggered to his feet. He still had the knife. He circled in for the kill. Pony remembered Devlin's warning about blows to the head and face. They would never be enough to stop someone like Messina.

Messina spat out blood. He was bigger. He was stronger. And he was going to bury his knife in Pony's skull.

He charged with the knife poised overhead to stab down. Pony stood his ground, met Messina's charge, blocking the downward thrust with two crossed hands. He quickly grabbed Messina's wrist with his left hand and redirected the knife with his right, at the same time turning into Messina and aiming his left elbow into the man's ribs. He rammed another elbow smash into Messina's solar plexus. He reached back, grabbed Messina's crotch in a powerful grip, and lifted him off his feet. Messina screamed and hit the ground hard. Pony spun around facing him and stomped his heel into Messina's crotch once, twice, and Messina was down for good, twitching in pain.

Pony stepped over Messina and pulled the knife out of his hand. He turned Messina over and plunged the knife deep into the back of Messina's leg, cutting the large hamstring muscle.

And then Pony replayed Wexler's words, which he had heard sitting at the bar, and pulled Messina's hand out from under him, knelt on the big man's arm and slowly bent back the little finger twisting and bending until the tendons and ligaments tore and metacarpophalangeal joint broke with a sickening, satisfying crack.

#

Back in the peaceful Oak Room bar, Wexler watched the distinguished black bartender pour him another orange juice and club soda. He swirled the drink in his glass and took a sip. Devlin sat patiently. He didn't mind letting Wexler play his games now that Susan and Daryl were gone, and hopefully safe.

Finally, Wexler spoke. "You've caused me considerable trouble, Mr. Devlin. You ruined two of my strongest men. You caused a great deal of damage and trouble at several of my properties. Not to mention you've interrupted the pleasure I took from Miss Susan's services." He leaned forward. "I want to know why."

"Because you hurt my brother."

"Don't be ridiculous."

"And because you hurt Daryl Austen. And you came after Susan Ferlinghetti and me."

Wexler started to speak, but Devlin kept talking.

"And because you think you can hurt whoever you want because you have some money and a crooked cop protecting you."

"That's your answer?"

"Yeah."

"But you're going to prove me wrong. You're going to prove to me that I can't do those things. Is that it?"

"That's it."

"Does this macho thing of yours make you stupid, or is it that you just don't care what happens to you?"

"You've used up all your questions, Wexler."

"Fine. Then I'll ask the question and give you the answer. The question, Mr. Devlin, is how do you propose to pay me for all the damage you've done. And the answer is with your life. Over a bit of time. And quite painfully. You disappoint me, Devlin. I thought you'd be more of a challenge."

"So stop talking about it, Wexler. Come on—kill me."

"I wouldn't dirty my hands on you."

"Then who's going to do it for you?" Devlin motioned with his head toward the others in the room. "These flunkies of Kelly's?"

Devlin stood up. Wexler looked around expecting to see Kelly's men moving in on Devlin.

Devlin came around to Wexler's side of the table. Kelly's men still hadn't moved. He asked, "When does it happen, Wexler?"

For the first time, Wexler's composure cracked. He stammered slightly as he said, "Sit down. You aren't going anywhere."

Devlin leaned close to him and said, "Who's going to stop me? You? C'mon, tough guy, stop me." Devlin waited. Wexler didn't move. Devlin said, "I think you're the one who's dead, Wexler. You just haven't hit the ground yet."

Wexler had no idea why Kelly's men weren't stopping Devlin, but he couldn't let him get away. He reached under his suit jacket, but Devlin rammed his fist into Wexler's chest. Wexler bent over, barely able to breathe, unable to say a word.

Devlin reached under Wexler's jacket and pulled out a small, silver-plated pistol, a .25 caliber Targa automatic with a pearl handle. He slid the gun into the side pocket of his jacket and stood looking at the back of Wexler's head. Suddenly, Devlin's entire body tensed as the fury of it all poured through him. He thought of his brother and Susan and Daryl. He thought of all the pain Wexler had caused. He had an overwhelming urge to smash Wexler's head like his brother's had been smashed. To hit Wexler so hard that his brain would crash back and forth against his skull.

He balled his right hand into a fist, and just as he was about to strike, Devlin heard a soft Irish voice in his ear and felt the hard muzzle of a gun pushed insistently between his sore ribs.

Sean McKay told him, "Now, Mr. Devlin, settle down, please. We can't have any more violence in public, now, can we?

Devlin's vision cleared, and he saw Sean on his left, and the smaller brother William on his right. William pushed the gun firmly into Devlin's side. Behind them and farther to his right stood Deputy Inspector Patrick Kelly holding up his badge announcing in a calm voice, "Sorry for the interruption, folks. Police business. Just stay where you are and we'll be out of here in a moment."

Sean said, "Any scenes now and we'll have to shoot you first. I'm not disposed to warn you twice, Mr. Devlin. You're a dangerous fellow you are."

Devlin relaxed and let the fury ebb away.

Kelly stepped forward and told Devlin, "You've caused us enough trouble, my friend. Now don't muck up your little scheme. Step aside, and let me and my men handle this."

Devlin spread his arms slightly, palms showing, and stepped back three paces, moving away from William McKay and his gun.

Wexler had recovered from Devlin's punch and stood up suddenly. He snarled at Kelly, "What the hell are you doing?"

The McKay brothers moved in on Wexler. Sean grabbed Wexler's right arm, and William stood on Wexler's left with his gun inches away. Several of Kelly's detectives moved closer to join them. The rest of the people in the bar saw Wexler being surrounded, but no one saw William's gun.

Wexler ignored everyone except Kelly. He carefully bit off each word, barely able to keep control of his icy voice. "What are you doing, Patrick? What the hell are you doing?"

"Seems you and your thugs have made quite a mess of things, Robert. Caused too much trouble. Old Devlin got the goods on you, and I can't let you jeopardize the operation. We're going to have to clean up some loose ends."

"Yes," said Sean McKay. "We're going to have to take you straight to hell, old boy. You can walk out like a man, or we'll shoot you right here, and you can shit yourself and bleed on the nice carpet. Choice is yours."

Wexler slowly turned to him and said, "Take your hand off my arm. I don't like you touching me. And I don't need to be led anywhere by you."

McKay smiled and released Wexler. "Certainly. Go ahead and act the boss one last time."

Wexler said, "Thank you. Now tell your smaller brother to stop pointing his gun at me."

"Give the old man a bit of room, William. Let him try to be brave. It might be fun."

William moved a step away. Wexler shifted his gaze to Kelly, who turned, ready to lead the group toward the lobby exit. His two men near that exit waited to fall in with the others.

Kelly said, "Let's go."

Sean waited for Wexler to follow Kelly and fell in next to Wexler.

Devlin stood where he was and watched them leave. Kelly, the man in charge, Sean and William with Wexler between them, and the four cops straggling behind. In a moment, they would all be gone. Wexler to his grave. A rogue cop and his private army, answerable to no person or law.

Suddenly Devlin called out, "Wexler!"

Everyone stopped as Wexler turned toward Devlin.

"Who would you rather kill right now, Wexler? Me or Kelly?"

Wexler stared at Devlin for a second, then said, "Well now—that's the first interesting thing you've managed to say to me, and damned if I know the answer."

Devlin reached into his coat pocket and said, "Let's find out."

Before anyone could react, Devlin pulled out the silver-plated Targa and tossed it to Wexler. Time seemed to freeze as the small gun arced through the air, heading toward Wexler as if he were a magnet. In two seconds the gun was in Wexler's hands, and then everyone moved at once.

Kelly turned away from Wexler just before Wexler's first shot hit him directly in his left temple, sending the small caliber bullet tumbling around inside his skull destroying Kelly's brain.

Sean McKay lunged to grab Wexler from his left, making William hesitate just long enough so that Wexler got off a second shot at the same time William pulled his trigger. Wexler might have been turning to shoot at Devlin, but his bullet angled up into William's throat, and exited out the back—tearing through William's brain stem and spinal cord. William's bullet hit Wexler right in the center of his chest, blowing apart most of his heart.

Four of Kelly's six detectives shot at the dying Wexler, blasting pieces out of him and killing Sean McKay, who was still going for Wexler's gun.

By the time the last shot was fired, no more than five seconds had passed, but it was time enough for Devlin to grab the nearest detective by the throat and pull him in front of him as a shield. Before anyone could stop him, Devlin had his Caspian .45 pressed firmly to the side of the man's head.

Everybody's ears were ringing from the gunshots, patrons were screaming, and running for cover, but Devlin yelled loud enough to be heard.

"Fingers off the triggers, guns on the ground, now. Drop 'em and don't move. Now!"

The room was filled with smoke and the acrid stench of gunpowder. Reality started to slowly come into focus, and all eyes shifted to the shouting Devlin and his hostage. Some of the detectives were so accustomed to taking orders that they lowered guns, but nobody dropped them.

It was a dangerous standoff until Sam Zitter strolled out of the kitchen near the bar area and walked over to Devlin. He had a gun in each hand and stood between Devlin and Kelly's men.

Zitter calmly told them, "Game's over, gents. Nobody shoots now without getting shot back. In about two minutes, this room is gonna be filled with real cops. You dumb fucks have a choice. Get the hell out now and try to convince the higher-ups you were never here, or put your goddamn guns in your holsters, sit down and get some bullshit story figured out before the brass arrives. I suggest you sit down."

Devlin took his .45 away from the cop he was using as a shield, pointed it at the other cops, and gently pushed the man down on a chair. Devlin and Zitter held their guns and watched as each of Kelly's men sat down, one by one.

They didn't need to be pushed.

EPiLOGUE

It took most of the night to even begin sorting out the mess.

Four dead bodies, one of which was an NYPD Deputy Inspector, made for a long night of questioning at Manhattan's Midtown North Precinct. Zitter and Devlin said they would cooperate, but only with their lawyers present. Zitter's attorney arrived first. Ten minutes later three lawyers from Pacific Rim showed up. For five hours, Zitter, Devlin, and the lawyers played the delicate game of letting the police and assistant D.A.'s know what they had to know about the bad guys, without hurting the good guys.

By the time they released Devlin and Zitter, it was clear that a lot of dirt was going to be swept under the right carpet, and a lot of cops connected to Kelly would either be in jail or off the force.

Once again, Devlin found himself at the end of a long night walking out into another New York dawn. While he and Zitter stood outside 54th Street saying goodbye to their lawyers, James Pony quietly walked over and stood next to them. Devlin smiled and said, "What'd you do, wait out here for us?"

Pony said, "Yes."

Devlin turned to Zitter and said, "Sam, this is James Pony. He's a very remarkable man. A true fighter. If you ever need one, there aren't many like him."

Zitter shook Pony's hand and said, "Nice to meet you."

Devlin asked Pony, "Are you okay?"

Pony nodded. "Yes, thanks to your advice about the vest."

Pony unbuttoned his shirt enough to show the bruise from Messina's bullet on his chest.

Devlin said, "Wexler's bouncer."

Pony said, "He won't be hurting anybody for quite some time."

"Good. And for a long time after that. The cops want him out of the picture. Susan and Daryl get away okay?"

"Yes."

"Good."

Devlin looked at Zitter and Pony. "I owe both of you a great deal."

Zitter said, "Damn right you do. Wait until you see my bill."

"You know what I mean, Sam. You guys did this like George was your brother. Like I was your brother."

Pony nodded but said nothing.

Zitter shrugged and said, "Don't forget I hate bad cops worse than you do. Especially that fuck Kelly. Come on, shake my hand and let me get out of here. I hate this goodbye shit."

They shook hands all around. Pony and Zitter walked off together. Pony in his effortless way. Zitter with a rolling shuffle. Devlin headed for a payphone on the corner.

Susan had left a message for him at the Carlyle. She had remembered to use the name Johnson. He found her in the waiting room of the trauma ward at New York University Hospital.

Susan had taken immediate and absolute control of Daryl, like a super-protective older sister. She'd never returned to the Carlyle that night. Instead, she'd taken Daryl straight to the hospital.

Hours before Devlin arrived, Susan had rousted the top hand surgeon on staff and pushed and cajoled and demanded until Daryl was admitted, X-rayed, and prepped for surgery. By the time Susan was done with him, the surgeon would have promised her anything, but she settled for his vow that he would fix everything wrong with Daryl's hand.

It took most of the night. When Daryl woke up, she saw Devlin and Susan standing at her bedside and started to cry.

Devlin stood back while Susan stroked her hair and told her to cry all she wanted. "It's all right, honey," she kept telling her, "it's all right. The doctor said your hand would be fine. It's all right."

Finally, Daryl settled down, and Susan stopped comforting her. Devlin stepped up to the bed. Susan looked at him, then at Daryl. She left the room without another word.

Daryl said, "You look tired."

"I am."

"Thanks for getting me back."

"Thank Susan. I couldn't have done it without her. I'm sorry I got you into it. I should have kept you someplace safe until the whole thing was over."

"No. No. You tried. You warned me. I'm just glad you got me out of it. I couldn't have stood much more."

"It's over."

"Am I ever going to be bothered by that guy?"

"No. He's dead."

"What about the one who hurt me?"

"No. It's over, Daryl."

She closed her eyes for a moment and seemed to be ready to go back to sleep. Then she opened them and looked at Devlin. She reached for his hand and said, "Jack, I have to forget about every-thing. Somehow. I can't be reminded of it, ever. Right now, I just want to say goodbye. I can't do anything else. Maybe later, way later, but not now. Is that all right?"

Devlin stared at Daryl for a few moments before he spoke. She looked raw and thin and vulnerable. Daryl Austen had been exposed to what existed out there beneath society's polite veneer, and she didn't want any part of it anymore. The thrill was gone. Long gone.

Devlin held her good hand and said, "Whatever you want, that's the way it will be. But the hell with goodbye. I'll leave you alone. For as long as you want. But you'll see me again. I owe you too much."

Daryl smiled, nodded, and closed her eyes. She slid back into a healing sleep. Devlin let go of her hand and walked out of the room.

Susan sat in the waiting room at the end of the hallway. She was on her third Parliament. She put the cigarette out and met him outside Daryl's room.

"Now what?"

Devlin asked, "You going to stay with her for a while?"

"For a while."

"You're being wonderful to her."

"I'm feeling very protective of her. That fucking animal Wexler. It's unbelievable."

"Wexler is dead."

Susan stopped and stared at Devlin. "Did you kill him?"

"Does it matter who pulled the trigger?"

"He's really dead?"

"Yes."

"Good. I'm glad he's dead. He doesn't deserve to be alive. You're not going to tell me what happened?"

"No."

"Is James all right?"

"Yes. He's okay."

"What's he going to do?"

Devlin shrugged. "Just go on being James. It's over."

"It's over."

"Yes."

"With me, too?"

"No, it's not over with you."

"Why? You going to stay and take care of me?"

"You can take care of yourself."

"You think so, huh?"

"Yeah. I do."

"Well, I guess we'll see about that."

Devlin said, "I guess we will."

"When?" she said.

"What do you mean, when?"

"When? When will you see if I take care of myself?"

"Name it."

Susan pursed he lips, thinking about her answer. "Six months."

"All right. Six months."

"How will you find me?"

"I'll look in the phone book."

"Under what name?" Susan asked.

"Under Ferlinghetti."

She smiled. They embraced once. Hard. Then Devlin turned and walked out of the hospital. He'd had enough of hospitals to last a long time.

He went downtown to the SoHo loft and called Pacific Rim. He gave William Chow a report, discussed how the lawyers would handle the police investigation, and made arrangements to meet Chow in Honolulu in three days.

He slept for fifteen hours, cleaned the loft, packed and took the shuttle to Boston. He rented a car and arrived in Truro on the Cape just as the sun was turning the sky a golden red. George was sitting on the porch of a big wooden house that had a view of the beach.

Marilyn and the kids stayed inside while they sat together on the porch.

George had lost so much weight that the skin sagged on his face, but when he saw Jack, he smiled a lopsided half-smile that showed he was genuinely glad to see him.

He sat in faded jeans and an old red Izod shirt with white paint stains on it. He wore no socks under his Sperry boat shoes. All his clothes were too big for him. He looked too fragile to be Devlin's big brother George, but he had the beginning of a tan that made him look almost healthy.

They embraced, gently. Devlin sat next to him, turned toward George, and asked, "How are you, bro?"

The right side of George's face didn't quite match the left, and the words came out slightly slurred as George answered, "Well, I look pretty pitiful I know, but I'm coming back. I'll be okay."

"Are you getting around all right?"

"Yeah, with the cane. Took a while to get one foot going in front of the other, but it's better every day. The doctor says in a year you won't notice it unless you look real close."

"George, I'm so goddamn sorry."

George nodded and said, "Yeah, I know. I knew you'd come up here all guilty and shit. It wasn't your fault, Jack. It really wasn't."

"I shouldn't have gone off and left you like that, George. I'm sorry."

George waved off the apology and said, "Marilyn told me you found out who did it."

"Yes."

"Did you tell the police? Can you prove anything?"

"It's all been taken care of, George."

"What do you mean?"

"We're not supposed to talk about it, George."

"You aren't going to tell me what you did?"

"The doctors don't want you thinking about it."

"I think about it all the time, Jack."

"They said you wouldn't remember anything."

"Oh, it took a little time for me to sort it out, but I remember it now. When I first woke up, I didn't know anything. The only thing I knew was that I hurt. I woke up in that hospital, and I just wanted to close my eyes and go back to sleep. For the longest time, I just wanted to stay asleep and not think about anything.

"Then when I did stay awake, I just wanted to figure out what was wrong with me. I couldn't walk. I couldn't sit up. I could hardly talk."

Devlin watched George, and all the guilt and pain of it swept over him. He sat motionless and listened as the sun continued to fade in the red sky. He couldn't think of any way to comfort his brother.

George continued, "But then when Marilyn and the kids showed up, and I finally got out of that hospital in the city, I started to come around. The clouds lifted, you know? The doctor in Connecticut got me up and walking. I started to sort things out. It came back pretty quickly. I remembered that guy telling those two big bastards to throw me out of his place. And I remembered what they did to me. And as soon as I did, all I kept thinking was how I could ever find those guys. How could I ever get any cops or anybody to do anything about it."

As the sun set under the horizon, casting a dazzling twilight over them, Devlin turned to his big brother and said, "George, I found them. All of them. And every last one of them paid for what they did to you. Believe me, George, every single last one of them paid."

George looked at his brother and nodded slowly. Some of the hurt and anger and confusion seemed to fade from his eyes. He nodded once more and said, "Good. I won't forget what happened, but at least now I can stop thinking about it. Now it really is over."